T0215519

Troubleshooting Java Performance

Detecting Anti-Patterns with Open Source Tools

Erik Ostermueller

Apress®

Troubleshooting Java Performance

Erik Ostermueller
Little Rock, Arkansas, USA

ISBN-13 (pbk): 978-1-4842-2978-1   ISBN-13 (electronic): 978-1-4842-2979-8
DOI 10.1007/978-1-4842-2979-8

Library of Congress Control Number: 2017954917

Cover image by Freepik (`www.freepik.com`)

Managing Director: Welmoed Spahr
Editorial Director: Todd Green
Acquisitions Editor: Jonathan Gennick
Development Editor: Laura Berendson
Technical Reviewer: Rick Wagner
Coordinating Editor: Jill Balzano
Copy Editor: James A. Compton, Compton Editorial Services

Distributed to the book trade worldwide by Springer Science+Business Media New York, 233 Spring Street, 6th Floor, New York, NY 10013. Phone 1-800-SPRINGER, fax (201) 348-4505, e-mail `orders-ny@springer-sbm.com`, or visit `www.springeronline.com`. Apress Media, LLC is a California LLC and the sole member (owner) is Springer Science + Business Media Finance Inc (SSBM Finance Inc). SSBM Finance Inc is a **Delaware** corporation.

For information on translations, please e-mail `rights@apress.com`, or visit `http://www.apress.com/rights-permissions`.

Apress titles may be purchased in bulk for academic, corporate, or promotional use. eBook versions and licenses are also available for most titles. For more information, reference our Print and eBook Bulk Sales web page at `http://www.apress.com/bulk-sales`.

Any source code or other supplementary material referenced by the author in this book is available to readers on GitHub via the book's product page, located at `www.apress.com/9781484229781`. For more detailed information, please visit `http://www.apress.com/source-code`.

Printed on acid-free paper

To John, Owen, and Joan.

Contents at a Glance

Contents

About the Author

Erik Ostermueller is a Java architect who is passionate about performance engineering. He has spent the last 10 years leading international performance engineering teams, tuning high-throughput Java financial systems in North and South America, Europe, and Asia. In 2011, he presented a paper entitled "How to Help Developers (Finally) Find Their Own Performance Defects" at the Computer Measurement Group's annual conference, where he won Best Paper and the Mullen Award for best speaker. The proceeds of this award financed an eight-city speaking tour in the US, Canada, the UK, and Italy.

Erik is the technical lead for the Performance Center of Excellence at FIS Global. He is the founder of heapSpank.org and wuqiSpank.org, and a contributor to jmeter-plugins.org and other open source projects. He lives in Little Rock, Arkansas and plays soccer, tennis, and the piano.

About the Technical Reviewer

Rick Wagner has been a software developer, architect, and maintenance engineer for 27 years. Rick has produced production applications in the mainframe era, through client/server, past the dawn of internet applications, and now into the age of containerization. Rick hopes a strict regimen of coding and reading of technical books will allow him to remain relevant as future generations of computer programming unfold.

Acknowledgments

Thanks to Apress for trusting me as a first time author; your support means everything to me.

Shawn McKinney of the Apache Foundation was the first person who thought I could write a book. Shawn, your early encouragement and honest feedback on crazy ideas have been invaluable, and you were always the first to provide feedback on any new code. Thanks. Mike Scheuter is one of the smartest people I know; he's a longtime friend, mentor, and colleague from FIS who first taught me to fall in love with stack traces and so many other things, work-related and otherwise. Thanks to my employer FIS and to our PerfCoE team. FIS' continued executive-level support for great performance throughout the enterprise is unique in the industry. Thank you for that.

Dr. Liz Pierce, the Chair of the Information Science department at UA Little Rock, orchestrated an 8-hour Java performance workshop that I gave in early June, 2017. Thanks, Dr. Liz for your support, and thanks to the 15 or so students, faculty, and others who gave up two Saturday afternoons to geek out on performance. Loved it. The CMG Canada group in Toronto was also kind enough the vet some of these ideas a month or two prior. Thanks.

In 2011, I won a best paper and best speaker award at a cmg.org international performance conference. The famous American computer scientist Jeff Buzen, who made many contributions to the field of queueing theory, led the committee that selected me for those awards. CMG's support (monetary and otherwise) way back then provided the confidence I needed to publish this book many years later. Thank you Jeff, thank you CMG.

There are many others who have helped in various ways: Joyce Fletcher and Rod Rowley who gave me my first tuning job way back in 2006. Thanks to Mike Dunlavey, Nick Seward, Stellus Pereira, David Humphrey, Dan Sobkoviak, and Mike McMillan for their support. To my Dad, Ralph Ostermueller, for your sustained interest and support over many, many months, and to Mom, too.

I'd also like to quickly mention just few of the particular open-source projects that I benefit from every day. Thanks to Trask at Glowroot.org for last minute fixes, to JMeter and JMeter-Plugins. You all rock.

Thanks to Walter Kuketz, Jeremiah Bentch, Erik Nilsson, and Juan Carlos Terrazas for reading late drafts of this book. Erik, your demands for clarity in the early chapters haunted me. Your input forced me to raise my standards a bit; I hope it shows, thanks. Jeremiah, your veteran commentary on SELECT N+1, JPA and other issues helped me fill in big gaps. Thanks. Lastly, to Walter: Your decades of performance/SDLC experience, succinctly imparted, really helped me avoid derailment at the end. Thanks.

To my technical reviewer, Rick Wagner: Rick, what I most loved about working with you, beyond your extensive Java/RedHat experience and beyond your unique experience reviewing so many technical books, was your ability to regularly guide me to paint a more complete picture of software performance for the reader, instead of the 1/2 painted I had started with. Thanks.

Lastly, thanks to my family. My older son Owen's editing skills are really on display in the introduction, Chapters 1 and 8, and other places as well. He's 20, knows nothing about programming, but gave me masterful lessons on how to gradually build complex ideas. Who'd a thunk it. Contact him before you write your next book. John, my younger son, helped test the code examples and put up with many brainstorming sessions that finally knocked the right idea out of my head. John's editing skills lie in smoothing out individual sentences. It turns out, there is a pattern here. My incredible wife Joan Dudley, who teaches college literature, is a-big picture editor for both this book and her students. Joan's editing contributions are "every paragraph is important" and "clarity takes a back seat to no one." Joan, you made many sacrifices, holding the fort down while I worked on this insanely long project. I love you and thank you for encouraging me to attempt great things.

Introduction

With just 30 minutes of troubleshooting, how close can you get to finding the root cause of a Java performance problem? What observability tools would you use? What subsystems would you investigate?

This book is a short curriculum in Java performance tuning for Java server-side developers. It explores one methodical approach to getting the most out of your 30 minutes and aims to show that much more is possible than is generally thought, even for Java developers with little exposure to performance tuning.

The brevity of this book is attributed to a sharp focus on only the worst problems seen in the author's 10 years of working exclusively as a lead Java performance engineer with Java distributed systems. That said, the tools and techniques can be used to find pretty much any defect.

This book is heavy on walkthroughs of performance problems that you can download from github.com and run on your own machine. The hands-on examples provide a rich, in-the-trenches experience that a book-only approach can't provide, not even a much larger book.

The reader will learn a methodical, easy-to-remember four-step tuning approach, called the P.A.t.h. Checklist, that directs the reader's attention to the right parts of the system and the right tools to find the performance defects. If you're wondering why I've chosen to capitalize the acronym that way, you'll find out in Chapter 4. Only open-source and freely available tools are used. In most cases, you will even see how the monitoring data looks before and after a performance fix is applied. Here is the checklist:

- P: Persistence. Learn how to recognize and fix the most common JDBC performance issues, ones that also apply to the NoSQL world.

- A: Alien systems. Detect when network calls to other systems cause slowdowns.

- t: threads. Learn how to identify CPU and response time issues using a low overhead tool that can be used in any environment, even production.

- h: heap. With the Quick GC Health Check, the reader will use a red-yellow green approach to assess whether GC performance is healthy. It also provides direction for more advanced techniques like finding/fixing memory leaks.

Generating a production-like workload is required to identify these defects, so there are a few chapters to get you up and going quickly to create load scripts to stress out your system. Among other topics like load scripting priorities and avoiding common pitfalls, the reader will learn a unique approach to deciding exactly how many threads of load to apply to show whether your system is scalable.

Themes

There are a number of recurring themes that we bump into while tuning software.

Dark Environments

Performance defects thrive in "Dark" Environments, ones without the right monitoring. This is a problem because so many of our environments are "Dark"—the QA environment, the demo environment, and the desktop of the developer on your team that has never used a Java profiler.

Using low-overhead tools that mostly come with the JDK, this book will help flush the performance defects out of any environment, dark or not.

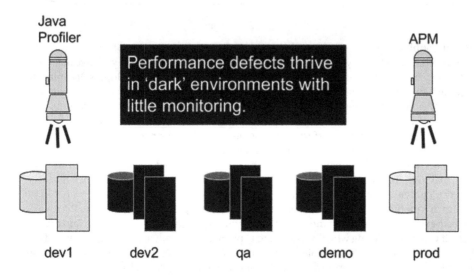

Figure 1. *"Dark" environments with little monitoring. APM = Application Performance Management tools.*

Plug-it-in-now

There are many outdated and productivity-draining monitoring tools that force us to reconfigure and restart a JVM before gleaning performance data. The dozen or more JVM parameters required for verbose garbage collection (GC) performance data are one such example. Wherever possible, this book uses metrics that you capture from any running JVM anywhere, without reconfiguration, without a JVM restart. I call this the plug-it-in-now approach.

Code First

Most performance engineers would love to have massive amounts of hardware for the software tuning process. Personally, I can't stand it. Having countless CPUs and unlimited RAM sounds nice, but in reality, once you have lots of hardware, you can't escape Big Environment Paralysis (my term), which includes:

- Reduced monitoring/visibility because of heightened security that limits access to machines.

- Infrequent test runs due to slower ops processes. Initial environment build is complex and takes weeks. Code redeploys take multiple hours. Cluster-wide restarts take 20-30 minutes. System backups and maintenance cause hours of downtime. Most individual load tests run > 60 minutes.

- Large environments have a ton of extra components with questionable performance: load balancers, firewalls, content switches, clusters, application server configuration, and so on.

- Larger staffing costs to babysit the extra infrastructure.

All of these things keep me from getting excited about large environments. I'm a little surprised anyone chooses to work like this because progress is excruciatingly slow. Ultimately, what really gets me excited is more tuning in less time.

What if we could get 5-10 fix-test tuning cycles completed a day, instead of the traditional 2-3? That would be a faster and more impressive way to tackle poor performance.

What if we could carefully design a tuning environment that minimized the Big Environment Paralysis? This would enable us developers to shift focus away from managing an environment and towards the performance of our deliverable, the Java code itself. I call this the Code First approach to tuning, and it's important because it's the fastest way to tune a system.

Chapter **2** lays out a very detailed design for such a tuning environment, one with a very special mystery feature that really minimizes Big Environment Paralysis. But aside from all of this, one particular requirement for this environment is key: when tuning here, we must be be able to reproduce most of the defects that we'd normally find in production. The environment would be worthless without it. So to concretely demonstrate that production-like performance defects can be found (and fixed) in this environment, I have coded two sets of server-side Java code examples that demonstrate these performance defects (under load) and their fixes.

Write Once Run Anywhere (WORA) Performance Defects

When Java was first released in the mid 1990s, compiling and running a 'C' program on multiple operating systems (OSs) was a royal pain. In response, the Java platform went to great lengths to ensure that Java code written on one OS could easily compile and run on all other OSs where Java was available. Sun Microsystems called this Write Once Run Anywhere (WORA).

But it just so happens that WORA has an undesirable and little-known side-effect: if there is a performance defect in your code, then that defect manifests itself not only on multiple platforms, but also in environments of different sizes, large and small.

Of course there are exceptions, but this has proven out repeatedly in my ten years as a Java performance engineer. Since I expect this will be hard for most readers to believe, I have coded more than a dozen performance defects to prove the point. Chapter 2 provides a quick overview of the performance results of these load tests. Chapter 8 details the architecture of the tests and describes how to run these examples on your own machine, with whatever capacity it might have.

Because most performance defects are reproducible in both large and small environments, we have an critical choice to make of where we do our performance tuning. This part is very important: Why tune in a big environment and suffer through all the 'Big Environment Paralysis' problems, when we could be much more productive and get 5-10 fix test cycles a day in a small environment?

Keep in mind that even though most tuning is done in a small environment for expediency, a larger environment is often required to demonstrate the full throughput and other performance requirements. What are performance requirements? We'll get to that real soon.

Three Threads of Load, Zero Think Time (3t0tt)

Part of my day job is training developers to tune their code. One of the most frequent mistakes I see is people stressing out their Java server-side systems with unrealistically large amounts of load. There are so many guys in this field, perhaps this is a testosterone thing?

Both sets of code that come with this book execute small load tests that apply stress to a server-side system. Each one of these tests is configured to launch exactly three Java threads that are simultaneously and perpetually submitting HTTP network requests. No 'think time' is configured between the HTTP requests. I call this amount of load 3t0tt, because it is 3 threads of load with zero think time. This is pronounced 'three tot.' It is used as a quantity of load, like this: How much load are you applying? 3t0tt.

This particular level of load is designed to have small enough CPU and RAM consumption to run on just about any workstation, but large enough to reproduce most multithreaded / synchronization problems. Even though this small amount of load is rarely enough stress to cause a system to go bezerk, throughout this book, the reader is encouraged to evaluate a few specific parts of the system and determine which one is causing the largest slowdown. This is called 'the lowest hanging fruit.' After identifying the issue, a fix is deployed and re-tested. If performance improves, the next lowest hanging-fruit issue is investigated and the process repeats.

Choosing the right amount of load to apply is tough for newcomers to performance. 3t0tt provides a very easy starting point to a difficult training problem. In Chapter 6, you will learn the next lesson in this realm, which is determining how much load to apply to quickly assess scalability.

The Discipline of Performance Engineering

This book is more of a troubleshooting guide than a guide to the entire discipline of performance tuning. This little section provides a brief look at how the performance process should work and how to know when you're done tuning a system.

If we're building a software system, the specs that define precisely what we're going to code are called the 'functional requirements.' They detail the items of data entry on each screen and the results that should be displayed when the user hits the 'submit' button. When all functionality in the requirements has been delivered, the application is functionally complete.

Performance requirements, on the other hand, define how quickly the application must respond, and how many business processes the system must handle in a particular time interval (like in an hour) in order to satisfy client needs. These are called, respectively, response time and throughput requirements. A performance requirements document starts by listing all/most of the business processes (from the function requirements) and then assigning response time and throughput requirements to each.

For example, if the response time requirement for your funds transfer is 2 seconds and its throughput requirement is 3,600 an hour, then a steady state load test (see Chapters 4, 5, 6, and 7 for details on load testing) must demonstrate that 90% of funds transfer response times are less than 2 seconds and that at least 3,600 of them were successfully executed in 60 minutes.

Sometimes performance requirements even place a cap on how much money can be spent on hardware. If five nodes in a cluster were required to meet the above goals, and the performance requirements said we could buy at most four nodes, then more tuning would need to be done (probably to lower CPU consumption) so that the response time and throughput goals could be met with just four nodes.

It is also common to stipulate that all performance requirements must be met while keeping CPU consumption below X, where X is whatever the operations folks feel comfortable with in production.

One of the most common mistakes in this area is not having any performance requirements at all. Of course these requirements are imprecise and imperfect. Start with something and refine them over time to best approximate client performance and stability needs without wasting time over-tuning the system.

Here is an example of the kind of refinement I'm talking about. Time should be spent understanding how closely the performance requirements match up to response time and throughput data gathered from production. If production data shows that the system processes 7,200 funds transfers on the busiest hour of the busiest day of the year, and the throughput requirement is less than that, then the throughput requirement should be raised to at least this number (7,200) and probably a little (perhaps 25%) higher, just to be safe.

For a more detailed look at the process, there is a great 20 page pdf whitepaper on the topic by Walter Kuketz on the `www.cgi.com` website. Walter actually helped me develop the above little section. To find his whitepaper, do an internet search using these search criteria:

"Walter Kuketz" "Guidebook for the Systems Development Life Cycle"

Draw the Line

Whose responsibility is it to make the system perform? The developers who coded it, or a performance engineer? If the performance engineer is your answer, then who is going to keep the developer from littering other code bases with the same kind of performance defects that caused the first system to tank? Keep in mind that laziness that drives automation is good. Laziness that avoids accountability for performance is bad.

This turns developers into performance defect progenitors, and the small cadre performance engineers don't have a chance of keeping up with such a huge number of defects.

Finally, if a performance engineer is brought in at the end of the development cycle to discover/fix performance issues, then there isn't time to tune, much less replace, a poorly performing technical approach that was months or years in the making.

Organization of Chapters

This book is divided into three parts.

Part I: Getting Started with Performance Tuning

The three chapters in Part I set the stage for performance testing:

Chapter 1 details four performance anti-patterns that lie at the heart of most performance defects. Understanding these anti-patterns makes the defects much easier to recognize when we're looking at raw performance metrics.

Chapter 2 makes the case that a very small computing environment, like a developer workstation, is the most productive place to tune a Java server-side system. It also details all the steps necessary to essentially collapse all the parts of a larger system into the smaller one.

Chapter 3 is about the vast sea of performance metrics and how to choose the right ones. If you've ever been confused about which metrics to use during performance testing, this chapter is for you.

Part II: Creating Load Scripts and Load Testing

Part II of this book is about creating load scripts and load testing in general:

Chapter 4 details both a "First Priority" and a "Second Priority" approach to creating network load scripts, ones that simulate a production load. The First Priority gets you up and testing quickly. The Second Priority shows how to enhance your scripts to more closely model the production load of real users.

Chapter 5 details all the right criteria you need to evaluate objectively whether the script you built in Chapter 4 simulates a "valid" test or not. This chapter helps you understand quickly whether you messed up your load test and the results must be discarded. No one wants to make big tuning/development decisions based on invalid results.

Chapter 6 details the fastest approach ever to assessing scalability. It describes a test called the Scalability Yardstick. If scalability is important to you, you should run this test once a week or more to help steer your app's performance in the right direction.

Chapter 7 is my love letter to the JMeter, the open-source load generator. jmeter-plugins.org is important, too! Commercial load generators can't keep up with all of JMeter's great features.

Part III: The P.A.t.h. Checklist and Performance Troubleshooting

The chapters in Part III are about performance troubleshooting. They detail the tools and techniques used to identify the root causes of Java server-side performance issues.

Chapter 8 provides the overview to that P.A.t.h. Checklist and provides an architectural overview of the two sample applications that you can run on your own machine. Downloadable from github.com, these sample applications provide a hands-on experience for collecting the right performance data and locating the root cause of the problem.

The items in the P.A.t.h. Checklist were described above so I won't repeat the descriptions, but here are the chapters for each one:

- P: Persistence. **Chapter 9**

- A: Alien systems. **Chapter 10**

- t: threads. **Chapter 11**

- h: heap. **Chapter 12**

PART I

Getting Started with Performance Tuning

CHAPTER 1

Performance Anti-Patterns

Before getting into the details of performance troubleshooting and tuning, it is helpful to have a high-level understanding of how performance defects make it into code in the first place. The four anti-patterns presented in this chapter illustrate the main kinds of defects you will encounter in Java server-side software. Throughout the book, we will refer back to the performance anti-patterns described in this chapter.

The objectives of this chapter are:

- Learn how to start with unfamiliar-looking, raw data from a performance monitoring tool and create a story (aka hypothesis) around it that describes how the code got to be so slow.

- Recognize the striking similarities between most performance defects.

- Commit to memory the names of the four Main Performance Anti-Patterns, or perhaps define your own anti-patterns.

- Learn how to assess whether a given defect is a large or small processing challenge.

When you first start investigating a performance problem, you know very little—perhaps you have a scrap or two of suspicious-looking data from one of the monitoring tools mentioned in the four P.A.t.h. chapters later in this book—but there is no smoking gun, no fix-in-the-waiting. This is the problem: you are stuck with just a sketch of the slowdown and you need a detailed picture to identify the culprit.

To fill in those details and to better understand the full story behind your defect, this chapter provides dossiers on the four most common types of performance defects—I call them the Main Performance Anti-Patterns.

Main Performance Anti-Patterns

Here are the Main Performance Anti-Patterns. As you are investigating a performance problem, ask yourself which of these anti-patterns your defect most closely resembles.

1. **Unnecessary Initialization**: While initializing some larger process, the system frequently reprocesses a small result that has already been processed. The accumulated effect of the many executions is extra CPU/RAM consumption and/ or slower execution that can all be avoided. Caching the small result is the main antidote.

2. **Strategy/Algorithm Inefficiency**: A misconfigured or poorly chosen algorithm or coding strategy is causing performance problems. A strategy is a technique used throughout a code base and an algorithm is a plan used to implement a single component.

© Erik Ostermueller 2017
E. Ostermueller, *Troubleshooting Java Performance*, DOI 10.1007/978-1-4842-2979-8_1

3. **Overprocessing**: The system is doing unnecessary work. Removing that work provides measurable performance benefit. One example is retrieving too much data, where most of the data is discarded. Another example is including in your load test the wrong resource-hungry use case—one that is seldom used in production.

4. **Large Processing Challenge**: Attempting to process and conquer a massive amount of data. Very few applications legitimately have such a need, but they do exist. Querying 4 billion rows of data. Transferring 10MB of data repeatedly over a slow network, and so on.

Unfortunately, there is overlap between these main anti-patterns, where one performance defect might fit two or more different main anti-patterns. To get around this fuzzy categorization issue, I have sorted these four issues from the most to least common (based on my own experience). This enables you to walk down the list in order and choose the first one that has the best fit to the problem you are faced with.

Main Anti-Pattern #1: Unnecessary Initialization

This anti-pattern frequently shows up in initialization, prior to actually doing something. This is a type of inefficient, CPU- and I/O-intensive coding in which certain tasks that have already been processed are unnecessarily reprocessed, often ad nauseum, causing unnecessary overhead. For example, rereading and reparsing an XML Schema .xsd file for every schema validation is unnecessary because the data in the .xsd file rarely changes. Instead of rereading/reparsing the .xsd, store and use a cached version that is already parsed.

Well, .xslt files are static too, and they have the same issue as .xsd files—they must be read from the file system (or network) and parsed before the transformation party begins, but most systems incur the reread and reparse overhead for every single transformation.

It turns out that static data, like .xsd and .xslt files, is everywhere, and there is a performance penalty to rereading or reparsing all that data. Here are examples of application-level data with this same problem:

- Authorization data. Which user has been granted which roles, and which roles have permissions to which resources? If you decide to cache this data to get a nice performance boost, the cache can easily be evicted-on-demand to accommodate time-sensitive security changes, like revoking privileges from your favorite disgruntled ex-employee.

- Product data. Yes, it would be tough for Wal-Mart and Amazon to fit their modest product offerings in RAM, but many organizations whose product offerings can fit nicely into a half gigabyte of RAM can boost performance by loading product configuration into memory at system startup.

- Organizational data, like physical plant locations, lists of countries of the world, states in the USA, and so on.

- Processing configuration data, like various transaction codes that orchestrate the flow of debits and credits in a banking system.

Repeatedly reloading any of those kinds of static application data causes measurable and problematic overhead. However, these improvements are not limited to application data, because there are even lower-level objects that are costly to repeatedly reload, as well. For example, many XML processing APIs sure seem like 100% of their processing is done in-memory, until you discover large, heaping portions of file system reads, jar-file-unzipping, and synchronization. Part of the problem is that the majority of Internet XML how-to articles advocate coding idioms that are insensitive to performance concerns. All of this nasty I/O can be avoided by an alternative idiom to consuming the API. Lots of room for optimization here. So, try these suggestions. You can find the code for these on my eostermueller repo on github.com—it's named crazyFastXml:

https://github.com/eostermueller/crazyFastXml

- For XSLT, cache and reuse the output of `javax.xml.transform.TransformerFactory.newTransformer()`

- For SAX parsing, cache and reuse the output of `javax.xml.parsers.SAXParserFactory.newSAXParser()`

- For StAX parsing, cache and reuse the output of `javax.xml.stream.XMLInputFactory.newInstance()` and `javax.xml.stream.XMLOutputFactory.newInstance()`

- For XPath, instead of using `javax.xml.xpath.XPathFactory.newXPath()`, use `org.apache.xpath.CachedXPathAPI`.

We will talk more about how to detect and fix these issues, especially in Chapter 11.

Caching the right objects helps avoid this first anti-pattern (Unnecessary Initialization). Exactly the same thing applies to networking: caching and reusing a network connection (aka TCP socket) is many times more efficient than shutting down and re-creating it for every request. For example:

- Consider using the pooling in the Apache HTTP Client to avoid the overhead of re-creating the TCP Socket. An Internet search for "apache client connection management" will get you to the right place.

- Some server-side JDBC apps still incur the overhead of using `javax.sql.DriverManager.getConnection()` to re-create the TCP socket for the database connection for every SQL request. Instead, consider using Hikari, C3P0 or a JDBC connection pool provided by your container, whether it is JBoss, WebSphere, Jetty, Tomcat or some other container.

Now that we have a good picture of several of the culprits, let's talk about a few more of the common traits that will help you recognize this Unnecessary Initialization anti-pattern when you are looking at performance data:

- Many small I/O hits. These examples are not about large I/O hits (say, 50ms or longer) but many small I/O hits (perhaps a few ms each) executed frequently by a handful of subsystems (application initialization, XML processing, HTTP requests, and so on), incurring overhead for every round trip.

- Performance Insensitive Idiom. The four problems with the XML APIs show that Unnecessary Initialization can be caused by using the wrong idiom to consume a particular API. Some of the most popular idioms available on the Internet, in the four XML cases, just happen to be fraught with performance problems. This is a problem.

As a performance recommendation, "avoid unnecessary I/O" is a cliché and banal, but it also happens to be the root cause of this bountiful class of performance defects. Ouch. Let's pay closer attention to the "avoid unnecessary I/O" recommendation and minimize requests to the disk and over the network.

Main Anti-Pattern #2: Strategy/Algorithm Inefficiency

This Main Anti-Pattern is about choosing an algorithm or strategy that doesn't perform well. Also included, though, is choosing the right algorithm with the wrong algorithm configuration/parameterization. Comparing the complexity of algorithms (using "Big O" notation) is out of scope for this small book.

It is not about fawning over your favorite sorting algorithms or using "Big O" notation to compare worst-case complexity. Why not? Because most enterprise software is considerably less complex. It is more about moving data from point A to point B. This book is about all the performance trouble that we regularly get ourselves into before even attempting to tackle more complex things, like algorithms.

This anti-pattern is about algorithms (structured plans of attack for processing some data), but also strategies, like a data access strategy that is an application's approach to sculpting SQL statements to retrieve/update data. An algorithm's implementation is normally in a single place. A strategy, on the other hand, is much more difficult to tune and/or replace because its code is scattered throughout the system.

You can use performance testing early in the development cycle to avoid investing in an ill-performing code strategy that is cost-prohibitive to replace. For example, you could discover early on whether executing a lot (say more than 25) of database or other back-end requests will perform well (it won't).

In Chapter 9 on Persistence, I will talk about the "Biggest Performance Problem Ever" in server-side software. This problem is so big that it stretches into anti-patterns 1 and 2. Stay tuned—it's really big and there is a good chance you have seen this already. Can you guess what it is?

Main Anti-Pattern #3: Overprocessing

This anti-pattern is about misguided attempts to embrace resource-intensive use cases, ones that are only marginally valid. One common example is where more data is processed than a single end user could possibly make use of in a single screen-full or webpage of information. In other words, expecting 50 pages of data in a single HTML table to load in 100ms is not going to happen. But 3 pages of data with a "next page" button could perform quite nicely. Another example is expecting a particularly complex use case to perform well under high throughput, even though it will see only light throughput in production.

While assessing this anti-pattern requires some technical expertise, it falls more so on business expertise. You specifically need to know which business processes are, or will be, used in production, and it would be helpful to know the rough percentages of each.

As a convenience to both developers and QA, often test databases contain a few "super customers" configured to demonstrate a large, dizzying array of business functionality, even though customers never get that large or complicated in production. Data like this in a load test is a frequent cause of the Overprocessing anti-pattern.

Here is one way this unfortunate scenario will play out: you create a load test that stresses out your system (Chapter 4). The four chapters in the P.A.t.h. section of this book will then walk you through hooking up monitoring tools and finding the slowest parts of your code and the highest CPU consumers. This is all good and well—no anti-pattern here. The problem happens if you get eager and spend lots of time tuning a particular section of code that users rarely traverse, but just happens to be inadvertently included in your load tests. This is time wasted.

Here is another example. Consider an inadvertently oversized RDBMS result set that takes extra time to process. An overly-broad WHERE clause in a SELECT could cause this, like a misplaced wild card that retrieves all customers matching anything. But unexpected and invalid data in the database could be at fault, too. And do not forget about the quintessential example mentioned earlier, where your system wastes resources cramming huge amounts of data into a single web page, more data than a single user will be able to digest.

So remember: performance tuning is as much about sculpting code to go faster as it is about making smart choices about which business processes to load-test. It is also about trade-offs between performance and user interface design—like keeping web page sizes small to accommodate performance concerns.

This means that when your head is stuck under the hood of your system looking at questionable performance from a large result set, you have to reorient your thinking and consider more abstract things, like performance/usability trade-offs and the throughput needs of the business. This human context switching is not easy, but consider how helpful it is: some tuning challenges can be avoided altogether because the underlying use case was so unrealistic that it shouldn't have been included in the load test in the first place.

Main Anti-Pattern #4: Large Processing Challenge

This anti-pattern describes I/O and other hardware limitations to big performance challenges, like lookups on a few billion rows of data or repeatedly pushing several megabytes over a really slow network. Enterprise software development has very few of these large, difficult challenges. But when you do encounter one, I recommend extra design and testing care, respect, and a healthy dose of trepidation. Optimizing everything else is almost trivial.

"Large Processing Challenge" is the last of the four Main Anti-Patterns. As I mentioned, anti-pattern 1 shows up the most, and anti-pattern 4 shows up the least. You can count yourself as an exception if you are on the bleeding edge and trying new things, and regularly encounter many of these big challenges. Congratulations. But for the rest of us writing enterprise web applications, there are very few big processing challenges that inspire this kind of fear. Here are a few examples of these large challenges:

- Lookups on just a few records in a table with 200 million records.

- Transferring a lot of data (say more than a megabyte) repeatedly over a slow network, especially over long distances.

- Multi-threaded performance is tough to get right, but there are many readily available APIs and solutions, where someone else already got performance right.

How will you know which processing challenges are "Large?" These kinds of challenges are so enormous, they will show up regardless of

- Language (Java, C#, C++, ...)

- Operating System

- Selection of API (like StAX vs SAX for XML parsing)

- Idiom your code uses to access the API, like Xalan vs. Saxon for XSLT transformation

Preparing for these large challenges takes so much work, it seems that preparations should begin back when the design document is created. If you truly fear a large processing challenge, invest the time to test its feasibility early in the project; perhaps hardware experts could contribute here.

Its common for developers to mistake an inadvertant glut of data for a large processing challenge. For example, why suffer slow responses from queries through 10 years of historical data when queries through 2 years of data would perform quite nicely, and the business side would be happy retaining a single year of data?

The troubleshooting techniques in this book will certainly identify performance issues with large processing challenges, both real and imagined. However, I must admit that creating solutions for large challenges is out of scope for this book, mostly because genuine issues of this type are rare.

Assessing the Size of a Processing Challenge

It makes perfect sense why large processing challenges (Main Anti-Pattern 4) show up on some kind of a performance radar that highlights performance problems, especially when troubleshooting online, Java server-side systems—the main topic of this book.

Because of the hard work it takes to tackle large processing challenges like this, development teams should anticipate the extra work and, in scheduling, increase the priority of the performance tuning effort. However, when smaller performance challenges show up on performance radar, they get in the way of other priorities like tuning large performance challenges. They steal time from other parts of the development lifecycle as well: design, development, QA, and so on.

Tuning small performance challenges is essentially a nuisance; in my experience, slowdowns in small performance challenges make up an unexpectedly large portion of the pool of all performance defects.

So when looking at any piece of data that might indicate a slowdown, do this:

> **Make a rough, mental assessment of whether the processing at hand is a large, medium, or small processing challenge.**

Here is an important hint to help find small challenges to tune: generally, when tasked to code something like an SOA service or a web request, there is one main task to be processed. An order must be placed; the query results must be returned; the store closing must commence. Almost by definition, processing that happens before or after the "main task" is a small challenge, and any corresponding slowdown is a nuisance to be eradicated. Likewise, so called "cross-cutting concerns" like logging, auditing, and security and even monitoring itself are likely candidates for small processing challenges.

Furthermore:

> **When a slow-looking, small processing challenge involves a publicly available API, that API's user community is highly likely to have experience with the slowdown for you to learn from.**

Take the time to seek out this performance experience—on doc pages, Internet searches, wherever. Just tack the word "performance" to the name of the API in your search criteria and search away. Ask questions in user forums. Also, when I say "publicly available API," certainly anything available from github.com and mvnrepository.com falls in this category. I have seen a great many performance defects in my ten years of tuning experience, and the good people of the Internet always seem to beat me to the punch. When the size of the processing challenge is small and the API in use is publicly available, others have already documented the issues and discovered reasonable workarounds.

Using the Main Performance Anti-Patterns

Here is walkthrough of how to put these anti-patterns to work.

1. Start by collecting data using the P.A.t.h. Checklist, which begins in Chapter 8. Of all the P.A.t.h. data, choose the measurement/result that looks the most problematic, whose fix would make the most positive impact on performance.

2. Ask whether this "most problematic" measurement looks like main anti-pattern 1.

    - Does it deal with static data, or at least no dynamic data?

    - Is the static data reprocessed for every system request?

    - Is a small amount of I/O involved each time the static data is reprocessed?

    - ...and so on

3. If the data seems to fit main anti-pattern 1, then congratulations, you have built a nice hypothesis for the problem. To test the hypothesis, apply a fix to your system and retest and reassess performance. This is how to "build a case" for a performance defect.

4. If the "most problematic" measurement data does not seem to fit 1, then move on to main anti-pattern 2.

5. Continue to evaluate all four main anti-patterns. It's highly unlikely that none of them will fit.

Don't Forget

A large portion of today's server-side performance problems are generally caused by a handful of trivially small processing tasks whose performance could and should be good, but in actuality is not. These "trivially small processing tasks" mostly show up in Main Performance Anti-Patterns 1 and 2, "Unnecessary Initialization" and "Inefficient Algorithm/Strategy." Actually, anti-pattern 1 is a special case of 2.

Keep in mind that an inefficient algorithm is a lot easier to refactor or replace than a strategy, whose details are scattered throughout the code base. The most typical example is a really chatty database strategy that executes dozens of SQL statements for each request: it performs poorly and is very costly to refactor.

Although seen less frequently, the other two Main Performance Anti-Patterns (3 and 4) are "Overprocessing" and "Large Processing Challenge." Large processing challenges should be identified (and feared) in design. As you start to find parts of the system that might be slow, don't forget to ask whether "overprocessing" is the cause. This is when you apply unrealistically large amounts of load to an infrequently used business process, or when your code casts a wide net and processes a large amount of data, only to discard a large portion of it.

Throughout the rest of this book, we will continually refer back to these Main Performance Anti-Patterns as a quick way to communicate and understand the root of cause of the various problems that really drag down server-side Java performance.

What's Next

Having trouble finding the right environment to performance test in? The next chapter is just for you. The code examples that come with this book (not discussed in detail until Chapter 8) demonstrate more than a dozen very commonly found write-once-run-anywhere (WORA) performance problems. Chapter 2, coming up next, will show you how to create an inexpensive, modest-sized tuning environment where you can get started right away finding these and other performance defects, ones that would likely cause problems in production.

## CHAPTER 2

A Modest-sized Tuning Environment

This chapter shows how you can spend less time tuning in a larger performance environment by first tuning in a modest-sized, smaller environment. In this smaller environment, you can complete more fix-test cycles per day, which greatly accelerates the overall tuning process.

The objectives of this chapter are:

- Learn how to design load tests that will run in a very small computing environment (like your desktop), effectively turning it into an economical performance tuning lab.

- Learn how to graph CPU/RAM consumption of individual processes over time.

- Learn how to replace back-end systems with a stub server that returns prerecorded responses.

Scheduling the performance-tuning phase of a project in the rough vicinity of a code freeze is a bad idea, but that is precisely where we schedule it. The code freezers say, "No more changes" and the tuners reply back, grunting "must fix code." The argument ends in a slap fight outside on the playground next to the slide. This is productivity, SDLC-style. Even after witnessing this entire kerfuffle, management can't seem to figure out why system performance ends up being so awful. The perennial conflict between "code freeze" and "code change" goes unnoticed, again.

This chapter explores a set of techniques that will enable you to use a small, developer tuning environment to boost performance early and throughout the SDLC. A final performance vetting in a large, production-like environment will likely still be required, but the early vetting will keep it from devolving into a more traditional, angst-ridden rush-job crammed into the closing moments before production.

Rapid Tuning

Many will rightfully object that a small tuning environment with just a few CPUs is too small to meet final performance goals for a high-throughput system. That is a fair objection. But reaching maximum throughput is not the immediate goal. Instead, the small environment provides an easy-to-access and easy-to-monitor system where we can complete many fix-test cycles, perhaps as many as 10 a day.

In a single fix-cycle, you run a load test for a few minutes, use monitoring tools to identify the biggest performance issue, code and deploy a code fix, validate the improvement, and then repeat.

Traditionally, after the code is finished and Quality Assurance has tested all the code, performance testing is tightly crammed into the schedule right before production. This is particularly challenging for a number reasons. First, there is so little time to create the expensive, large computing environment that most feel is required for tuning. Second, for stability's sake, it makes sense to institute a code freeze as production draws near. However, the culture of the code freeze makes it particularly difficult for performance engineers to test and deploy the changes required to make the system perform. Lastly, there is little time to retreat from poorly performing technical approaches that were tightly baked into the product from day 1. This is a last minute rush-job.

To contrast, this "rapid tuning" approach helps keep tuning from consuming your budget and helps avoid a last-minute performance rush-job. With the bulk of the performance defects addressed early on, demonstrating the full throughput goal in the full environment is a smaller, more manageable task.

Write-Once-Run-Anywhere Performance Defects

The code samples that accompany this book are available in these two github repositories:

```
https://github.com/eostermueller/javaPerformanceTroubleshooting
https://github.com/eostermueller/littleMock
```

I'll refer to the first one as "jpt" and the second one as "littleMock." This section briefly enumerates the performance defects in the first set of examples—jpt. There is more detail on both sets of examples in Chapter 8. Chapters 1, 2, and 3 are introductory in nature, so I can understand why the hard performance data from load tests in Table 2-1 seems out of place. I have included this data to provide tangible proof that commonly found performance defects can be easily detected in a modest-sized tuning environment, like a workstation.

Each row in Table 2-1 details two tests—one with and the other without a particular performance defect. From row-to-row, it varies on whether the A or the B test has the defect. The test with the higher RPM has the better performance, although there are a few exceptions where other factors besides RPM determine best performance.

Table 2-1. *Throughput results from jpt Sample Performance Defects That You Can Run on Your Own Machine. RPM = Requsts per Minute, as measured by Glowroot.org.*

Test #	A Test RPM	B Test RPM	Performance Defect	Comments
01	119	394	Slow HTTP back-end	
02	2973	14000	Multiple reads to 1MB data file	
03	15269	10596	Uncached queries to static data	
04	6390	15313	Slow result set iteration	
05	3801	12	Missing database index	
06	10573	10101	Over-allocation of RAM on heap	No significant throughput difference, but essential for avoiding waste.
07	18150	26784	SELECT N+1	
08	354	354	Runaway thread with heavy CPU	Extra CPU consumption did not impact throughput.
09	N/A	N/A	Multiple Issues	09b.jmx does not exist. Try this yourself.
10	N/A	N/A	Uncompressed HTTPS response over WAN	Results only interesting when tested over a WAN.
11	N/A	N/A	Memory leak	11a throughput degrades, but only after the slow leak fills the heap.
12	7157	9001	Undersized Young Generation	

Like this set of examples, most performance defects are "Write-Once-Run-Anywhere" (WORA) defects, because regardless of whether you run them on a massive, clustered environment or a small laptop, the defect will still be there and it will be detectable.

I don't expect others to reproduce the exact numbers that I've included in this table. Rather, the main idea is to understand that there are concrete and repeatable performance differences between the a and b tests for any test number, like 05a and 05b.

I selected this particular set of defects based on my experience as a full-time Java server-side performance engineer over the last ten years. In the fifteen years prior to that as a developer, team lead, and architect, I saw basically the same issues.

Whether this list will exactly match what you see is up for debate; your mileage will vary. But I'm fairly confident these defects will be pretty familiar to server-side Java developers. More importantly, the tools and techniques that uncover the causes of these problems are even more universal than this listing of defects. This toolset will help detect a great many issues absent from this list.

Again, the 12 examples just shown are part of the first set of examples—jpt. We'll talk about the second set of examples (littleMock) in Chapter 8. Stay tuned.

Tuning Environment for Developers

Because these defects can be detected on both large and small environments, we no longer have to wait for a large environment to tune our systems. We can tune in just about any environment we want. This means we have choices, attractive ones, when we brainstorm what our tuning environment looks like. So what would be on your wish list for a great tuning environment? These things are at the top of my list:

- Lots of RAM.

- Having root or administrative access (or at least really good security access) to the system. In Linux, sudo can be used to grant access to some root commands and not others. This makes everything easier—monitoring, deploying code, viewing log files, and so on.

- The ability to quickly change/compile/build/package and redeploy the code.

After that, I need a good project manager to keep my schedule clear. But outside of this, surprisingly little is needed. With this simple list of things and the tuning approach presented in this book, you can make great progress tuning your system.

Most large, production-sized environments (Figure 2-1) are missing important things from this wish-list: code redeploys are slow (they take hours or days and lots of red tape). Then, the people tuning the system rarely get enough security access to allow a thorough but quick inspection of the key system components. This is the Big Environment Paralysis that we talked about in the Introduction.

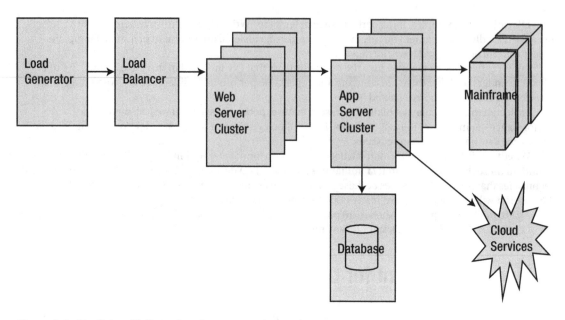

Figure 2-1. *Traditional full-sized performance tuning environment*

The environment shown here probably has redundancy and tons of CPU; those are great things, but I will happily sacrifice them for a tiny environment that I have full access to, like my laptop or desktop. Figure 2-2 shows one way to collapse almost everything in Figure 2-1 onto just two machines.

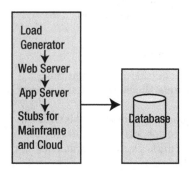

Figure 2-2. *Modest performance tuning environment with just two machines*

At first glance, it looks like concessions have been made in the design of this small environment. The live mainframe and live cloud services are gone. Redundancy is gone. Furthermore, since we are collapsing multiple components (load generator, web server, app server and stubs) on a single machine, running out of RAM is a big concern. These are all concerns, but calling them concessions is like faulting a baby for learning to crawl before learning to walk. This small developer tuning environment is where we get our footing, where we understand how to make a system perform, so we can avoid building the rest of the system on a shaky foundation, the one we are all too familiar with.

To bring this dreamy goal down to earth, the twelve "run-on-your-own-machine" performance defects distributed with this book will help to make all this tangible. Each of the example load tests is actually a pair of tests—one with the performance defect and then a refactored version with measurably better performance.

But we have yet to talk about all the back-end systems that we integrate with—the mainframes, the systems from third parties, there are many. The effort to make those real systems available in our modest tuning environment is so great that it isn't cost effective. So how can we tune without those systems?

In a modest tuning environment, those back-end systems are replaced with simple "stand-in" programs that accept real requests from your system. But instead of actually processing the input, these stand-ins simply return prerecorded or preconfigured responses.

In the remaining parts of this chapter, you will find an overview of some very nice toolsets that help quickly create these stand-in programs, a process we call "stubbing out" your back-ends.

To help stay abreast of whether these stand-in programs (I'll start calling them *stub servers*) have modest resource consumption, it's helpful to be able to graph the live CPU and RAM consumption of the processes on your machine. We will discuss a toolset for that graphing, but in the next section we will talk about the risks involved with any network segment you use in your modest load test environment. I personally wouldn't tolerate any more than about 10–15% of consumption (either RAM or CPU) from any one of these stub servers.

Network

I would have drawn Figure 2-2 with just a single machine, but I thought it might be difficult to find a machine with enough RAM to hold all components. So if you have enough RAM, I recommend putting all components on a single machine to further the Code First approach to tuning.

This section shows some of the benefits of collapsing multiple components in a larger environment into a single machine or two.

Let's say that every part of your test is in a single data center—server, database, testing machines, everything. If you relocate the load generator machine (like a little VM guest with JMeter on it) to a different data center (invariably over a slower network) and run exactly the same load test, the response time will skyrocket and throughput will plummet. Even when the load generation is in the same data center, generating load over the network exposes you to risk, because you are playing on someone else's turf. And on that turf, someone else owns the performance of the network. Think of all the components involved in maintaining the performance of a network:

- Firewalls

- Bandwidth limitation software (like NetLimiter) that runs as a security measure

- The HTTP proxy server, if accessing the Internet

- The hardware—routers, content switches, CAT5, and so on

- Load balancers, especially their configuration that manages concurrency

When my boss is breathing down my neck to make sure my code performs, none of the owners of these network components are readily available on the clock to help me out. So, I write them out of the script, so to speak. Whenever possible, I design my load tests to avoid network. One way of doing this is to run more processes on the same machine as the Java Container.

I concede that co-locating these components on the same machine is a bit nonstandard, like when your friends laughed at you when they saw you couldn't ride a bike without training wheels. I embrace chickenhearted strategies, like using training wheels, when it serves a strategic purpose: addressing performance angst, which is very real. Let's use training wheels to focus on tuning the code and build a little confidence in the application.

Once your team builds a little more confidence in performance in a developer tuning environment, take off the training wheels and start load-testing and tuning in more production-like network configurations. But to start out, there is a ton of risk we can happily eliminate by avoiding the network in our tuning environments, thus furthering our Code First strategy.

Stubbing Out Back-end Systems

If you are personally ready to start tuning, but one of your back-end systems isn't available for a load test, you are a bit stuck creating your environment. But there are options. Simply commenting out a network call in your code to the unavailable system and replacing it with a hard-coded response can be very helpful. The resulting view of how the rest of the system performs will be helpful, but the approach is a bit of a hack. Why? Because altering the content of the hard-coded response would require a restart. Additionally, none of network API gets vetted under load because you commented out the call. Also, any monitoring in place for the back-end's network calls will also go untested.

Instead of hard-coding, I recommend running a dummy program, which I'll refer to as a network stub server. This general practice also goes by the name of *service virtualization*.[1] The stub server program acts as a stand-in for the unavailable system, accepting network requests and returning prerecorded (or perhaps just preconfigured) responses.

You configure the network stub to return a particular response message based on what's in the input request. For example, "If the stub server is sent an HTTP request, and the URL path ends with /backend/fraudCheck then return a particular json or XML response."

If there are many (perhaps dozens or hundreds) request-response pairs in the system, network record and playback approaches can be used to capture most of the data required to configure everything.

When you are evaluating which network stub server to use, be sure to look for one with these features:

- Lets you reconfigure requests/responses without restarting the network stub program.

- Lets you configure response time delay, in order to simulate a back-end with response time similar to your own back-end.

- Allows custom java code to customize responses. For instance, perhaps the system calling the stub requires a current timestamp or a generated unique ID in a response.

- Allows you to configure a particular response based on what's in the input URL and/or POST data.

- Offers record and playback.

- Similar to record and playback, it is also nice to be able to do a lookup of recent request-response pairs.

- Network stub program can be launched from a unit test or as a stand-alone program.

- Can be configured to listen on any TCP port.

If your back-end system has an HTTP/S entry point, you're in luck because there are a number of mature open-source network stub servers designed to work with HTTP:

- Wiremock: wiremock.org

- Hoverfly: https://hoverfly.io/

- Mock Server: http://www.mock-server.com/

- Betamax: http://betamax.software/

---

[1]If you'd like more detail, there are more service virtualization tools. See http://blog.trafficparrot.com/2015/05/service-virtualization-and-stubbing.html
And this book: http://www.growing-object-oriented-software.com/.

But similar stub servers of the same maturity are not yet available for other protocols, such as RMI, JMS, IRC, SMS, WebSockets and plain-old-sockets. As such, for these and especially proprietary protocols and message formats, you might have to resort to the old hack of just commenting out the call to the back-end system and coding up a hard-coded response. But here is one last option: you could consider writing your own stub server, customized for your protocol and proprietary message format. Before dismissing this as too large an effort, take a quick look at these three mature, open source networking APIs:

- Netty: `https://netty.io/`

- Grizzly: `https://grizzly.java.net/`

- Mina: `https://mina.apache.org/`

All three were specifically designed to build networking applications quickly. In fact, here is one demo of how to build a custom TCP socket server using Netty in less than 250 lines of Java:

`http://shengwangi.blogspot.com/2016/03/netty-tutorial-hello-world-example.html`

This could be a great start to building a stub server for your in-house TCP socket server that uses proprietary message format.

Stubbing Out HTTP Back-ends with Wiremock

Figures 2-3 and 2-4 show a quick example of how to launch, configure, and submit a request to Wiremock, my favorite HTTP stub server.

```
#~/Documents/src/jdist/wiremock/wiremock-2.1.7/standalone: java -jar wiremock-standalone-2.1.7.jar
SLF4J: Failed to load class "org.slf4j.impl.StaticLoggerBinder".
SLF4J: Defaulting to no-operation (NOP) logger implementation
SLF4J: See http://www.slf4j.org/codes.html#StaticLoggerBinder for further details.
  /$$       /$$ /$$                      /$$      /$$                     /$$
 | $$   /$ | $$|__/                     | $$$    /$$$                    | $$
 | $$  /$$$| $$ /$$  /$$$$$$   /$$$$$$$  | $$$$  /$$$$  /$$$$$$   /$$$$$$$| $$   /$$
 | $$ /$$ $$ $$| $$ /$$__  $$ /$$_____/  | $$ $$/$$ $$ /$$__  $$ /$$_____/| $$  /$$/
 | $$$$_  $$$$| $$| $$  \__/| $$$$$$$$$  | $$  $$$| $$| $$  \ $$| $$      | $$$$$$/
 | $$$/ \  $$$| $$| $$       | $$_____/  | $$\  $ | $$| $$  | $$| $$      | $$_  $$
 | $$/   \  $$| $$| $$       |  $$$$$$$  | $$ \/  | $$|  $$$$$$/|  $$$$$$$| $$ \  $$
 |__/     \__/|__/|__/        _____/ |__/     |__/ _____/  _____/|__/  \__/

port:                     8080
enable-browser-proxying:  false
no-request-journal:       false
verbose:                  false

■
```

Figure 2-3. *Startup banner running the wiremock.org stub server with the java -jar option*

```
{
    "request": {
        "method": "GET",
        "url": "/some/thing"
    },
    "response": {
        "status": 200,
        "fixedDelayMilliseconds": 5000,
        "body": "Hello world!",
        "headers": {
            "Content-Type": "text/plain"
        }
    }
}
```

Figure 2-4. *The json body of an HTTP POST used to configure wiremock to return a predetermined HTTP response*

It is incredibly easy to launch Wiremock with a simple java -jar approach: Just execute java -jar wiremock.jar, and it starts right up listening for HTTP requests on port 8080 (which is configurable).

Once it is started, you can make HTTP/json calls to configure the request-response pairs to mimic your back-end. You POST the json to http://<host>:<port>/__admin/mappings/new. Then you can save those calls in a SOAP UI, Chrome Postman, or JMeter script and execute them right before the load test. In Figure 2-4 json says, "If Wiremock receives a GET to /some/thing, then return 'Hello world!' as the response, but only after waiting 5 seconds."

Once you have POSTed the preceding code to http://localhost:8080/__admin/mappings/new, you should try out the new stub as shown in Figure 2-5.

Figure 2-5. *Using Chrome to test the newly created wiremock configuration (Figure 2-4)*

… and sure enough, the browser doesn't paint "Hello world!" until Wiremock waits the 5000 milliseconds that we asked for using the fixedDelayMilliseconds attribute in the json.

That wasn't too difficult, right? To summarize, download the Wiremock jar and run it as java -jar. Then submit Wiremock json-over-HTTP configuration messages to essentially teach Wiremock which responses to return for each HTTP request supported by your back-end. Lastly, start your app and watch it submit requests to Wiremock, and Wiremock will return the responses that you configured. That's it.

Local Load Generation

With the Code First approach in mind, the heart of the two-machine developer tuning environment (Figure 2-2) is your code—a single JVM for the web tier that makes calls to a single JVM for the application tier.

Here are the other parts we are concerned with.

First are the stub servers we just talked about. They replace the mainframe and the cloud services. Vetting the actual systems for performance will have to wait for later, probably in an integration testing environment.

Ultimately, some monitoring will be sprinkled in, but the last component to go into the developer tuning environment is the load generator, the topic of this section.

Quick Overview of Load Generation

A load generator is a network traffic generator. We use it to stress a network-enabled software application, like a SOA or the server-side portion of a web-application, to see if the responses are fast enough and to make sure it doesn't crash.

Of course, it wouldn't be helpful to sling random traffic at a web application—we'd need to submit the exact kind of web requests the web app was designed to process. For this purpose, most load generators, like JMeter, use a record-and-playback approach to get the traffic just right. It works like this: on an otherwise idle system, you manually traverse your application using a web browser while a special tool (which comes with a load generator) records the network requests made by your browser.

The output of that recording is a tool-specific script that can replay, verbatim, that single user's traffic, thus stressing out the SUT a little bit. Then, to model a dynamic workload and move away from the verbatim recording, you enhance the script to log on a (data-driven) variety of users and operate on a (data-driven) variety of "things" in the SUT—whatever things the SUT deals in—shopping for kayaks, a dating service for manatees, delivering news stories, whatever. Hardware permitting, load generators can spin up as many threads as you like to simulate a larger number of users.

Load Generator Responsibilities

A load generator has these main responsibilities:

1. To record network traffic as you traverse a system, and save the navigation details to a script.

2. To allow you to edit/debug/enhance the script, so that it more closely resembles a production load.

3. To run the script in a single thread, and to enable multiple threads to run the same script concurrently, thus applying load to your system. This is "load generation."

4. To display the response time, throughput and other test results via live graphs/displays and/or via post-test reports.

The "Load Generator" in Figure 2-2 specifically refers to responsibility 3, load generation. You can take care of responsibilities 1, 2 and 4 wherever and however you need to.

In fact, the startup banner for the JMeter load generator addresses this very concern (Figure 2-6).

```
■ C:\Windows\System32\cmd.exe

========================================================================
Don't use GUI mode for load testing, only for Test creation and Test debugging !
For load testing, use NON GUI Mode:
   jmeter -n -t [jmx file] -l [results file] -e -o [Path to output folder]
& adapt Java Heap to your test requirements:
   Modify HEAP="-Xms512m -Xmx512m" in the JMeter batch file
========================================================================
```

Figure 2-6. *Warning from JMeter not to use the GUI during a load test*

The idea is to create, record, and refine your load script using JMeter GUI Mode. Running a small amount of load, perhaps less than ten requests per second is acceptable, too. Do all of this with the JMeter GUI Mode. But when it comes to running more than 10RPS, your safest best to avoiding performance problems in the load generator itself is by running JMeter in NON GUI Mode, aka from the command line, or headless. The JMeter startup banner in Figure 2-6 even shows how to do this. Here is an example:

1. First start the JMeter GUI and create your load plan and save it to myLoadPlan.jmx.

2. Copy the myLoadPlan.jmx file to your developer tuning environment, where JMeter needs to be installed.

3. Run this command:

    $JMETER_HOME/bin/jmeter -n -t myLoadPlan.jmx -l test001.jtl -e -o dirTest001

    where test001.jtl is a text data file in which JMeter will write results from the test and dirTest001 is a folder that JMeter will create and use to hold a performance report after the test finishes.

As long as RAM and CPU consumption for the JMeter process stay relatively low, perhaps below 20% for both, then I have had no problems running JMeter on the same machine as the SUT. If you are still skeptical, see if performance dramatically improves by moving the load generation to another box on the same subnet.

CPU Consumption by PID

Having just a single person on a team care about performance is a tough, uphill battle. But when you have a few (or all) coworkers watching out for problems, making sure results are reported, researching performance solutions, and so on, then performance is much more manageable.

So to get (and keep) others on-board and interested, a certain amount of performance transparency is required to better keep others up-to-date. For example, everyone knows how to use top and TaskMgr to watch for CPU consumption. But did you watch it for the duration of the test, or did you take your eyes off it while looking at the flood of other metrics? We should all be good skeptics for each other when troubleshooting, and a basic CPU consumption graph for the duration of the test really helps answer these questions before they're asked.

But the task of watching CPU is more work when you're trying to watch it on multiple machines, or as well in our case, trying to distinguish which of the many processes on a single machine has high/spiky CPU. My point here is that it is worth the time to regularly create and share easy-to-understand graphs and metrics, and furthermore in the special case of CPU consumption, there is a void of open-source/free tools that will graph CPU consumption over time for individual process IDs (PIDs).

I would like to quickly highlight one of the few tools that can do this, and it just so happens that this tool not only works with JMeter, but its results can be displayed on the same graph as any other JMeter metrics. The tool is called PerfMon and it comes from jmeter-plugins.org at `https://jmetr-plugins.org/wiki/PerfMon/` (see Figure 2-7).

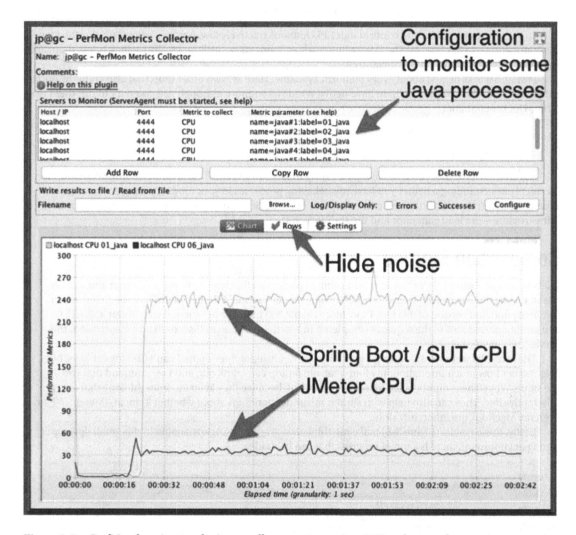

Figure 2-7. *. PerfMon from jmeter-plugins.org allows you to monitor CPU andmany other metrics*

Here are a few notes:

- Because the i7 processor for this test has eight cores, if a single line reached 800, that would mean the system is 100% consumed. For six cores, 600 is the max. In this graph, we have two lines, 240 and 40. 240+40=280, and 280/800 = 35% CPU.

- In the pane at the top, I have configured PerfMon to capture CPU metrics for six different Java processes. Unfortunately, I had to use `top` on my MacBook to confirm which process was using ~240 and which was ~40.

- Sometimes there are many lines with low CPU consumption that get in the way. The "hide noise" label in Figure 2-3 shows one way to temporarily remove lines with very low consumption that make the graph noisy. Auto scaling, color selection, hiding lines, and other great graph refinement features are documented here:

```
https://jmeter-plugins.org/wiki/SettingsPanel/
```

I use these graphs mainly to confirm that CPU remains relatively low, perhaps below 20%, for the load generator and any stub servers. The JMeter line reads at about 40, so 40/800=5% CPU, which is less than 20%, so JMeter CPU consumption is sufficiently low.

PerfMon works on just about every platform available. Here are two other tools that also graph resource consumption by PID. Neither of them have native Windows support, although you could try to run them in a Linux/Docker container:

- ```
  https://nmonvisualizer.github.io/nmonvisualizer/
  ```

- ```
  https://github.com/google/cadvisor
  ```

Regardless of the tool you use, having PID-level metrics to show CPU and other resource consumption is critical understanding whether you have misbehaving processes in your modest tuning environment. When reporting on your results, remember to point out the portion of consumption that comes from test infrastructure—the load generator and the stub server(s).

Comparison Metrics

A few years ago, I ran a JMeter test on a do-nothing Java servlet that was deployed to Tomcat and was on the same machine as JMeter. Had I seen 1,000 requests-per-second, I think I would have been impressed. But in my updated version of this test, I saw more than 2,800 requests per second with about 35% CPU consumption. And 99% of the requests completed in less than 1.3 ms (milliseconds), as measured at the servlet (by glowroot.org).

These results were so astoundingly good that I actually remember them. I can't find my car keys, but I remember how much throughput my four-year-old laptop can crank out, and I recommend that you do the same. Why? These numbers are incredibly powerful, because they keep me from thinking that Java is inherently slow. They can also help with similar misunderstandings about whether Tomcat, JMeter, TCP or even my MacBook are inherently slow.

Lastly, these results (Figure 2-8) make me think that even on a single machine in this small developer tuning environment, there is a ton of progress that can be made.

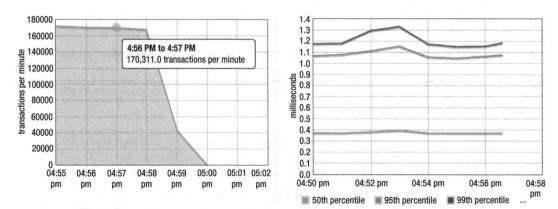

Figure 2-8. *Response time and throughput metrics for a do-nothing Java servlet. Metrics from Glowroot.org. Intel(R) Core(TM) i7-3615QM CPU @ 2.30GHz, Java 1.8.0_92-b14.*

Don't Forget

The environments in Figure 2-1 and Figure 2-2 are substantially different! This chapter has discussed all the things that were excluded from the design of the developer modest tuning environment (Figure 2-1). We are cutting scope so we can vet the performance of the part of the system that we developers are responsible for—the code. Hence the Code First mantra.

I can appreciate that the small developer tuning environment I'm proposing looks unconventional, so much so that you might wonder whether it reproduces realistic enough conditions to make tuning worthwhile. In short, the appearances of this environment design seem wildly artificial.

In response, I will say that this particular environment design addresses a longstanding specific strategic need that helps avoid last-minute rush-job performance tuning efforts that have left our systems, and perhaps even our industry, a bit unstable. The modest tuning environment also helps us identify and abandon poorly performing design approaches earlier in the SDLC.

Few question the efficacy of a wind tunnel to vet aerodynamics or a scale-model bridge to assess stability. The wind tunnel and the model bridge are wildly artificial, yet widely accepted test structures inserted into the development process to achieve strategic purposes. This small developer tuning environment design is our technology offering to address long standing, industry-wide performance issues.

There will be skeptics that say that a small environment can never provide a close enough approximation of a production workload. These are generally the same people that feel that performance problems are only rarely reproducible. To this group I would say that the modest tuning environment is a reference environment that we use to demonstrate how to make our systems perform. We won't fix everything, but we have to begin to demonstrate our resilience somewhere and somehow.

What's Next

In the Introduction, I talked about how performance defects thrive in Dark Environments. Well, not all environments are Dark. Sometimes there is an unending sea of metrics and it's tough to know which to use to achieve performance goals. The next chapter breaks down metrics into a few high-level categories and talks about high to use each to achieve performance goals. There are also a few creative solutions to restructuring your load tests that can help avoid wandering around lost in a completely Dark Environment.

CHAPTER 3

■ ■ ■

Metrics: The Antidote to Guesswork

The Introduction talked about the concept of Dark Environments, the problem where the right monitoring is rarely available when and where you need it. This is indeed a problem that we as an industry are long overdue to talk about and address, but there are two sides to this story. If we forget about all the practical problems (security, access, licensing, overhead, training, and so on) of getting the right tool plugged into the right environment, the tables are completely turned around. For some, instead of a being starved for data with too few metrics, many are frightened by the vast sea of all possible metrics, and how easily one could be duped by selecting the wrong one.

The objectives of this chapter are:

- Understand which types of metrics should be used to determine whether to keep or discard tuning changes.

- Understand which types of metrics are used to identify components responsible for a particular slowdown.

- Remember that tracking, graphing, and sharing your system's tuning progress over time helps people on your team care more about performance.

This chapter breaks down this vast sea of metrics into three loose categories and shows how to put each category to work to accomplish key performance goals.

Which Metric?

When wrestling with performance issues, we spend a lot of time asking these three questions:

- The Resource Question: How much of the hardware resources is the system using (CPU, RAM, network, disk)? 35%? 98%?

- The Blame Question: What components of the system-under-test (SUT) are to blame for a particular performance problem? A "component" needs to be something specific that we can investigate, like a single Java method in a specific source code file, or perhaps a single DB query or other network request.

- The User Benefit Question: Will the end users notice the response time impact of a particular tuning enhancement? And which code or configuration change performs better?

© Erik Ostermueller 2017
E. Ostermueller, *Troubleshooting Java Performance*, DOI 10.1007/978-1-4842-2979-8_3

On a good day tuning a system, I am capable of doing the right thing, "following the data" instead of guessing at the answers to these three all-important questions. That means taking the time to capture certain metrics from carefully planned load tests. But when firefighting a really stressful production problem, or perhaps just on a bad day when my socks don't match, all bets are off and my explanations for things are a nasty tangle of unsubstantiated guesswork. The Dark Environments issue makes this even harder because conjecture rules when the right metrics aren't available, which unfortunately is pretty frequently.

As such, this chapter aims to make it easier to find a helpful metric by first focusing on answering these key questions with metrics. In short, Table 3-1 shows the metrics I suggest for answering each of our questions.

Table 3-1. *Metrics for Common Performance Questions*

Performance Question	Answered by:
1 Are resources (CPU/RAM/etc...) available?	The basics: PerfMon, TypePerf, ActivityMonitor, top/htop/topas/nnon/sar, and so on
2 Which component is to blame for slowing things down?	Server-side data like thread dumps, Profiler data, verbose GC data, SQL throughput/response time, and so on
3 Does the end user benefit? Which code change performs better?	Response time and throughput metrics from the load generator.

Some metrics help answer more than one of these questions. For example, questions 2 and 3 both deal with response times, to some extent. My point is not to forge tight metric classifications without overlap, but to give you a reasonably good starting point for what metrics to use to answer each of these key questions.

Later in the book, the four chapters on the P.A.t.h. Checklist answer question 2 (what is to blame?). Question 1 (are there available resources?) uses metrics from tools everyone is familiar with, right? Top, PerfMon, nnon, and so on. Brendan Gregg's USE method is a great way to avoid forgetting to watch resource consumption. Here is the link:

http://www.brendangregg.com/usemethod.html

If a machine is part of your load test and you don't have access to resource consumption metrics, beware or blaming it for any of your problems.

I really think that learning the troubleshooting techniques in the four P.A.t.h. chapters is a do-able thing. It might be more of a challenge to stay abreast of all three of these metrics questions for the duration of the tuning process—forgetting just one of them is so easy.

The rest of this chapter is devoted to answering question 3, determining whether your end users will benefit from various proposed performance changes.

Setting Direction for Tuning

Deciding which tuning enhancements to keep sets a lot of the direction for the tuning process. Generally, faster response time and higher throughput metrics from your load generator should provide the final say on whether to keep a particular change. Lower resource (CPU/RAM) consumption is also key, but normally it is a secondary factor.

All of this advice sounds a bit trivial, so let me zero in on this point: only decide to keep a performance tuning change once the load generator tests shows it will benefit the end user or reduce resource consumption. Just because a code or config change benefitted some other environment doesn't mean it will benefit your environment. Furthermore, unsubstantiated guessing deflates confidence in a tuning project. Avoid it when you can.

Consider this example: a code change that buys you a 10ms response time improvement can do magical, transformational things to a system with 30ms response time, but the likelihood of making a big performance splash is pretty low if you apply that same 10ms-improvement-change to a system with 3000ms response time. Let the load generator metrics drive the bus; let them guide which code/config changes to keep.

But tuning guidance doesn't come solely from load generator metrics, because tuning conspicuously high CPU consumption out of the system is pretty important, too. CPU plays an even larger role than getting rid of CPU-heavy routines—it provides us with a handy yardstick, of sorts, that we can use to determine whether a system will scale. Chapter 6 provides very specific guidance on the matter, stay tuned.

Many different metrics, like those to be discussed in the P.A.t.h. chapters, contribute to deciding what change to keep: server-side verbose GC metrics, SQL response time metrics, micro-benchmark results. But ultimately, these changes should only be kept in the code base if the load generator results show benefit for the end user. Remember: load generator metrics drive the bus. CPU and RAM consumption metrics are important too—they ride shotgun.

The Backup Plan: Indirect Performance Assessment with Load Generator Metrics

The P.A.t.h. chapters show how to directly assess and single out what parts of the system are the slowest, and the four performance anti-patterns in Chapter 1 help you conjure up what changes are likely to improve performance. After deploying a change, if the load generator response time and throughput metrics (and resource consumption) show sufficient improvement, then you keep the change; otherwise you revert it (I do). You return to the P.A.t.h. Checklist to reassess the performance landscape after your brilliant change (because the landscape changes in interesting ways; check it out) and then you deploy another change and repeat. That's how tuning works. Mostly.

Before I got into a groove of using the P.A.t.h. Checklist and a modest tuning environment, discovering root cause was a bit tougher. I sought out ways to dislodge extra hints and clues from the load generator metrics. These "indirect" techniques are still helpful today, but they're much less necessary when you can directly observe performance problems with P.A.t.h.

But I will share some of these techniques here, because sometimes you don't have access to the system for a quick run through P.A.t.h., like when you're looking at someone else's load generator report. Likewise, sometimes it takes a second supporting opinion from a different metric to make the case for a particular optimization sufficiently compelling to the team, and convincing the team is a surprisingly large part of it all.

Large Payloads are a Red Flag

Logically interrogate the requests in your load test with the largest payloads, asking whether all of those bytes are really necessary? For example, have a look at Figure 3-1.

Label	# Samples	Average	Min	Max	Std. Dev.	Error %	Throughput	KB/sec	Avg. Bytes
/JPetStoreApp	36099	0	0	100	1.54	0.00%	149.8/sec	275.31	1882.0
/JPetStoreApp/shop/signonForm.shtml	36099	0	0	264	1.63	0.00%	149.8/sec	575.93	3937.0
/JPetStoreApp/shop/newAccountForm.shtml	36099	0	0	98	0.71	0.00%	149.8/sec	835.91	5714.0
/JPetStoreApp/shop/newAccount.shtml	36099	3	1	99	2.08	0.00%	149.8/sec	914.86	6253.7
/JPetStoreApp/shop/viewCategory.shtml	108290	1	0	99	1.43	0.00%	449.4/sec	1743.83	3973.6
/JPetStoreApp/shop/viewProduct.shtml	108288	1	1	99	1.35	0.00%	449.4/sec	1864.10	4247.8
/JPetStoreApp/shop/viewItem.shtml	108285	1	1	265	1.81	0.00%	449.4/sec	1782.34	4061.5

Figure 3-1. The rightmost column, Avg. Bytes, shows the size of HTTP responses for each process (leftmost column). Large outliers in this column (there are none in this figure) would be prime suspects for performance issues. Data from JMeter Summary Report.

The request with the most bytes in the Avg. Bytes column is newAccount.shtml, which has 6253.7 bytes on average. This number does not scare me, especially in relation to the Avg. Bytes numbers for the other rows in the table. But if one Avg. Bytes value is a few times bigger or more than the others—that's something to investigate. At a minimum, the extra bytes will take extra time to transfer, but it can get a lot worse. What if the system spent precious time assembling this large page? One time I saw this, a flood of disabled accounts (that no client wanted to see) were accidentally enabled and plumbed all the way from backend to browser, wasting a ton of time/resources. A separate time, not only was the client repeatedly requesting data that could have been cached on the server, but the XML format was needlessly large and no one cared enough to insure the payload was compressed. Zipping text files often shrinks a file by 90%. Use this to minimize the bytes transferred. If you application hails from 1999, perhaps the large size is from all the data being crammed onto a single page instead of having nice "first page / next page / last page" support.

Variability Is a Red Flag

One semi-obvious sign of a fixable performance problem in response time metrics is variability. In most cases, the more jittery the response time, the worse the performance. So, pay attention to the HTTP requests with the highest standard deviation (the Std. Dev column), showing highly variable response time. Of course, highly variable response time could be attributed to certain benign things, like occasionally complex data or other processing.

The three rows in Figure 3-2 show slightly different XSLT process transforming the exact same .xslt files with the same .xml files—you can tell by the exact same values for Avg. Bytes (the rightmost column) for each row. The data is from three different tests, each a 60 second steady state run with 8 threads of load, and each shows dramatically different performance.

Label	# Samples	Average	Min	Max	[res_ke...	Std. Dev.	Error %	Throughput	KB/sec	Avg. Bytes
03 Reinstantiate	61286	7	4	133	8	3.44	0.00%	1021.6/sec	7728.74	7747.0
05 Reinstantiate with DTMManager	76391	6	3	46	7	1.95	0.00%	1273.3/sec	9632.98	7747.0
10 Pool with DTMManager	319475	1	0	33	2	0.51	0.00%	5325.8/sec	40292.34	7747.0

Figure 3-2. *Results from load tests with three implementations of XLST processing. Data from jmeter-plugins. org Synthesis Report.*

Note that response time (Average) and standard deviation (Std. Dev.) are roughly proportional to each other. Throughput is inversely proportional to both of these. In other words, performance/throughput is great when both response time and variability are low.

If the very low .51 standard deviation with 400+% throughput improvement (1273.3 instead of 5325.8) is not compelling for you, perhaps the time series graphs of the same data in Figure 3-3 will convince you.

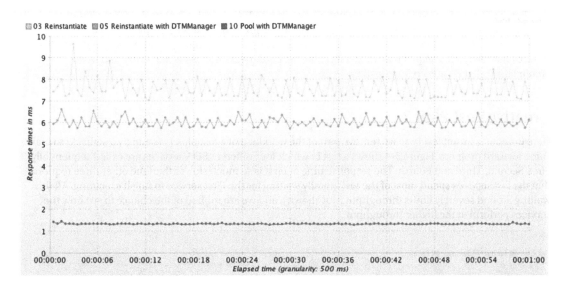

Figure 3-3. *From top to bottom, good, better, and best XSLT response time with 3 different XSLT API idioms. The faster the test, the less zig-zaggy variability.*

Extra variability in response time, as shown in the graphs here, can help point you to which system request could use some optimization. Variability in other metrics, like throughput and CPU consumption can help point out issues.

Creatively Setting Direction for Tuning

Yes, the load generator metrics should drive the bus and call the shots on what optimizations to keep. But also keep in mind there is much room for creativity here. This section provides a few examples of creatively restructuring tests and test plans to provide performance insights.

Two chapters in this book help you run load tests that model (aka imitate) a regular production load. Chapter 4 describes how to evolve a load script from an inflexible, stiff recording of a single user's traffic into a dynamic workload simulation. Chapter 5 helps you detect some performance characteristics of an invalid load test, which can help you avoid making bad tuning decisions based on invalid load generator data.

The gist, here, is that making the load test more real is a good thing. As preposterous as it might sound, though, there are a lot of fantastic insights to be gained by making your load test less real. Let me explain this insanity by way of two examples.

Creative Test Plan 1

Once upon a time I was on a tuning project and sure enough, I was wandering aimlessly in some Dark Environments. I was lacking security access or licenses (geez, it could have been anything) to all my favorite monitoring tools. How was I supposed to tune without metrics? This was a middle tier system, and I was trying to figure out whether all the time was being spent calling non-Java back-end systems or perhaps within the Java tier itself. To find out how fast the Java side was, I decided to comment out all calls to databases and back-end systems, leaving a fully neutered system except for entry into and exit from the Java architecture. It should have been pretty quick, since most of the real work was commented out, right?

Response time in a load test of the neutered system was 100ms. Is that fast or slow? For a point of comparison to this 100ms, the "do nothing" example in the previous chapter took just about a single millisecond. I had two different systems that did about the same thing (nothing), and one was dramatically slower. Ultimately, this helped us find and fix some big bottlenecks that pervaded every part of the architecture. That's some creative testing.

Creative Test Plan 2

Here is another example where we remove part of the workload of a test plan (seemingly a setback) to make some forward progress. Figure 3-4 shows a test in which four different SOA services are called sequentially: First, Second, Third and Fourth. The response time of First is so much slower than the other three requests that the fast services spend most of the test literally waiting for the First service to finish executing. All this waiting around severely limits throughput (not shown), and we are robbed of the chance to see how the services perform at the higher throughput.

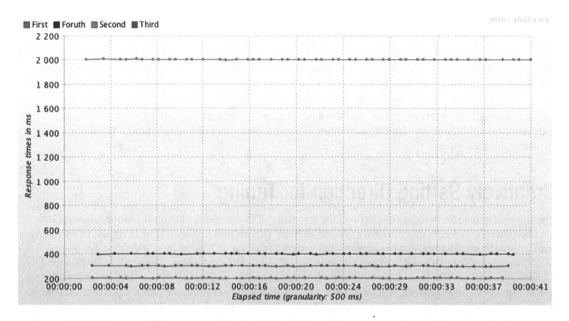

Figure 3-4. *The three fast services in this test mostly wait around for the slower service*

To get around this problem, we need to divide and conquer and enlist the help of another technician. One developer works on improving the performance of the slow service (First) by itself in one environment, while the three fast services are tested by themselves with a different load script in a different environment. Without this approach, the three fast services would miss out on testing at much higher throughput. When just about any environment can be a tuning environment, this is much easier. Having a single monolithic tuning environment makes this standard "divide and conquer" approach very difficult.

Tracking Performance Progress

Load generator response time and throughput metrics are so important, a weeks- or months-long tuning effort should march to their beat. Chapter 2 on Modest-sized Tuning Environments encourages us to complete more fix-test cycles every day, by using smaller, easier to manage and more accessible computing environments. As that testing happens, on each day of tuning you will have many more results, good and bad, and both the results and the test configurations become easy to forget because there are so many. To remember which changes/tests make the most performance impact, put the results of each test on a wiki page in a nice, clean table (such as in Table 3-2) to share with your team. Some wiki tables even allow you to paste a little thumbnail image (expandable, of course) of a performance graph right in a table cell. Put the most recent tests at the top, for convenience.

Table 3-2. Example of Load Test Results That Document Which Changes Had the Biggest Impact

Test ID	Start / Duration	Purpose	Results	RPS	RT (ms)	CPU
3	July 4, 6:25pm, 10 min	Added DB index	Huge boost!	105	440	68%
2	July 4, 11:30am, 10min	Test perf change to AccountMgr.java	performance improved	63	1000	49%
1	July 4, 9am, 10 min	Baseline		53	1420	40%

Remember that the role of the project manager of a performance tuning project is to be the four year old kid in the back of the family car, pestering us with the question, "Are we there yet?" Have we met our performance targets? A table like this one mollifies them, but it is for you too. I am not sure why, but wallowing in a performance crisis makes it very easy to forget the list of changes that need to migrate to production. Keeping the table regularly updated takes discipline, but the table documents and justifies (or not) money spent on better performance. It is essential.

At first, it seems like the rows of the table should compare results from one, unchanged load plan, applying exactly the same amount of load. Is this what we mean by an apples-to-apples comparison? Not quite. Instead, the table captures the best throughput to date for a particular set of business processes, regardless of the load plan, although this would be a great place to document changes in that load plan. Once your tuning efforts produce more throughput, you will need to dial in to your load plan more threads of load to get closer to your throughput goals.

To create a compelling performance tuning narrative, convert the requests per second (RPS) and date columns of this table into a "throughput improvements over time graph." This quickly communicates the ups and downs of your hard tuning work (Figure 3-5).

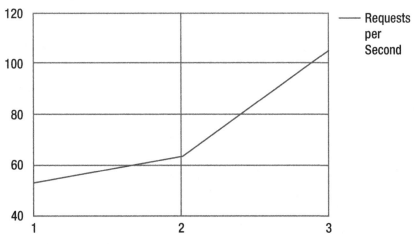

Figure 3-5. Use graphs like this to help communicate performance progress

Don't Forget

If you are stuck trying to fix a performance problem from the outside of the system using just resource consumption metrics and load generator metrics, it can become frustrating because there isn't enough information to identify which parts of the system need to be changed to fix the performance issues. This is where "Blame" metrics come into play. The P.A.t.h. Checklist, which we begin to use in Chapter 8, is specifically designed to fill this gap.

Also remember that one of the main purposes of modest-sized tuning environments is to get more fix-test cycles run in a single day, helping you make more performance progress. But more tests mean more results, and more results are easy to lose track of, so spend some time to find a nice wiki-like solution for documenting performance test results with your team, especially the project manager. To address all those issues surfaced in your performance tests, it helps to triage the problems so your team knows what to focus on.

There are 3 'parts' in this book and you've just finished the first one about getting started with performance tuning. Chapters 4, 5, 6 and 7 make up the next part, which is all about load generation—how to stress out your system in a test environment, as if it were undergoing the real stress of a production load.

What's Next

Getting started quickly tuning your system is a lot easier knowing that you can find real performance defects in just about any environment. Perhaps the next biggest impediment to getting started is the need to create load scripts.

The first part of the next chapter is a road map for getting up and going quickly with your first load script. The second part details how to enhance the first script to create/model a load that better resembles production.

PART II

Creating Load Scripts and Load Testing

CHAPTER 4

■ ■ ■

Load Generation Overview

We have all seen brief glimpses of concern during meetings and other discussions about whether your product will be able to handle a production workload. This is performance angst. It's like a big, red bubble of uncertainty that hovers over the team of an unreleased server-side software product.

Validating whether the architecture of a system performs well is a great way to pop the big, red bubble, and this chapter helps you get started doing that early in the software development life cycle (SDLC).

This chapter presents a two-part plan for creating load scripts, which are essential for understanding how your application behaves under stress. The first part of the plan helps you create your first script quickly, so you can understand the performance of your architecture.

The objectives of this chapter are:

- Understand that load testing the architecture of the system can be done with a very basic, no-frills load script with just a few business processes.

- Understand how tuning architecture-wide performance problems can provide quick performance boost to all business processes.

- Understand the load gen script enhancements required to more realistically model production business processes.

As if developing and testing software weren't hard enough already, learning how to generate load for a load test takes extra work. Here are just a few of the tasks involved in load testing:

- Creating and maintaining scripts for a load generator that apply stress to the system under test (SUT).

- Creating and maintaining a production-sized data set for your database.

- Creating and maintaining user IDs and passwords that your load test will use to sign on to the SUT.

Because of all this and other work, load testing 100% of the SUT's business processes is rarely, if ever done. It just is not cost-effective. My fall-back approach is to first load test the basic architecture with a simple First Priority script, and then later enhance the script to cover the most critical processes (the Second Priority script). Tuning your system with these two scripts educates you on the techniques required to make the other SUT business processes perform, as long as those processes are underpinned by roughly the same architecture, libraries, container, logging, the same authentication and authorization mechanisms, and so on.

This chapter provides an overview of the enhancements required to create First and Second Priority load scripts for your SUT. The First Priority script helps you quickly discover architecture-wide performance defects. The Second Priority script provides a little more workload realism. But first, there are some basic skills you will need for enhancing load scripts. We will cover those skills in the next section, which also includes a brief introduction to the load generator.

© Erik Ostermueller 2017

E. Ostermueller, *Troubleshooting Java Performance*, DOI 10.1007/978-1-4842-2979-8_4

The Load Generator

In Chapter 2 when we talked about the modest tuning environment, we said that a load generator is basically a network traffic generator used to see whether your SUT can handle the stress of a production-like load. It is possible to assemble a script manually, but they are normally created by a "record-and-playback" process. This section talks about all the enhancement you'll normally need to make after that initial recording has been done and it is tested.

Performance problems can be fixed in code or in data or in configuration, but there are also many things that need to be corrected inside a load script to best approximate your production workload.

Correlation Variables

Of all enhancements you make to a load script, creating *correlation variables* is used more frequently than any of the others, so everyone should be familiar with it. We create these variables in the load generator's scripting language. Then, you use the variable to hold a particular piece of data from the output of an HTTP request, so it can later be presented as an input parameter or perhaps in the POST body for a subsequent request.

Here is a quick example: let's say you used your browser to create a new customer in a web app, and the web app generated a new customer ID (custId=2360 in this case). Then you chose to update the customer details with a new street address. The "customer update" URL looked like this:

```
http://mybox.com/startCustUpdate?custId=2360
```

If you were recording this with your load generator, this URL would be recorded and saved into your script, verbatim. Days and weeks later when you run this script again, use of this particular custId of 2360 will be quite inappropriate as new custId values are created. As such, we don't want hard coded values like this encoded in the script files.

So, we carefully replace a hard-coded value with a correlation variable. You are responsible for updating the script to locate custId=2360 in the response, storing it in the correlation variable, and then using that variable on some subsequent request(s).

I went over that pretty quickly, so Table 4-1 summarizes the required changes.

Table 4-1. *Enhancements Required to Convert a Hard-Coded ID from Your System with a Correlation Variable*

Order	Load Script Behavior, as initially recorded	Enhancement required to add a Correlation Variable
1	The load script calls some URL to create a new customer.	no Changes.
2	The response to the previous request is returned to the load generator, and somewhere inside the response is the newly generated customer ID 2360.	Enhance the load script to locate/grab the newly created unique customer ID from inside the HTTP response. Store the value in a load script variable; CUST_ID would be a good name. With JMeter, you can accomplish this with a Regular Expression Extractor.
3	The load script submits a URL to update the customer details; the recorded cust ID 2360 is passed as a URL parameter: `http://mybox.com/startCustUpdate?custId=2360.`	Instead of passing the hard-coded cust ID of 2360, enhance the script to pass the number stored in the CUST_ID variable.

This correlation variable technique can and should be used in much more complicated load scripts, especially ones that are recorded. The trick for you, a troubleshooting trick, is to find exactly where in the scripts the technique needs to be applied. At a minimum, you should carefully consider applying this technique at least in these places in your scripts:

- As shown earlier, anywhere the server-side code generates a unique ID.

- Anywhere you typed in data or selected some option during the script recording.

- All parts of the application that store HTML hidden variables.

- Any other place, as with hidden variables, where JavaScript will move data from the output of one server-side request to the input of another.

- All places where CSRF tokens (`https://stackoverflow.com/questions/5207160/what-is-a-csrf-token-what-is-its-importance-and-how-does-it-work`) are used. These unguessable tokens are generated on the fly and stored in URL parameters. They make it tough for malicious web pages in one tab on your browser to execute requests to other sites (like your bank) in a different tab on your browser.

- When using JMeter, correlation variables are **not** required for JSESSIONID support. Instead, just make sure your JMeter script has one Cookie Manager.

To repeat, you are on the hook for finding where correlation variables need to be added. Start with the previous list and then yours is an ugly task after that: carefully assess whether each HTTP request is returning the right data, and add this technique as necessary. Another way to find the locations in the script for Correlation Variables is to think about all the data items you typed into the browser: searching for particular customer name, selecting a particular item to purchase, selecting that special manatee that you'd like to see in a singles bar.

Regardless of which load generator is used, correlation variables are critical to applying real production load. But if you're using JMeter, Chapter 7 provides a step-by-step guide to creating correlation variables based on an example JMeter .jmx plan in the github.com repo for this book. Look for `jpt_ch07_correlationVariables.jmx`.

Sequencing Steps in a Load Script

When you record a load script, you log on to the SUT, navigate around a handful of web pages executing business processes (like the "create customer" detailed earlier) and then you log off.

Load generators let you choose to play a recorded script once, or repeat the script a specific number of times, or repeat it for a particular duration of time. These options are available in JMeter in something called a *thread group*, which is also where you dial in the number of threads that should be replaying the script at a time. The default one that comes with JMeter is fine for basic tasks, but I really like the Concurrency Thread Group from Blaze Meter. It has a nice visual display of how quickly your threads will ramp up to full load. You can download it from jmeter-plugins.org.

Often, you want two (or more) sets of users executing different business processes at the same time. The not-so-obvious approach to scripting this is to make two separate recordings, one for each task, and then combine the two scripts into one. To do this in JMeter, create two separate thread groups in a new/blank/empty JMeter script, and perhaps name them A and B.

Then record and test the two load scripts separately, and copy all the activity in one into the A thread group and the other into the B.

There are some very compelling reasons for this organization. It lets you dial in, for example, a higher count of threads (more load) with one thread group and a lower volume with the other, which enables you reflect the actual volumes (roughly) used by your end users in production.

Furthermore, this helps you to model the activity of a web application that helps two different groups of people coordinate activity. Say, for example, one group creates orders for widgets while the other approves each order. It's pretty straightforward to implement one thread group that repeatedly creates orders. To implement the other thread group with the order approval activity, start by writing a script that repeatedly checks for new orders. Load generators, JMeter included, allow you to add conditional tests that would check in the response HTML for tags or attributes that indicate whether any new orders were created. Once a new order is detected, you can add the recorded steps to approve the order. See the JMeter If Controller and While Controller for details. The Loop Controller can be helpful, as well as the Setup and Teardown thread groups.

With these load generator basics under your belt, the next two sections lay out a two-step plan, "First Priority" and "Second Priority," that helps you balance the conflicting concerns of creating a load script quickly and creating a script that applies load somewhat realistically.

The First Priority Script

Performance angst is a real; consider these tough-to-answer questions: How many defects must we fix before our performance goals are met? How long will that take? Have we invested in the wrong Java architecture, one that will never perform well enough? Taunting project planners with these kinds of angst-ridden and unanswerable questions is a bit fun, try it some time.

The First Priority script helps you get up and going quickly to fix some of the most obvious performance defects quickly and to curtail some of this performance angst. This section provides a minimum check-list of "must have" load script enhancements, the ones required to convince you and your team of the validity of your load test. But also, look at the "First Priority" version as a cap: Once you have added these First Priority enhancements, stop. Focus on addressing the main performance defects uncovered by the P.A.t.h. Checklist in Chapter 8. Once you have the biggest issues under control, then you can jump to the Second Priority load scripting enhancements, later in this chapter, to finish off the job, and deliver some great performance.

Load Scripts and SUT Logons

The third performance anti-pattern discussed in Chapter 1 is "Overprocessing." It says, in part, that trying to load-test and tune a seldom-used business process is a waste of time. Instead, we should focus on the most important and frequently used processes.

When first creating a load script, it is very easy to run into this exact situation, and have your users log in and out of the system much more frequently than would happen in production.

So, the main goal of a First Priority load script is to make sure the SUT logon activity in your script is somewhat realistic, especially for SUTs with processing-intensive logons.

The intensive activity I'm talking about includes things like creating resources for a user session, single sign-on, authorization of hundreds of permissions, password authentication, and more. The more complex the logon process, the more care that needs to be put into getting your load script to emulate realistic logon scenarios. Why? Because it is a waste of time to tune something that isn't executed that often.

If you don't have good data from production to understand logon frequency (for example, that says how many logons happen system-wide in an hour as compared to other business processes), you will have to make a judgement call. In most systems, real users do not logon, perform two business processes, and then log off—a 1 to 2 ratio. Instead, they do more work before logging out. Perhaps users do 1 logon for every 10 other business processes is a more reasonable ratio. My numbers are completely rough here—in the end you need to make the call.

Using JMeter, one easy way to implement a roughly 1-to-10 ratio of logon to other business processes would be to use a Loop Controller (mentioned earlier) like this:

1. User logs on.

2. JMeter Loop Controller repeats five times.

    a. Business process 1 (often requires a handful of HTTP requests).

    b. Business process 2 (often requires a handful of HTTP requests).

3. Logoff.

Once your script has a somewhat realistic number of SUT logons as compared to other business processes, it is time to start applying load and using the P.A.t.h. Checklist to find defects.

Using the Same SUT User in Multiple Threads

The suggestions in this section can be done either the First or Second Priority load script—your choice. I have included them here because they are also logon issues, akin to the ones discussed earlier.

If your SUT disallows the same user to be logged in from two different browsers at the same time, you get logon failures when logging on two or more concurrent users in your load test.

To avoid this problem, you can read your user IDs and passwords from a text file, instead of hardcoding a single user ID in the load script. Picture a .csv file with one user ID and password per line. Here is Jmeter's component for reading from the file:

```
http://jmeter.apache.org/usermanual/component_reference.html#CSV_Data_Set_Config
```

Most load generators, including JMeter, have features to keep two threads from using the same user (really just a line of text) at the same time. Default behavior normally wraps to the beginning of the .csv file after that last record is read/used. You could create the .csv file by hand in a text editor, or you could manually export the results of a SQL statement like SELECT MY_USER_NAME FROM MY_USER_TABLE.

There are other motivations to use a more realistic number of users. Let's talk straight about this. Memory leaks and multi-threaded defects keep performance engineers very well employed, and generally, session management code is imbued with plenty of each type of defect. Load testing with one solitary SUT user ID, as with a freshly recorded and mostly unmodified load script, will not sufficiently stress your SUT's session management.[1]

Let's say your scripts are still logging on the same user repeatedly. If the SUT cached this user's permissions, your hit/miss ratio would be unusually large (one miss at app server startup followed by hit hit hit hit...), because that same user would always remain in cache while a load test was running. This means your SUT would always be taking the fast code path, loading the user's permissions from fast cache instead of the database (slower), and thereby underestimating the actual amount of processing.

When testing with just a single user, you also miss out on understanding how much memory is required to keep a large number of users in session. So, be sure to take a stab at how many users will be logged on at any one time, and include that many users in your load testing.

Lastly, while we are on the subject of users and session memory, don't forget to validate that your system's auto logout functionality works. You may want to make a one-off version of your load test and comment out all logoff activity. Run the test, wait 30 minutes or so (or however long it takes your SUT to auto-logout users) and verify that the session count drops down to zero.

---

[1]The kind of session management I am talking about uses these interfaces:
```
http://docs.oracle.com/javaee/7/api/javax/servlet/http/HttpServletRequestWrapper.
html#getSession--
https://docs.oracle.com/javaee/7/api/javax/servlet/http/HttpSession.html
```

Second Priority

To fully and accurately model business processes and workloads, you need a full-featured load generator like JMeter. However, as I said earlier, most performance defects can be found using the small subset of functionality I've detailed in the "First Priority" section. Of course there are critical bugs to be discovered with the "Second Priority" enhancements, but there tend to be fewer of them. Those defects also tend to be part of a single business process, instead of the SUT architecture as a whole.

The following various load script stages show a typical progression of enhancements that are made to scripts. Each stage shows enhancements you can make.

Load Script Stage 1

When you are at Load Script Stage 1, you have recently recorded a load script of yourself using a web browser to traverse the latest/greatest version of the SUT. Instead of being recorded, of course, perhaps you are working with a manually collected set of requests to an SOA. You have added to the scripts some processes that validate that all HTTP/S responses are error free and contain a few key bits of response text. A few correlation variables have been added to the script that will ferry a single data item (like a generated new customer ID or a shipping confirmation number) from the output of one HTML response to some needy web page in a subsequent part of the script's business workflow. Aside from that, few other modifications have been made.

Details

Load generation is a record-and-playback technology and it is a little bit fragile, like most things code generated. So keep a backup of the full, detailed HTTP log of the most recent record process; perhaps keep the most recent recorded log and load script in source code control. The log must include all the HTTP request URLs, any POST data, HTTP response codes, and for sure the HTTP response text. When subsequent "refinements" to the scripts break something, you can return to your pristine, pseudo-canonical original log of the entire conversation to figure out what went wrong.

In fact, with the right load generator, a simple but very careful text file diff/comparison between the canonical and the broken HTTP log will guide you to your directly to your functional script problems. There is an example of how to do this in JMeter in Chapter 7. Look for the section "Debugging an HTTP Recording."

Validating HTTP Responses

Validating that HTTP responses contain the "right" response data is critical. Cumulatively, I have wasted weeks and weeks of time analyzing and trusting tests whose responses were, unbeknownst to me, riddled with errors. So I implore you to please take some time to enhance your scripts to tally an error if the right HTTP response is absent. In addition, you should also check to see if the wrong response (exceptions, error messages, and so on) is present.

Chapter 7 on JMeter shows a feature that does this, called an Assertion. There are all kinds of JMeter reports and graphs that show error counts. When your JMeter Assertion flags an issue, those JMeter reports reflect those errors. Without this essential visibility, you, too, could waste weeks of time as I have.

Load Script Stage 2

Load scripts log many different users on in a single test, instead of the same user over and over. Hard-coded hostnames or IP addresses and TCP port numbers are replaced with variables, whose value you will change when using the scripts in a different environment. The script executes the business processes in the rough proportions seen in production.

Details

This script deals with workload proportions. To get a more production-like workload, you need to enhance your load scripts to execute various business processes in more realistic proportions. At a very high level, for many purposes, the breakdown of business processes is 70% inquiry, 30% update/insert/delete. All too seldom, our proportions are unrealistic, because we don't take the time to collect quality data from production to learn how often each type of BP is executed.

But before jumping head-first into finding which services are used the most/least in production (and tweaking your load scripts to apply load in those proportions), I recommend, first, to focus on a more imperfect approach, where you apply three or more threads of load (with zero think time) to all services. This is the 3t0tt mentioned in the introduction. Of course, we do this to shake the multithreaded bugs out of that old dormitory room couch. Getting more persnickety and perfecting realistic load proportions buys you two different things. One, you avoid wasting time troubleshooting problems with a never-to-be-used workload, and two, you find compatibility/contention problems with the go-to, production workload. Of course these are both important concerns, but in my experience, their incidence is noticeably eclipsed by that of the multithreaded bugs, which can be evicted from that lovely couch even with imprecise load proportions. Aim for the right workload proportions and load script think times, but start out with at least three threads of load with zero think time.

With JMeter, you implement your workload proportions/percentages by assigning different numbers of threads to your various scripts. For instance, if you wanted to model the 70%/30% split detailed earlier, you would start by recording two separate scripts, one for account inquiry and the other for account update. With a single simple script like this, all the HTTP requests are stored under a single JMeter Thread Group— the place where you specify the number of threads of load to apply, and the duration of the test.

So to implement the 70/30 workload proportions, you might start with a blank script with two blank Thread Groups that are siblings in the JMeter tree configuration. In the first Thread Group, you might assign seven threads, and the other three threads. Then you would copy/paste all the HTTP requests from the account inquiry into the Thread Group with the seven threads, and the account update HTTP requests into the other Thread Group.

This blog post details three alternative JMeter approaches to getting workload proportions right:

https://www.blazemeter.com/blog/running-jmeter-samplers-defined-percentage-probability

Load Script Stage 3

Instead of inquiring upon or modifying the exact customer or accounts used to record the script, the load scripts are enhanced to read account/customer/other identifiers from a data file and then input those to the SUT.

Details

In this stage, the load scripts move beyond reading user IDs from .csv files and on to reading other important data from .csv files, like customer and account data. But come to think about it, why bother? We are most certainly getting ahead of ourselves. Beefy-sized data must actually exist in these customer, account, and other tables before we spend the time to enhance our load scripts to apply traffic with .csv or data-driven samples.

Yes, this chapter is about load scripts, but I cannot keep myself from reminding everyone that my dog has the skills to design a great-performing database, if the row counts are low enough. Just about any query you can dream up will perform very well with fewer than about ten thousand records. So, "performance complacency" is high when row counts are low.

To get around this complacency, it seems like a nice idea to use the load generator scripts to drive the SUT to grow the table counts of your big tables. But unfortunately, the SUT, at this point in the tuning process, is generally so slow that you will start collecting retirement checks before the SUT adds enough data, even if left to run for many hours.

If this is the case, consider using JMeter as a quick RDBMS data-populator. Create a separate script that uses the JMeter JDBC Sampler (Figure 4-1):

```
http://jmeter.apache.org/usermanual/component_reference.html#JDBC_Request
```

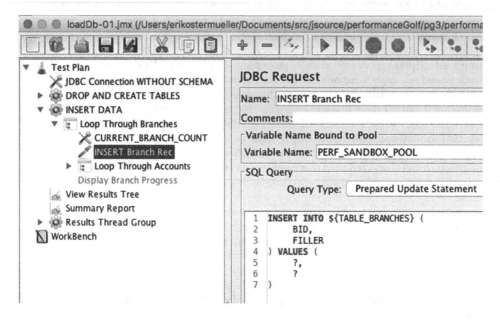

Figure 4-1. *JMeter can execute SQL using your JDBC driver. This file was used to populate more than 2 million rows in well under 10 minutes on my 2012 MacBook. This file,* loadDb-01.jmx, *is available in the src/test/jmeter folder in the jpt examples.*

It should fire multiple threads that execute massive numbers of INSERTs (carefully ordered to align with foreign key dependencies), with VALUES taken from either random variables:

```
http://jmeter.apache.org/usermanual/component_reference.html#Random_Variable
```

Or from .csv text files:

```
http://jmeter.apache.org/usermanual/component_reference.html#CSV_Data_Set_Config
```

And that concludes my little detour discussion of how to quickly get production-sized table counts. Let's get back to the original discussion, where the initial recorded load script inquires upon or modifies data from one or a few particular customers or accounts. Whatever data you used in the script recording is hard-coded in the load script file. Inquire on customer 101. Update the balance of account number 393900. The "101" and "393900" are stored in the script file.

Now that your table counts are sufficiently beefed up, you can enhance your load scripts to, for example, do account inquiries based on account numbers found in a .csv file. So instead of having 101 and 393900 in the load script file, those values are instead stored in the .csv file.

A great place to start is with a text file containing tens of thousands of different account numbers, one account number per line in the text file. This is the most common format of input file for load generators. But do not stop there with just a single column in your .csv file; there is some great low-hanging fruit here. If you add a second column in your .csv file with corresponding account balances, you can easily enhance the load generator script to validate that the SUT is returning the right balance for each inquiry.

Load Script Stage 4

As more tuning happens, the SUT becomes a formidable data-producing beast, and repeated load tests INSERT massive amounts of data into SUT tables. Don't forget to keep an eye on growing row counts, for reasons you might not expect:

- Yes, unrealistically large table counts are bad, but undersized table counts are bad, too. If your load test, which lasted 300 seconds, created 10 orders per second, there should be some concrete proof somewhere in that database. Shouldn't there be roughly 3000 (300x10) somethings INSERTed, that you can easily verify with SELECT COUNT(*) queries? As I mentioned earlier, invite skepticism in your load scripts, and capture table counts before and after your tests to prove that real work has been completed.

- Make sure table counts do not grow unreasonably large, causing performance to degrade unnecessarily. Spend the time to work with business analysts (the ones that have the most experience with your customer's data as well as regulatory requirements) and agree on retention requirements and how they impact table counts. If your live, primary database must keep ten years of transaction history, calculate how many records that translates into.

- Have a plan for keeping your tables trimmed to the right sizes. When tables get unreasonably large, we have generally restored a backup to a known state/size, but that takes time/management/discipline to acquire disk space for the backup file(s), time to actually create a backup (and keep it up-to-date). Ad-hoc DELETEs are simpler, but can be very slow because rarely is time spent to get indexes for ad-hoc queries in place, plus anything ad-hoc just sounds bad—it seems like you are unnecessarily introducing variance and risk. Yes, TRUNCATE is faster, but we are here to validate performance with realistic table counts. Zero is not realistic.

Invite Skepticism

I'd like to leave you with a small warning: invite skepticism from yourself and your coworkers as to whether the load generated by your scripts resembles that in production. Perhaps even block out some time on your team's calendar for a "load script skepticism" meeting. Of course this requires a lot of transparency, communication, and sharing of performance test data. Let me explain why this is important. The propeller on my colorful propeller-head beanie gets all excited and spins gleefully when watching a load script exercise the SUT. Look at all the load generator threads, like happy, little robots, navigating the pages of my big web application! How fun! The outward appearance is impressive. A freshly recorded load script, with dozens of captured URLs/parameters, appears to be impressive. Watching the script apply load for the first time also appears to be impressive, with busy log files and throughput and CPU metrics that really seem to be impressive.

But do not be fooled. Temper your excitement. Check for errors. Make a skeptical, sober assessment of whether all of that "activity" really approximates production-like workload. If your load script cranks out individual little results, perhaps a row in a database table to represent a single completed internet shopping order placed, then enhance your script to validate that final result. Even if free of errors and exceptions, your script might still not be returning the right data, say account balances for an account inquiry.

If your application is already in production, perhaps compare some production metrics (like hit counts per URL) to those captured during a load test.

Project Lifecycle Hints

The obstacles to getting started performance testing can be formidable. So many things take a lot of time: hardware purchase and setup, installation of the SUT, installation of monitoring tools, creation of the JMeter or other load scripts, creation of test users for the SUT, enhancing the data in the database to look more like production (especially the row counts), and so on. Just typing that list wore me out, but bear with me because I can show you some nice opportunities that most people miss.

Unfortunately, most of the previous prep work is required for a thorough performance vetting before you usher your SUT into production. But please understand that you must not wait for the perfect, unicorn-like performance environment to get started tuning. With the traffic of just a single lucky user (you), you can actually get started right now finding beefy and meaningful performance defects, ones that degrade performance in production. Here is one of those opportunities I mentioned: start using the P. and A. items on the P.A.t.h. Checklist (P=Persistence, A=Alien systems) in any "no-load" environment you can find, where just a few people are leisurely traversing the SUT. So if you are ready to make things faster without having to invest time creating load scripts, jump right now to Chapters 9 and 10.

This is the sole reason the P and A are in uppercase in P.A.t.h., and the t.h. are in lowercase. The lower case ones are for load testing only—specifically, they are of no real use in a no-load environment. When under load, they can help tune synchronization, find the exact location of heavy CPU consumers, identify inefficient garbage collection, and the list goes on. The uppercase ones are for both load and no-load environments. Typographically, the mixed case is not attractive, but perhaps it will be a subtle reminder to get started now finding performance defects with the P. and the A.

The overly simplified schedule in Table 4-2 shows how two developers could both be productive at the same time, working on performance. Java Developer 1 gets started tuning right away, while Java Developer 2 creates the load scripts.

Table 4-2. *Rough Sketch of a 9-Day Schedule for the Start of a Performance Tuning Project*

Days	Java Developer 1 / Tasks	Java Developer 2 / Tasks
1-3	Explore performance issues with "no-load" using the P. and A. parts of the P.A.t.h. checklist	Load Script / V1: record, parameterize and test it.
4-6	Load Script / V2: record, parameterize, and test it.	Load Script / V1: apply load with it, locate defects using P.A.t.h. checklist.
7-9	Load Script / V1: apply load with it, locate defects using P.A.t.h. checklist.	Fix and deploy performance defects.

Don't Forget

The rationale for deciding which script enhancements get first priority and which get second is pretty straightforward. Because there is neither time nor money to performance test and tune all business processes, performance problems will happen in production, even if you do everything "right." As a fall-back position, you should therefore first aim to tune the overall architecture, so that the dozen or so business processes that do get a thorough performance vetting become blueprints of how to write a component that both functions and performs.

Many ask whether tuning during development is even worth it, considering that the code base will have to be performance tested again after more code changes. I agree this is a small problem. A much more important question is ask, though, is whether our current architecture will crash and burn under the projected load in production. That's the often-forgotten question I want answered, and the "First Priority" script in the chapter is exactly the tool you need to answer it.

Furthermore, fixing one architecture-wide defect affects most business processes, which helps to maximize the performance impact of your fixes. The other side of the coin is, of course, that some script enhancements that are second priority might be necessary to stabilize the performance functionally critical business processes. You will have to use your own judgment here. Perhaps your most critical business processes deserve both first and second priority enhancements at the outset.

What's Next

As this chapter demonstrates, load tests take some time to prepare and run, so I'm always hesitant to scrap the results of a test. But sometimes, the results are so wrong, the there is no other option. The next chapter is your detailed guide on when to acquiesce and scrap the results of a test.

CHAPTER 5

■ ■ ■

Invalid Load Tests

Performance tuning can get pretty complex; just think about all the various places in an environment that could have performance problems:

- The configuration of your container (WebSphere or Spring Boot or whatever)
- The network
- The operating system
- The hardware
- The load generator

Don't let all of this overwhelm you. To minimize the complexity of it all, we developers should first focus on the performance of the part we're responsible for—the code. This is the Code First approach. A healthy percentage of performance defects are write-once-run-anywhere issues that will thrive, regardless of the environment.

The objective of this chapter is:

- Learn about a half dozen things to check to make sure your load test is generating a healthy, production-like load.

This chapter highlights environmental and other performance problems that invalidate the results of the load test you've worked so hard to create. Getting around some of these invalid tests (which are often caused by environment issues) requires a bit of creativity; let's have a look.

Network Issues

In chapter 2, I gave you this list of things that contribute to network performance:

- Firewalls
- Bandwidth limitation software (like NetLimiter) that runs as a security measure
- The HTTP proxy server, if accessing the Internet.
- The hardware—routers, content switches, CAT5, and so on
- Load balancers, especially their configuration to manage concurrency

© Erik Ostermueller 2017

E. Ostermueller, *Troubleshooting Java Performance*, DOI 10.1007/978-1-4842-2979-8_5

Any time one or more of these cause a performance problem, your load test is invalid and the results need to be thrown away. Rarely do we have the tools, access or expertise to troubleshoot network problems, so why do we bother in the first place? I recommend designing tests to eliminate network hops, when possible. Integration tests and other larger environments are fine places to finally learn about full network performance.

Sometimes I get painted into a corner and I'm forced to use a particular network segment that I suspect of having problems. If like me you don't have the tools or expertise (or access) to solve a network performance there is one option: indirect measurement. Say you suspect a particular network segment to have issues. If you apply load to a static web page, one known to be fast, and the response time end up being really poor, then you have an issue.

Container Issues

One of the reasons I am qualified to write a book on performance is that I have wasted so many hours of my life messing up the configuration for JDBC connection pools and web container thread pools.

One upside of these pools, and there really are many upsides, is that they can keep the OS or database from seizing up if your Java app goes haywire for some reason. The pool does this by capping the count of threads or connections to the max value set in the configuration. But if the caps are configured too low, the pools will limit performance. Knowing whether the caps are set too low should be an ongoing concern for you.

Keeping your eye on the right monitoring will show whether the caps have sprung into action at an inopportune time, robbing your system of precious throughput. But believe me I know, that takes a ton of work and steals your attention away from the primary focus (Code First). A simple guideline helps avoid all of this:

"Raise resource caps before tuning and lower them before production."

Yes, I'm a bit jealous that way back in 2006, Steven Haines first suggested this idea of raising all the caps in his book *Pro Java EE 5 Performance Management and Optimization* (Apress, 2006):

https://www.amazon.com/Pro-Java-Performance-Management-Optimization/dp/1590596102

You can also find this suggestion in this online article of his:

https://www.infoq.com/articles/Wait-Based-Tuning-Steven-Haines

But I think I've phrased it more succinctly, so you'll be more likely to remember it.

When I say raise these caps, I mean raise them very high, like a value of 1999 for both max threads and max connections in the JDBC connection pool.

An example will help here, I think.

The graph in Figure 5-1 shows the number of concurrent users, over time, that will run in a JMeter load test against the littleMock server configured with an 8-second sleep time. littleMock is a small Java server-side test application that we will talk more about in Chapter 8. Here is the URL: https://github.com/eostermueller/littleMock

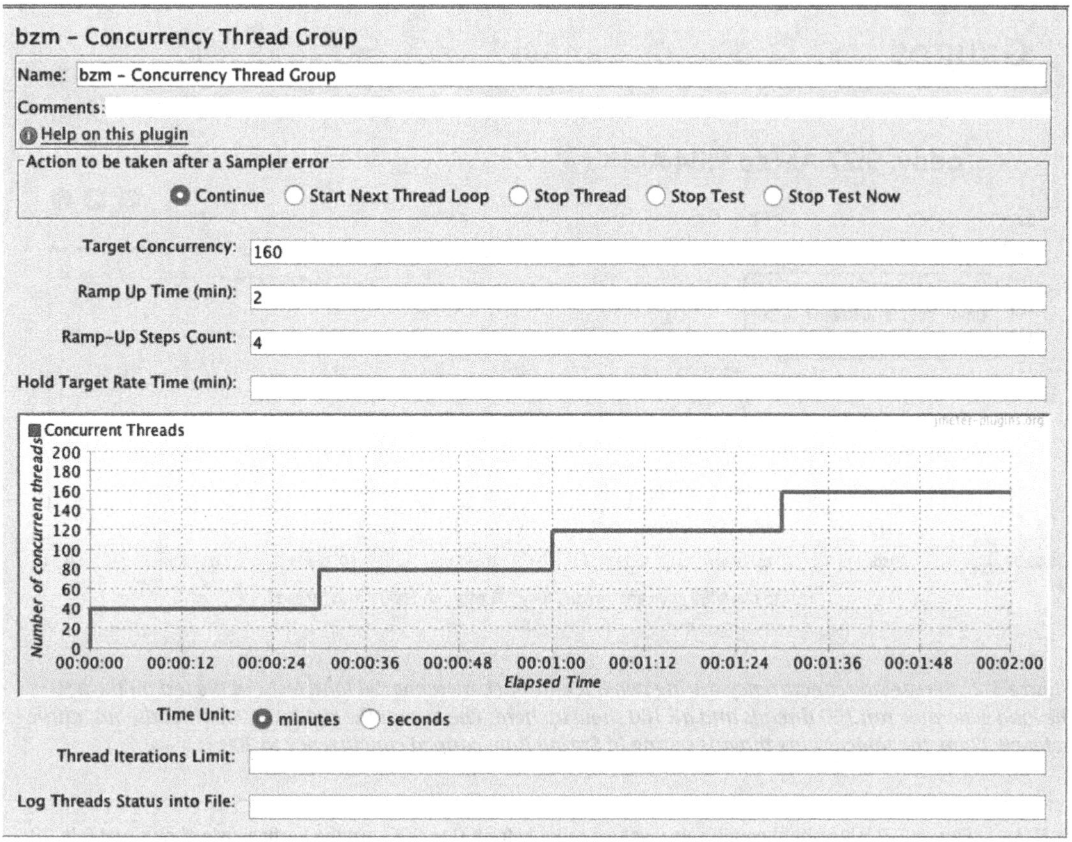

bzm – Concurrency Thread Group

Name: bzm – Concurrency Thread Group

Comments:

🛈 Help on this plugin

┌ Action to be taken after a Sampler error ─────────────────────────────
    ◉ Continue   ◯ Start Next Thread Loop   ◯ Stop Thread   ◯ Stop Test   ◯ Stop Test Now

Target Concurrency: 160

Ramp Up Time (min): 2

Ramp–Up Steps Count: 4

Hold Target Rate Time (min):

■ Concurrent Threads

Time Unit: ◉ minutes ◯ seconds

Thread Iterations Limit:

Log Threads Status into File:

Figure 5-1. Configuration for an incremental load test that shows the plan for applying load in a test. This thread group is a plugin for JMeter, downloadable from `https://jmeter-plugins.org/wiki/ConcurrencyThreadGroup/`.

The stair-stepped "ramp up" is the hallmark of an incremental load test, a test performance engineers have been using for many years. Each "step" adds 40 threads of load. At the one minute and 30 seconds into the test, all 160 users will be up and running. Got it?

Figure 5-1 shows what is referred to as a load plan, and I ran it two times. The first time, I used the configuration shown here. Just seconds after the first test finished, I changed the Target Concurrency from 160 to 240 and ran it again. So instead of 160/4=40 threads per step, the second test had 240/4=60 threads per step.

All that configuration is on the load generator side, aka the client side. To check out the number of threads on the server-side (the count of active threads is called the *concurrency*), in Figure 5-2 I used Glowroot, an open source APM tool from glowroot.org.

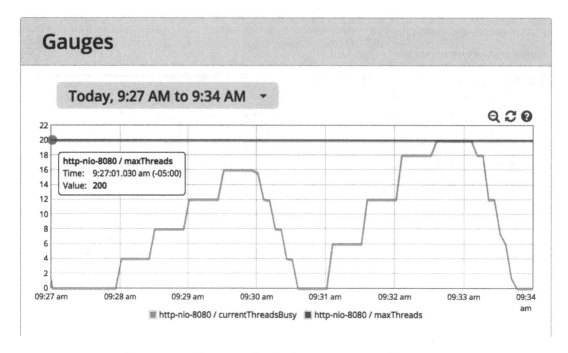

Figure 5-2. Server-side concurrency during two back-to-back incremental load tests. In the test on the left, the load generator ran 160 threads and all 160 show up here. The test on the right ran 240 threads, but a little before 9:33am, the tomcat max threads setting in Spring Boot capped concurrency to 200.

■ **Note**   Figure 5-2 talks about concurrency values roughly from 0 to 200, but the vertical axis shows just 0 to 20, why the discrepancy? The roundtangle in the upper left shows that the actual value of maxThreads is 200. Glowroot "auto-scaled" the vertical axis and ended up with 0-20.

Avoiding this cap problem in the test on the right would have been simple, had I followed the recommendation to "raise caps before tuning, lower them before production." Since the SUT is littleMock, which runs under Spring Boot and Tomcat, I could have easily added this property:

```
server.tomcat.max-threads=1999
```

to the application.properties file, as documented here:

```
https://docs.spring.io/spring-boot/docs/current/reference/html/common-application-properties.html
```

Don't forget to do the same for JDBC connection pool settings. Most importantly, before you move the app into production, you need to lower the caps to avoid the seizing/haywire case I mentioned earlier. How much lower? Lower them to a point that is about 25% above the number of threads or connections you will use in production. For example, if your load tests show (using the metrics in Figure 5-2) that you will use no more than 240 threads in production, set the cap to 300 (1.25×240).

So load tests that bump into resource caps are invalid tests, but now you know how to easily avoid this problem: raise resource caps before tuning and lower them before production.

Insufficient Warmup

Performance engineers could argue without end about the right amount of time required to warm up a system before running a steady-state load test. 5 minutes? 15 minutes? For me, every system is different. I warm up a system until its metrics stabilize for a few minutes. If metrics never stabilize, then the length of the warmup is irrelevant. In that case, one thing I do is simplify the load scripts to isolate which part of the workload contributes most to the chaos.

So, if you are making performance assessments before metrics like response time and throughput stabilize, you are looking at an invalid test.

Maxed-Out Hardware Resources

It should go without saying that it is your job to make sure there is enough CPU/RAM on your systems when you test. Keep in mind that it is easy to forget to check. It is also helpful to look at the two main subdivisions of CPU. Kernel CPU (aka system CPU) is the percentage of CPU used by the operating system. User CPU is the percentage of CPU used by our Java and other applications, including the database. Some people think that 0% kernel CPU is achievable. That would be grand, but I sure don't know how to make that happen. Generally, if kernel CPU is 10% or less than the user CPU, there are no issues. So if user CPU is 75%, then 7.5% or less of kernel does not raise any red flags. When kernel CPU is much more than this, it's time to get a system admin involved—because this load test is probably invalid. When working in virtualized environments, sometimes adding a CPU or two can fix this.

Capturing metrics from remote systems is much easier these days. Having those metrics graphed right there in your load generator is a great gentle reminder to pay attention to them. PerfMon will do that for you. It is the tool we used in Chapter 2 to graph CPU of individual PIDs. Here is the link again:

```
https://jmeter-plugins.org/wiki/PerfMon/
```

The JMeter plugin Composite Graph will even display CPU (and other environment metrics) on the exact same graph as JMeter metrics, like response time and throughput.

```
https://jmeter-plugins.org/wiki/CompositeGraph/
```

When your test eats up all the CPU/RAM, you have a few choices. Either add more CPU/RAM, or use the P.A.t.h. Checklist to lower consumption. That discussion begins in Chapter 8.

By now, you have probably figured out there is some overlap in my approaches. In Chapter 3, of the three types of metrics, one type is for understanding resource consumption. In this chapter, I'm saying too much consumption makes a test invalid. There are no subtle differences between these two—just two reminders to have your eye on consumption.

The same thing goes for functional errors in load tests. I mentioned these in Chapter 4 on load scripts and again here, when talking about invalid tests. I believe the message is warranted in both places, but I wanted to make sure you know these are two references to the same issue.

Virtualization Issues

I love the idea of virtualization—being able to create a new "guest" machine (for load testing, of course) whenever I need one. But the performance metrics for the "parent" VM that runs the whole show are often off-limits for mere mortals like me. How can you know whether the guest is healthy if you don't have access to the metrics?

Gil Tene of Azul Systems (https://www.azul.com/) has the answer. He wrote a little Java utility called jHiccup. The tool is based on an interesting question: If you schedule a thread to sleep for a specific number of milliseconds, will that thread wake up on time if the entire operating system is experiencing pauses or hiccups? The answer is no, the thread will not wake up on time, and jHiccup measures the differences between expected and actual wake times for threads.

Look at this URL for the latest releases of jHiccup:

https://github.com/giltene/jHiccup/releases

and the home page is here:

https://github.com/giltene/jHiccup

Download and unzip the release zip file to a new folder. Then cd to the same folder as jHiccup.jar and execute the following:

```
java -javaagent:jHiccup.jar="-d 4000" org.jhiccup.Idle -t 30000
```

The console will appear to hang for 30 seconds (the -t parameter). When it finishes, it will have created a file like Figure 5-3; this will be located in the current folder and named like this: hiccup.170709.1303.20680.hlog.

```
#[Logged with jHiccup version 2.0.7]
#[Histogram log format version 1.3]
#[StartTime: 1499623397.272 (seconds since epoch), Sun Jul 09 13:03:17 CDT 2017]
"StartTimestamp","Interval_Length","Interval_Max","Interval_Compressed_Histogram"
4.050,5.001,0.393,HISTFAAAAEF42pNpmSzMwMAgywABTBDKT4GBgdnNYMcCBvsPEBEOFi4RHjE5GSE7I7I
9.051,5.000,0.426,HISTFAAAAEF42pNpmSzMwMAgzwABTBDKT4GBgdnNYMcCBvsPMBkhESkVPgU+CTGZCY:
14.051,5.000,0.393,HISTFAAAAD542pNpmSzMwMAgzQABTBDKT4GBgdnNYMcCBvsPUBk2Di42Hh4xPjE+H:
19.051,5.000,0.393,HISTFAAAAD942pNpmSzMwMAgwwABTBDKT4GBgdnNYMcCBvsPUBk2DgEeLh4eHj4uF:
24.051,5.000,0.573,HISTFAAAAEB42pNpmSzMwMAgywABTBDKT4GBgdnNYMcCBvsPEBEWDg4RKTkpDQE1F:
```

Figure 5-3. *Output from jHiccup. The third column, Interval_Max shows the maximum time in milliseconds over the last 5 second interval (second column) that your OS was paused. The last measurement of 0.573ms is the largest pause in 30 seconds.*

In the Introduction, I mentioned the need for "plug-it-in-now" tools so we can more quickly diagnose and fix performance issues. jHiccup is a great example of that. Yes, you do have to download a jar file, but outside of that it is easy. You don't need security/access for the parent VM. You don't need to restart any programs to capture the metrics.

Getting more detailed metrics, like actual pause times instead of just the Interval_Max ones, takes a bit more work (using jHiccupLogProcessor). But that work is only necessary if the max times show concern. Personally, I'd be concerned if the parent VM regularly paused my guest for more than 2% of the time. So if any of those Interval_Max times regularly move from the current 0.573 in Figure 5-3 to 100 or more, then I'd be concerned (100ms / 5000 interval = 2%) and I'd do two things:

1. Research how to use jHiccupLogProcessor to get and graph the detailed data instead of just the max values above.

2. Pass along my findings to the administrator of the VM parent, the one who has access to all the performance metrics.

jHiccup measurements are also sensitive to garbage collection (GC) pauses. Chapter 12 will talk more about the tools used for assessing GC health, but if you need a second opinion that GC pauses are slowing things down, jHiccup is your tool. My example, above, plugs jHiccup into a do-nothing program named org.jhiccup.Idle. You will need to seek out the alternate syntax for to plug jHiccup into the JVM whose metrics you're questioning.

The point of this story is that unhealthy virtualization infrastructure is yet another cause of an invalid load test, whose results really need to be discarded.

Generally, I would only spend the time collecting jHiccup data if no explanations on the table (or in the P.A.t.h. Checklist) could explain a particular performance problem.

Wrong Workload Issues

The section delves into a little more detail on the Performance Anti-Pattern Number 3:

> **Overprocessing**: The system is doing unnecessary work and removing that work provides measurable performance benefit. One example is retrieving too much data, where most of the data is discarded. Another example is including in your load test the wrong resource-hungry use case—one that is seldom used in production.

I am very thankful for developers who take the time to create both data and tests for an application's complicated edge cases. Thank you. We need exactly these kinds of tests, these reminders, to show the functionality we expect from the system.

All that said, it is a waste of time to pummel your system with edge cases (and try to tune them) if just a slow trickle of such cases will ever traverse your production system. Often, these edge cases rear their heads unexpectedly. Once, after performance on a system degraded unexpectedly and severely, I scoured the source code control system for any unexpected code or other changes. No obvious problems there.

After ten painfully unfruitful days of troubleshooting, we re-evaluated the load generation scripts for some of these pesky edge cases and we discovered one anomaly. The problem was not with the functionality we included in our load generation script (which is indeed something to watch out for), it was with the data.

What we found was that the average number of bytes for one of the HTTP responses (as shown by the load generator) was about 10 times larger than the rest. Why was one so much larger than the others? It turned out that a setting on our backend SUT was inadvertently changed and it started returning HTTP inquiry results for many hundreds of inactive (and unexpected) accounts, as well as the expected active ones. Oops. Sanity-checking the average sizes (in bytes) of the various parts of your load script is important for finding inefficiencies, so I also mentioned this in the chapter on Metrics—there is a nice screenshot there (Figure 3-1) if you need some detail to get the full picture.

The moral of the story is that edge cases show up not just in the functionality you choose to include in your load script, but also in your system's data and in other places. For example, performance almost always suffers when too much logging (like log4j) is turned on, and having so much logging could also be considered one of these edge cases. Sometimes the problem is you. You find performance defects, you deploy code, and you run some load tests and then run even more load tests until you have run the "add widget" use case 100 million times. If these repeated load tests make the count of records in the database very unrealistically high, then you, the load generator, are the problem. Problems can come from the funniest places.

So, take some time to understand the various types of traffic in your production workload. If you are not really sure about the load of each business process, how will you know what functionality should be in your load test? For example, if fewer than 1% of your account deposit traffic includes more than 10 items (checks, cash), it is a waste of time to hammer the system with deposits with thousands of checks from that one remaining pizza joint in town that still accepts checks. I bet they listen to 8-track tapes, as well.

There are a few angles here:

- Don't waste time tuning use cases that are seldom used.

- Validate that the main use cases in production are also in your load script. If you think you know which use cases are there, what data do you have to convince others?

A large percentage of performance defects that you would normally find in production can be found even when running a single business process with a few threads of load (like 3t0tt), without any of the other business processes in the system. So I consider a "single business process" load to be a "valid" test, even though it does not contain all the business processes in the production workload.

Of course there will be occasional issues where you can only reproduce a performance defect when two particular business processes run in the same workload—consider two processes that read/write to the same rows in a RDBMS table, like "Check order status" and "Update order status." Many applications use tables to monitor the state of a process in a workflow. These situations must also be load-tested together.

Lastly, I'd like to close this section on "Wrong Workload Issues" by mentioning a few other types of processing to watch out for. Sometimes when you are load-testing on a machine, that machine is not 100% "yours." Automated installs run in the background, backup jobs kick off unexpectedly, and who knows when virus scanners kick in.

If you suspect any of these, don't settle for traditional CPU metrics that show just CPU or CPU-Core level CPU consumption. Instead, take the time to find and graph the CPU consumption of each PID using PerfMon, as we did in Chapter 2 for the modest tuning environment.

https://jmeter-plugins.org/wiki/PerfMonMetrics/#Per-Process

Load Script Errors

When performance tuning, you are always rubbing shoulders with some interesting problems (my wife says that I am an interesting problem). Why is performance worse when nothing (seems to have) changed? Why do these two metrics contradict each other? Likewise, you have got to pack a lunch when trying to find the cause of a full catastrophic failure, when a JVM process dies—so that is kind of fun too. Jumping onto a sweaty wrestling mat with these kinds of problems is my kind of fun. But it is much less enjoyable to be bogged down with mundane, functional failures.

In fact, there is so little joy that ignoring functional errors, unfortunately, comes second nature to me. I often say to myself, "I didn't see any errors when recording the load generation script, so how could there be a problem when I'm replaying that same script?"

Several years ago, we were struggling to find out why performance was so horrible. I was refactoring a load script to read usernames and passwords (they were test passwords. honest, they really were) from a .csv file so that my load generator script would not log on to the SUT with the exact same user for every thread. We wanted to know whether the SQL caching code was working (and performing well). After I refactored the script, the load test successfully logged on hundreds of users (or so I thought) and response time was blazingly fast and throughput doubled (or did it triple?). I announced the great results to the team and a celebration ensued.

But what actually happened was that I forgot to put the right two-character prefix on the users' IDs in my newly-created .csv data file, so zero of my users even logged on successfully, and zero of the business processes I had scripted were getting put through their paces. When I corrected the user names in the data file (duh), our original crappy performance was fully restored. Yeah! Performance testing is littered with bittersweet, dubious victories like this. As such, I had been load testing a lot of SUT failure, which is certainly not a priority in our Grand Focus.

So please learn from my mistakes, spend the time to enhance your load scripts to not only check for functional errors in each HTTP or other SUT response, but also make sure that the correct response is present. I will repeat this because it is very important: Your load script must check for the absence of common errors, ("exception" and "error" and other error message text) as well as the presence of the expected results, like an account balance on an inquiry, or a generated unique ID when creating an order. Richard Feynman once said "The first principle is that you must not fool yourself—and you are the easiest person to fool."

Make skepticism in the performance results a team sport that will build team confidence in the whole tuning process. Error counts should get first-class billing, right alongside throughput and other metrics.

A reviewer once wrote the following about the Pixar animated movie "Wall-E":

"These robots, beings not usually considered to have emotions ... must convince the audience of their souls and personalities."

As performance engineers, it is our job to convince our audience (our dev/QA team and our client) that the load test is real, that the load test inflicts stress on the SUT very much like the stress in production. Why? So the team will be motivated to fix any performance problems that arise. Sometimes, I am so skeptical of load test results (really, just afraid of all the embarrassment) that I will count the rows in important SUT RDBMS tables. Generally, I pick the largest ones that change the most. I will then make sure that before-test and after-test table counts jibe with the throughput results from the load generator. For example, say that the load generator reported that ten "Create new account" processes executed every second of a 300 second test. After the test, I would then make darn well sure that the account table contained about 3,000 more records than it did before the test started.

You might think that these kinds of errors from the SUT can be detected and managed by getting the load generator to log the full HTTP request and response for all threads. I know I did, at one time. Chapter 7 shows that too much load generator logging kills load generator performance and skews the results of the entire test. This much verbosity is invaluable for troubleshooting problems with playback of a single thread, but gets in the way otherwise.

When your load generator is tallying test results, separating the wheat from the chaff, the success from the failure, most load generators provide a way for us specify what SUT responses indicate an error. I strongly encourage use of both techniques to flag errors. Chapter 7 will show you how to

- Flag errors because an important part of an HTML response (like an account balance on a balance inquiry) is missing.

- Flag errors when text for an exception shows up in an HTML response.

- Provide high-level overview of how many errors show up and when.

How much validation to add is up to you. I hope the earlier vignette shows the problems with too little validation that happen all too frequently. But adding too much validation takes up time that could be spent optimizing code. Too much validation can also cause load generator performance to degrade. For instance, validating 20 different data items on a single page is probably overkill for a performance test (but reasonable for a functional test). I've had no problems with load generator overhead while validating 3-5 data items per HTTP response while running 1,000 requests per second, generating load from a single, modern desktop-class machine. If you have overwhelmed the CPU/RAM of a load generator at this volume, then that is a problem worth your time to fix.

When a load test applies 3t0tt, it is applying three threads of load with zero think time. In my experience, this is more than enough load to flush out most errors in multi-threaded code. The classic signature of this kind of a problem is a small but steady flow of errors. If your tests have regularly have garden variety functional errors, your ability to detect multi-threaded errors will be diminished or gone altogether. Aim for zero errors in your load tests.

Don't Forget

Imagine a college entrance exam that was printed in a font so small that the test takers, even with young eyes, were squinting at their desks for the duration and could not really read the tiny print. We would call that an invalid test, and no one in their right mind would even look at the students' results, much less make life-changing college entrance decisions based on them. The lesson here is this: discard the results of invalid tests.

Likewise, before making decisions based on the results of a load test, you must first assess whether a test is valid, whether it approximates the conditions in your production environment closely enough. This chapter explored a number of criteria that, in my experience, make a test invalid. The validity of every single performance test should be carefully assessed before acting upon its results.

What's Next

Does your system scale? When was the last time you checked? Chapter 6 provides a specific and novel formula for testing scalability. It is so easy to follow, you can measure for scalability every day of the week, to help keep performance angst at bay. The test is called the Scalability Yardstick.

■ ■ ■

## CHAPTER 6

A Scalability Yardstick

Few systems achieve scalability these days, because scalability tests are run so infrequently. This chapter shows how to run a scalability test that is so quick-and-easy, you can run it every day of the week, providing much needed guidance to finally steer your SUT toward scalability.

The objectives of this chapter are:

- Learn a formula to determine exactly how many threads or load to apply so you can easily see how close your system is to scaling.

- Learn how to recognize when test data shows you have reproduced a performance problem that is an impediment to scalability.

Trying to fix a defect that you can't reproduce is daunting, and performance defects are no exception. This chapter walks you through a methodical approach to reproducing defects that keep your system from scaling. Chapter 8 is where we start using the P.A.t.h. Checklist to diagnose and fix the problems.

The Scalability Yardstick is a variant of the good old incremental load plan, often lost in the annals of performance best practices. This variation is built to show us exactly how much load to apply and how to recognize when we have reproduced a problem, an impediment to scalability.

Scalability is a system's ability to increase throughput as more hardware resources are added. This definition is accurate and concise, but it is also painfully unhelpful, especially if, like most technicians, you are looking for concrete direction on how to make your system scale.

To fill this void and provide a little direction, I use the following load test that I call the Scalability Yardstick:

1. Run an incremental load test with four equal steps of load, the first of which pushes the app server CPU to about 25%.

2. When this test produces four squared, chiseled steps of throughput, the last of which pushes the CPU to 100%, the SUT is scalable.

Let's start by seeing how to use the load generator to create a load plan for the Yardstick, and then we will talk about how scalability actually works. It takes a little bit to explain this approach, but it becomes second nature after you do it a few times.

Creating a Scalability Yardstick Load Plan

The Scalability Yardstick says that your first step of load needs to push the SUT to consume about 25% of the CPU. How many threads of load will it take to reach 25%? You need to run a quick test to find out. This essentially calibrates the Yardstick to the SUT and this environment.

The JMeter test plan shown in Figure 6-1 asks the question, "At which of these 10 steps will the SUT CPU consumption reach 25%?"

© Erik Ostermueller 2017
E. Ostermueller, *Troubleshooting Java Performance*, DOI 10.1007/978-1-4842-2979-8_6

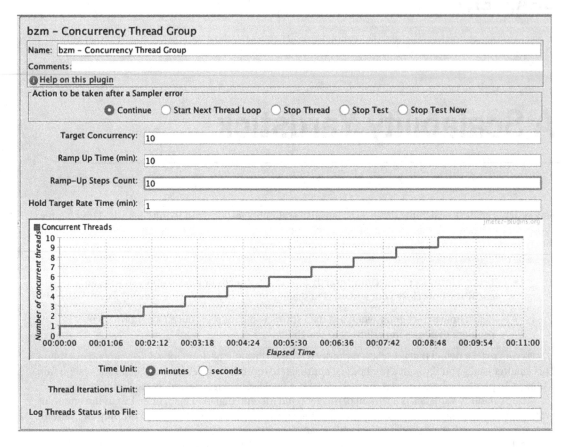

Figure 6-1. *JMeter load plan used to see how many threads of load it takes to push the application server CPU to 25%*

Here are some brief instructions for doing this:

1. Install JMeter from jmeter.apache.org.

2. Install the Concurrency Thread Group using one of these two options:

    1. Install the Plugin Manager into JMeter by downloading a jar from here:

        `https://jmeter-plugins.org/install/Install/`
        into the JMETER/home/ext directory. Restart JMeter and then select
        Custom Thread Groups from the Options / Plugins menu.

    2. Download the zip file directly from here:

        `https://jmeter-plugins.org/wiki/ConcurrencyThreadGroup/`
        ...and unzip the contents into JMETER_HOME/lib and lib/ext folders, as
        they are in the zip file.

3.   Restart JMeter.

4.   Add the Concurrency Thread Group using the menu options in Figure 6-2.

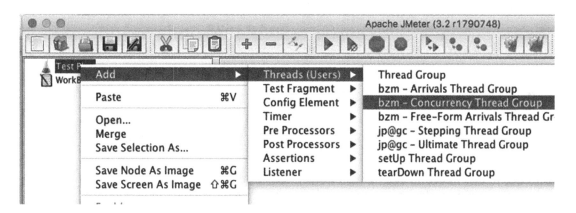

Figure 6-2. *Adding the Concurrency Thread Group to a new JMeter load plan.*

5.   Dial in the 10-10-10-1 options in Figure 6-1.

Figure 6-3 shows the results of this short little calibration test, or at least the very first part of it. By the time the test reached just the second of 10 steps, I had seen enough, so I stopped it.

The load plan in Figure 6-1 shows that each step of load should have lasted about 60 seconds, and it did. We know this because the black line (below Active Threads Over Time) travels at a Y axis value of 10 for 60 seconds, then at 20 for the rest of the test. The autoscaling on this graph is a big confusing. The (x10) that is displayed in the legend means the 10 and the 20 are magnified by 10 on the graph, and are actual values of 1 and 2 instead of 10 and 20.

The yellow line in Figure 6-3 shows that the first thread of load pushed the CPU to about 15% and the second thread (at the 60 second mark) pushed the CPU to about 28%. The whole purpose of the test was to push the SUT to at least 25%, so I stopped the load generator after the step that first hit 25%. The calibration is complete.

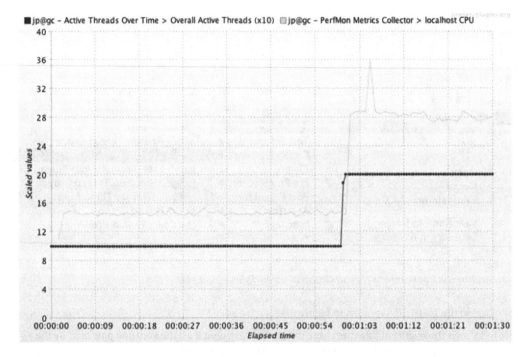

Figure 6-3. Discovering how many threads it takes to push the CPU to 25%. This graph with two different metrics (CPU and active threads) was made possible by Composite Graph and PerfMon, both from jmeter-plugins.org. Learn how to use them in Chapter 7 on JMeter.

The Yardstick says we need "four equal steps of load, the first of which pushes the CPU to about 25%." Since two threads pushed the SUT to about 25% CPU, 2 is the size of each of the four equal steps in the Yardstick. We now know enough to create our Yardstick load plan.

Interpreting Results

The calibration test is complete, and you know about how many threads of load it takes to push the SUT to about 25% CPU consumption. I took the result of 2 from the Calibration Test and put it into my load plan to create a Scalability Yardstick test with steps of 2-4-6-8. Every minute, two threads of load are added; for the last minute of the 4-minute test, eight threads are running. Staying at a single level of load for 1 minute works when a single iteration of your load script lasts, say, less than 10 seconds with zero think time. This is a very rough guideline to make sure your script repeats at least several times (six in this case) for each step of load.

Figure 6-4 shows the results of the test. This part takes a little thinking, so get ready for this: the x100 in the legend (top of screenshot) mean the black line values of 200, 400, 600 and 800 really mean 2, 4, 6, and 8 load generator threads. The jmeter-plugins.org auto-scale feature caused this. Read here for more details: https://jmeter-plugins.org/wiki/SettingsPanel/

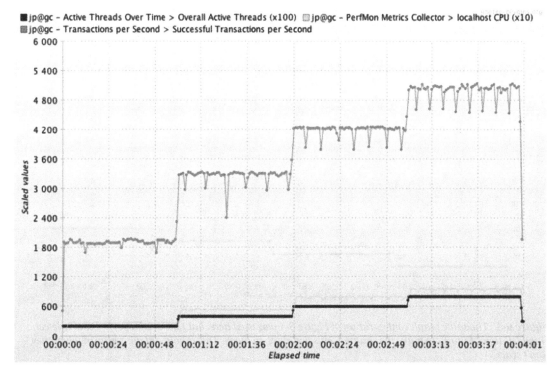

Figure 6-4. *The blue line shows squared, chiseled steps of throughput created by the Scalability Yardstick, meaning that this system will scale. To produce this graph, the Throughput metric was added to the same graph component used in Figure 6-3.*

The Scalability Yardstick aims to find the SUT's throughput at 25%, 50%, 75% and 100% CPU consumption, and Figure 6-4 shows that. The blue line shows these four throughput landmarks are (roughly) 1800, 3300, 4200 and 5100 requests per second. Because each of the four steps generates a nicely squared chunk of throughput, this particular SUT is very well tuned.

By contrast, Figure 6-5 shows an SUT with a performance defect. See how the squared, chiseled steps of load have been replaced by limp, faltering throughput?

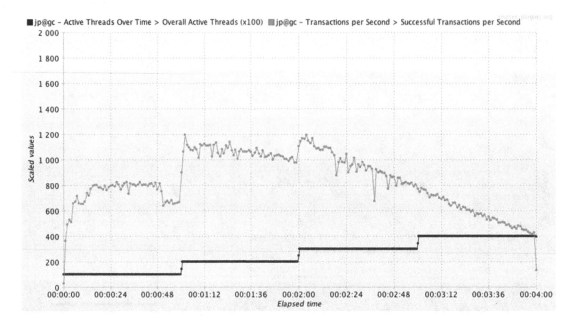

Figure 6-5. *The same graph configuration of Figure 6-4 was used here, but I induced a performance defect (high GC times I think) to make the squared, chiseled steps go away. This is how systems perform when they don't scale.*

To those who are hesitant to push the CPU to 100%, how else will we discover whether the system is capable of using an additional CPU, should one become available? We know that pushing the CPU to 100% is not going to hurt the machine, because anti-virus software has been doing that to desktop workstation CPUs for a decade.

Here are a few quotes from other Java performance authors that show that this approach is on the right track, especially the part about pushing to 100% CPU:

> *"The goal is to usually keep the processors fully utilized."*
>
> *Java Concurrency in Practice*, Brian Goetz, et al. (Addison-Wesley, 2006) p. 240

> *"For a well-behaved system, the throughput initially increases as the number of concurrent users increases while the response times of the requests stay relatively flat."*
>
> *Java Performance*, Charlie Hunt, Binu John (Addison-Wesley, 2011), p. 369

Driven by the black line in Figure 6-4, each of the four steps in the Yardstick acts as a request for the SUT to leap. The four steps in the blue throughput line shows that the SUT responded with a leap for each load step. Take the utmost care in noticing that a nice square, step/leap of additional CPU consumption (yellow) was required at each step. When the load generator said to leap, the SUT leapt, and only a well-tuned and scalable SUT will leap like this.

Of the four CPU landmarks in the Scalability Yardstick, we care the most about the 100% landmark. We ultimately want to know whether the SUT can utilize 100% of this CPU and 100% of all the subsequently added CPUs to produce more and more throughput leaps when the load generator applies additional steps of throughput. This is scalability.

Let's walk through a quick example of how to use these numbers. Let's say that our client is upgrading from someone else's system to our system. Data from peak hours of their previous system shows the client needs to reach 6,000 requests per second (RPS).

Let's use the graph from the Scalability Yardstick test in Figure 6-4. It shows that we are in trouble—the 5,100 RPS in the graph falls a bit short because we ran out of CPU before getting to the client's 6,000 RPS target. What is to be done? We need to do the impossible—to push from 100% to 101% CPU consumption and beyond. It is as if someone wanted the volume nob on their car radio to go past the max of 10 and on to 11.

To get to the 6,000 RPS, we have to add more machines to share the burden (to form a cluster), using a load balancer to distribute the load between the machines. Alternatively, we can add additional CPUs to the original machine. This is the classic and powerful concept of scalability.

When an application on a single machine can incrementally turn every bit of the CPU into a decent amount of throughput, it is straightforward to see how it would also be capable of using additional CPUs, once they were made available.

Figure 6-5 depicts the system without the squared, chiseled steps—it's the one that did not scale. Without more tuning, it has no hope of scaling, because the throughput won't approach 6000, no matter how many threads of load are applied.

If adding additional users won't buy extra throughput, the system will not scale. That is the lesson here.

Imperfect and Essential

I will never forget this painful story about tuning. We were beaten down and exhausted after 12 weeks of gruelling, long hours trying to reach an unprecedented amount of throughput for an especially demanding client. The crowded and stale conference room was so quiet, you might not have known we were actually celebrating, but we were—just too exhausted to get excited. The system finally scaled, or at least we thought it did. Doubling the hardware had doubled the throughput—that much was good. Tripling the hardware tripled the throughput, but that was the end of the scalability, and after that the quiet room got busy again. No one predicted this problem because the problem was not predictable.

The Scalability Yardstick test, like all forecasting tools, is imperfect; it cannot predict what has not been tested, just as in this little (and mostly true) anecdote. But even though scalability tests are imperfect, they are still essential. The Yardstick measures a key facet of all scalable systems: the ability to produce even steps of throughput at all levels of CPU consumption. Without such a tool, we stumble blindly through the development SDLC phase and beyond, knowing nothing of our progress towards the very goal we seek: scalability.

Back in the crowded conference room, there was progress. A concurrency cap, configured on the load balancer, had kept additional nodes from producing any more throughput. After fixing the configuration, adding a fourth node in our system quadrupled the throughput, pushing us past our difficult goal, and demonstrating great scalability.

Reproducing Bad Performance

As mentioned, the 100% CPU landmark is important for demonstrating scalability. The other three landmarks (25%, 50%, 75%) serve as little breakpoint tests for all those applications that do not perform as well as the SUT in Figure 6-4—which means most applications. The CPU landmarks show exactly how much load you need to apply to reproduce a performance problem. For example, let us say that you have nice chiseled and squared steps at the first two load increments (25% and 50% CPU), but throughput will not climb and the CPU will only push to, say, 55% in the third load increment. Bingo. You have reproduced the problem, which is the first part of "seeing" the problem. The second and last part of "seeing" the problem is to look at the right performance data using the right monitoring tools, as described in P.A.t.h. chapters, starting in Chapter 8.

When a seemingly formidable opponent is taken down by a lesser challenger, headlines are quick to hail the underdog and disgrace the dethroned champion. Likewise, if a seemingly robust SUT exhibits a monumental performance problem with very few threads of load, this is a critical problem, indeed. The smaller the amount of load required to reproduce a performance defect, the more critical the problem. As such, reproducing a problem at 25% CPU shows a much more critical problem than that same issue produced at a higher CPU percentage. Don't forget that the priority and/or criticality that you designate for an issue in a defect tracking system should somehow reflect this. Additionally, an unnecessarily high amount of load often introduces others issues (like the concurrency cap issues discussed in Chapter 5 on invalid load tests), that complicate an already difficult troubleshooting process. The lesson here is to apply only as much load as it takes to reproduce the problem—any more load than that unnecessarily complicates matters.

Once the Scalability Yardstick establishes the smallest amount of throughput required to transition from chiseled steps into erratic chaos and thus demonstrate a performance problem, it is helpful to switch from the Yardstick load plan to a steady-state load plan. You can then change the load plan to extend the duration of the test—the goal is to provide ample time to review the P.A.t.h. Checklist and start capturing data from the monitoring and tracing tools.

Once the problem has been identified and a fix deployed, a rerun of the steady-state test provides a great before-after comparison and a compelling story for your team. If the system change brings us closer to our performance goals (higher throughput and/or lower response time and/or lower CPU consumption), then the change is kept and the cycle begins again by rerunning the Yardstick to see where the next problem lies. Remember that the fix has changed the performance landscape and you will likely need to recalibrate the Yardstick by rerunning the Yardstick Calibration test.

We use the Scalability Yardstick for two purposes: measure the best throughput and reproduce performance defects. When the detect-reproduce-fix cycle all happens on a single machine/environment, the single-threaded workflow drags to a slow crawl: developers are forced to stand in line to run another test on the "golden" environment to get feedback on proposed code fixes. Comparing the performance of multiple code options is thus rendered infeasible, because access to the busy golden environment is in high demand. To get around this, the best performance engineers are skilled at enabling developers to work independently, to reproduce performance defects themselves, perhaps on their own desktops, and perhaps even comparing the performance of multiple design approaches. This is yet another benefit of the Modest Tuning Environment discussed back in Chapter 2.

Good and Bad CPU Consumption

Not all high CPU consumption is bad, especially when scalability is important. In fact, if building scalable systems is part of our goal, then we should actively drive systems to make leaps in throughput, while using all 100% of the CPU, at least in test environments. Of course, CPU that does not contribute to throughput is bad. For example, consider the case when the CPU hits 100% during application server start up when no load is applied. This is bad CPU.

One way to look at bad performance is that it is caused by either too little or too much CPU consumption. The first kind, "too little CPU," behaves like this: no matter how many threads of load are applied, the SUT throughput will not climb much, even though there is plenty of available CPU. The SUT acts as if an unimaginably heavy blanket, one that is many times heavier than the lead apron you wear to protect your body during a chest x-ray, has been cast on top of the frail throughput and CPU lines, holding them down, keeping them from making the responsive throughput leaps found in scalable systems.

As such, when that heavy blanket camps out on top of your SUT, using faster CPUs will provide only marginal benefits. Adding more of the same kind of CPU will just damage your pocketbook.

I will defend to the death the reasoning behind driving CPU consumption up to 100%, especially when throughput is bursting through the ceiling.

Why? If it is not proof of scalability, it is certainly a required attribute thereof. Flirting with 100% CPU like this is understandable, but there is no sense in applying more load if the CPU is already at 100%. As part of a negative test, this might be helpful, but it is a dead end when you are looking for more throughput.

Even when faced with really low throughput, technicians sometimes boast about their SUT's low CPU consumption. It takes work to help them figure out that, in this light, low CPU consumption is bad and not good. On the other hand, low CPU consumption is good when you are comparing two tests whose performance is alike in every way (especially throughput), except that CPU is lower on one.

With the second kind of poor performance, "too much CPU," the SUT burns through so much CPU that you would need an entire farm of busily grazing CPUs to generate enough throughput to meet requirements, when a better-tuned SUT would just require a few CPUs, slowly chewing cud. This is why its helpful to introduce a performance requirement that caps the amount of money spent on hardware.

"Too much CPU" should guide us to optimize code that is both unnecessary and CPU hungry. The tools to point out which code is CPU hungry are discussed in the P.A.t.h. Checklist for threads, Chapter 11. And whether code is unnecessary is of course subjective, but there are some great, concrete examples of unnecessary code in that same Chapter 11. "Too little CPU" indicates that contention or I/O or other response time issues are holding back the system from generating enough throughput. Guidance for addressing these problems is scattered throughout four chapters covering the P.A.t.h. Checklist, starting in Chapter 8.

Chapter 2 on Modest Tuning Environments encourages us to run more fix-test cycles every day, with the expectation that improvements will ensue. That means the performance landscape is fluid and needs to be re-evaluated between optimizations. Just an optimization or two can easily turn a "too much CPU" system into a "too little CPU" system. For instance, suppose a number of systems with complex security requirements query a database for hundreds of permissions for each user, and let's further say that a review of the entire P.A.t.h. Checklist shows this is the worst problem in the system. Once you add caching to this CPU-intensive approach, you will discover the next worst problem in the system, which very well might be contention (discussed in Chapter 11), which leaves us with a "too little CPU" system.

Be careful how others perceive your attempts to push CPU to 100%, as with the Scalability Yardstick. Rightfully, data center owners require plenty of assurances that production applications will meet throughput requirements while consuming modest portions of the allotted CPU. Ask them how much consumption they feel comfortable with. The risk of running out of CPU is too great, especially when human error and other operational blunders can unexpectedly drive up CPU consumption. Sometimes business processes get inadvertently left out of the tuning process altogether, and their CPU-hungry nature ambushes you in production. Sneak attack.

Don't Forget

I am not a carpenter, but even I know that you measure twice and cut once to fashion a board to the right dimensions. With software, we generally measure scalability zero times before checking into source code control. Zero times.

Once the clay has been baked, the sculptor is done. If you wanted that malformed mug to instead be a fancified chalice, you are out of luck. If that clay bust of your benefactor looks more like a sci-fi monster with three noses, sorry. The development process is our golden window of opportunity to sculpt and reshape the code, and we currently let that opportunity sail right on by without ever checking in on our progress towards our scalability goal. Does it have the right number of noses? Does it still look like a monster? Why do we never ask these obvious questions until it is way too late?

The Scalability Yardstick is quick and easy to use; it enables us to measure performance progress frequently during the development process, while our window of opportunity is open to set things right, before the clay is baked.

When our system scales, the load generator pushes the SUT to produce clean, chiseled leaps/steps of throughput. Instead of the squared and chiseled throughput (and other) metrics, poor performing SUTs have jagged, impotent and weighted down throughput because the code is littered with contention, as shown by the jagged variability in individual metrics.

I have mentioned that applying an unrealistically large amount of load is a common mistake, perhaps even an anti-pattern. 3t0tt helps address this problem—it is a nice, safe way to keep pretentious performance engineers like myself from lecturing about unrealistically high load. 3t0tt is a fantastic starting point, but it doesn't tell you whether your system scales—you need the Scalability Yardstick for that.

What's Next

This chapter focused on the interplay between throughput, CPU and the amount of load applied. Seeing these three metrics on the same graph was helpful to running the Scalability Yardstick test. In Chapter 7, coming up next, we will see how to put all these metrics on the exact same JMeter graph. Chapter 7 is a deep dive into the JMeter basics that deserve being repeated, and into important JMeter features and foibles that seem underdocumented.

CHAPTER 7

■ ■ ■

JMeter Must-Know Features

Because you can find a lot of documentation on the Internet about JMeter, the load generator, I have tried to limit this chapter to include either features with little documentation available, or features that newcomers rarely seem to pick up, even if they are well documented.

The objectives for this chapter are:

- Get comfortable using JMeter by creating small test scripts in a tiny sandbox environment using just your desktop.

- Understand that learning a few particular JMeter features can quickly advance you from a beginner to an intermediate/advanced user.

- Understand that once JMeter is installed, extra plugins from jmeter-plugins.org and other places are required to make it really useful.

I see a lot of people start to use JMeter and not get very far with it, and that is frustrating for me because I have seen what a capable load generator it is. To address this, the guided tours in this chapter will propel beginning JMeter users into the realm of intermediate and advanced users.

But wait, there is more.

"Hello World!" programming experiments are great for getting started learning a technology, and JMeter has exactly this kind of sandbox that you can use to try out its features. If you know about this sandbox (most don't), it takes just 20 seconds (I'm not exaggerating here) to create a little test in the sandbox and learn (and even perfect) your approach to answering these and many other JMeter questions:

- How do you increase load?

- How do you graph throughput?

- How do you conditionally execute something based on a value in a script variable?

- How do you read data (like SUT user names/passwords) from a .csv text file into JMeter script variables?

So keep an eye out for the sandbox later in the chapter.

This is a JMeter-only chapter, so if you are already sold on your own load generator, then by all means, proceed to the next chapter. But before you leave, please read my "love letter to JMeter" and see if your load generator has all of these features, ones that I rely on for tackling difficult performance problems. It is tough for me to imagine how other load generators (and other software developers) make do without this fantastically broad set of features, all open source. I sure hope the commercial (and other) load generator competition takes note of this high bar. For reference, here are some other popular load generators; the last three are commercial ones.

© Erik Ostermueller 2017
E. Ostermueller, *Troubleshooting Java Performance*, DOI 10.1007/978-1-4842-2979-8_7

Faban

The Grinder

Gatling

Tsung

jmh

HP Performance Center (aka 'Load Runner')

Load UI

Silk Performer

Since a single chapter does not a training plan make, I recommend using this chapter to supplement other JMeter training you might find at jmeter.apache.org or in JMeter books (*Performance Testing with JMeter*, by Bayo Erinle (Packt Books, 2015; ISBN-13 = 978-1787285774) or *JMeter Cookbook*, by Bayo Erinle (Packt Books, 2014; ISBN-13 = 978-1783988280). The good citizens of the Internet, God bless them, also have their own compendium of training material, which is an irrefutable sign that JMeter is a vital organ in the body of the performance discipline at large:

"Load Testing with JMeter: Part 1 - Getting Started," (`https://lincolnloop.com/blog/load-testing-jmeter-part-1-getting-started/`)

"Learn JMETER from Scratch -(Performance + Load) Testing" (`https://www.udemy.com/learn-jmeter-from-scratch-performance-load-testing-tool/`)

"Introduction to JMeter" (`https://www.guru99.com/introduction-to-jmeter.html`)

"JMeter - Quick Guide" (`http://www.tutorialspoint.com/jmeter/jmeter_quick_guide.htm`)

"JMeter getting started" (`https://www.youtube.com/watch?v=KI6u5pclYIw`)

"Getting Started WIth JMeter" (`https://www.youtube.com/watch?v=dJw8sBk_wSo`)

"How To Use Apache JMeter To Perform Load Testing on a Web Server" (`https://www.digitalocean.com/community/tutorials/how-to-use-apache-jmeter-to-perform-load-testing-on-a-web-server`)

"A quick howto to setup JMeter" (`http://zacster.blogspot.com/2008/03/quick-howto-to-setup-jmeter.html`)

Love Letter to JMeter

Your load generator might have one or two of the following features, but JMeter is the only one that has them all, touting a feature set robust enough to be shared by QA and developers. It would take many volumes to show you all of this material, so this chapter will showcase just a few of the more important ones in this list.

- Right alongside standard load gen metrics (response time, throughput, and so on), JMeter can graph all kinds of other metrics:

  - JMX metrics from your SUT (`https://jmeter-plugins.org/wiki/JMXMon/`). For example, this will show you whether you are maxed on out your web container threads, as detailed in Chapter 4 on load anti-patterns.

- CPU, RAM, network, disk metrics from all popular OSes (using PerfMon (`https://jmeter-plugins.org/wiki/PerfMon/`) and SIGAR).

- SIGAR also enables you to graph CPU consumption per PID (operating system process ID). If you have more than one Java process on a machine, this will show which one is eating all the CPU.

- Load-test anything you want: simple Java programs, HTTP/S applications, JMS apps, a ton of SQL statements, TCP Socket servers, and many others (`http://jmeter.apache.org/usermanual/component_reference.html`). The JMeter term for the JMeter Test Element that knows how to test to each of these is a Sampler.

- WS-Security. If your client has to encrypt your WS-Security message, then your load generator must also (`https://github.com/tilln/jmeter-wssecurity`)

- Advanced Graphing:

  - Put any two (or more) metrics together on a single graph (`https://jmeter-plugins.org/wiki/CompositeGraph/`). Three metrics with three different units of measure with auto-scaling? No problem. This helps identify how one metric impacts another. You can even take metrics from two different tests and put them onto the same graph (`https://jmeter-plugins.org/wiki/MergeResults/`) for compelling before-after visualizations. For example if your throughput maxes out because you are out of CPU, you can get a single graph that contains the ugly throughput cap at the exact time the CPU hits 100%. That is a very compelling graph!

  - Do you distrust averages? You should. You can use Frequency distributions (`https://jmeter-plugins.org/wiki/RespTimesDistribution/`) and percentile graphs (`https://jmeter-plugins.org/wiki/RespTimePercentiles/`)to show response time metrics without "average lies."

  - On the Settings panel (`https://jmeter-plugins.org/wiki/SettingsPanel/`), you can tweak graph granularity, axis scale, colors, and more.

- Generate load from any OS with a JVM.

- Record JMeter test results locally to a text file or to a centralized database (`http://jmeter.apache.org/usermanual/realtime-results.html`).

- The following automated performance test platforms have JMeter integration and reporting:

  - Jenkins (`https://wiki.jenkins.io/display/JENKINS/Performance+Plugin`)

  - Taurus (`http://gettaurus.org/`)

  - Sonar (`http://testersinaction.blogspot.com/2013/05/v-behaviorurldefaultvmlo_24.html`)

- A variety of ways to deploy load generators:

  - From a single machine:

    - Quick and easy, default approach: Create a load script with Java UI and then generate load and view graphs.

- Generate load (`http://jmeter.apache.org/usermanual/get-started.html#non_gui`) on a headless machine, using a premade test plan. Transfer the raw results back to your desktop for analysis, or just generate the .png images of the graphs headlessly for later analysis.

- Distributed Testing (`http://jmeter.apache.org/usermanual/jmeter_distributed_testing_step_by_step.pdf`). From multiple machines, with a central JMeter controller. Load over a few thousand TPS might be too much for a single generator.

Using jmeter-plugins.org Is a Must

To be frank about it, I would have ditched JMeter long ago without Andrey Pohilko's [1] incredible jmeter-plugins.org, which is a set of additional tools and graphs and things that plug right into JMeter. I suppose I'm a little biased; I contributed a few hundred lines of code, myself.

The project started way back in 2009, so it's pretty stable. Chapter 6, on the Scalability Yardstick, relied heavily on JMeter Plugins. The CPU consumption was from JMeter Plugins, as well as the thread groups that draw the nice stair-steps for an incremental load plan. Remember when I mentioned the two approaches to installing this? I talked about installation using the Plugin Manager or by unzipping jar files for a single plugin into `JMETER_HOME/lib/ext`.

Here are two other installation approaches that I think are just as important as the first two:

- Use the "old style" releases. First surf to `https://jmeter-plugins.org/downloads/old/`. Then download both `JMeterPlugins-Standard-N.N.N.zip` and `JMeterPlugins-Extras-N.N.N.zip` and unzip them into JMETER_HOME. The jar files in the zip must end up in the same folders (/lib or /lib/ext) as specified in the .zip files.

- Use Maven. Not only does this approach install jmeter-plugins, it does a full JMeter install too! Look in the littleMock repository for `pom-load.xml`. Instead of launching JMeter with `JMETER_HOME/bin/jmeter.bat`, you use my trivial little loadGui.cmd / .sh (also in the littleMock repo). I borrowed most of `pom-load.xml` from some kind soul on the Internet. The maven plugin used is very well named: jmeter-maven-plugin. Thank you, Internet. You'll find `pom-load.xml` in the root folder of `https://github.com/eostermueller/littleMock`.

Please use the first technique ("old style") to install JMeterPlugins on your own workstation to view the .jmx scripts for this chapter. Those .jmx files are in the sampleJMeterScripts/ folder of this repo:

`https://github.com/eostermueller/javaPerformanceTroubleshooting`

I refer to this as the jpt repo.

Consider this everyday problem: Let's say you create a JMeter load script (a .jmx file) that uses a few jmeter-plugins. When your cube neighbor who does not have JMeter-Plugins installed tries to run your .jmx file, they will get cryptic errors that do very little to highlight the missing dependency.

---

[1]`http://jmeter-plugins.org/wiki/Contributors/`

The two install approaches above help with this. Maven is not always easy to use, but the above pom-load.xml is wonderful—it will download, on the fly, any dependent JMeter-Plugins specified as a <dependency> in the pom-load.xml file.

The moral of this story is that sharing your .jmx file, alone, is prone to cryptic dependency issues. Sharing both your .jmx file and your customized pom-load.xml file fixes all of that. But another way to discover JMeter is to use the JMeter Plugins Plugin Manager, one of the install techniques mentioned in Chapter 6. Here is the URL for quick reference:

```
https://jmeter-plugins.org/wiki/PluginsManager/
```

If you have the PluginsManager installed (see above), it will prompt you with "Your test plan requires the following plugins" when it discovers a .jmx file that references a JMeter Plugin you don't have installed. Then, it will give you the option to actually install in or abort.

The load-pom.xml mentioned above does a full JMeter install and also let's you specify the dependent Plugins in use. Alternatively, you can also use this script to install all plugins in a specific plan file:

```
PluginsManagerCMD install-for-jmx /home/username/jmx/testPlan.jmx
```

This is really helpful for automated, lights-out perf testing, but keep in mind that even the PluginsManagerCMD has its own install process here:

```
https://jmeter-plugins.org/wiki/PluginsManagerAutomated/
```

In Chapter 2, I showed you how to graph the CPU consumption of individual PIDs. To do that, download and install this plugin—this part enables just the graphs, not the collecting of CPU data:

```
https://jmeter-plugins.org/wiki/PerfMon/
```

Then use the ServerAgent to collect data that will display on the graphs: Download ServerAgent-N.N.N.zip from

```
https://jmeter-plugins.org/wiki/PerfMonAgent/#Download
```

Unzip it onto any machine (any platform) from which you want to collect metrics. When you start the startAgent.sh (or startAgent.bat), it listens for a connection on port 4444 from the JMeter GUI (or headless) process on your desktop. It is extremely well behaved, cross platform and easy to use.

The StartAgent captures RAM, network and other metrics—not just CPU. There are a number of other JMeterPlugins, detailed next.

PerfMon

In Chapter 3 I talked about how metrics answer three basic questions for us:

1. How utilized are our hardware resources?

2. Which component is to blame for a particular performance problem?

3. Does the end user benefit? Which code change performs better?

Load generators were specifically designed to answer the third question about meeting performance requirements. The jmeter-plugins.org PerfMon component also provides high-level answers to the first question. When I say high-level, I mean CPU, RAM, and network consumption and a little more than that (`https://jmeter-plugins.org/wiki/PerfMonMetrics/`). Here is how it works.

For starters, no administrative or root permissions are required to run `startAgent.bat` (Listing 7-1). This process consumes very few resources, so it is safe to launch this process and forget about it for days or months.

Listing 7-1. Startup banner for serverAgent, which provides hardware utilization data for JMeter

```
# ./startAgent.sh
INFO  2016-02-21 14:03:05.061 [kg.apc.p] (): Binding UDP to 4444
INFO  2016-02-21 14:03:06.064 [kg.apc.p] (): Binding TCP to 4444
INFO  2016-02-21 14:03:06.069 [kg.apc.p] (): JP@GC Agent v2.2.0 started
```

Figure 7-1 shows how to add a JMeter graph that connects to the serverAgent and display a CPU graph.

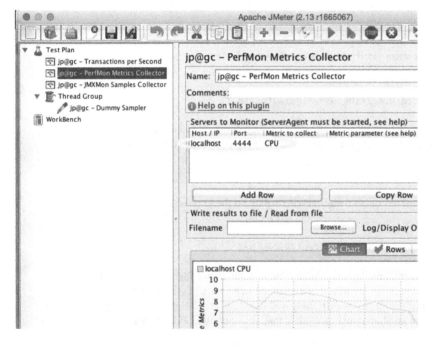

Figure 7-1. To capture great CPU, RAM, and other hardware metrics, just point PerfMon to the host and port *(default port is 4444) where you have unzipped and started the serverAgent*

So, JMeter helps answer two out of three of the metric questions. You can even make a case that it answers the remaining question, about which component is to blame for a particular performance problem. How? Check out these other metrics available that you can graph in JMeter.

The JMXMon plugin graphs JMX metrics in JMeter:

`https://jmeter-plugins.org/wiki/JMXMon/`

It is an unfortunate coincidence that the file extension for the JMeter load plan (.jmx) is the same three letters as the abbreviation for Java Management Extensions (JMX), a monitoring API. JMX the monitoring API isn't very popular right now, but Spring Boot's Actuator is. It delivers great JVM health metrics in json-over-http messages. The following page shows how you can enable Actuator in Spring Boot by adding a simple dependency to your Maven pom.xml Spring Boot file:

```
http://www.baeldung.com/spring-boot-actuators
```

Then, you can use the following JMeterPlugin to graph Actuator data in JMeter:

```
https://jmeter-plugins.org/wiki/PageDataExtractor/
```

JMX and Actuator data can point to a number of problems inside your JVM, thus helping answer the "which component is to blame" question. So JMeter and JMeterPlugins help provide all three kinds of metrics. Impressive.

JMeter user.properties Is Your Friend

From time to time, I discover JMeter properties that tweak JMeter's default configuration in some particular way. So that these property tweaks don't get lost in the 45KB (as of JMeter version 2.13) of other properties in JMETER_HOME/bin/jmeter.properties, I segregate them into JMETER_HOME/bin/user.properties, where they override those in jmeter.properties.

Having them separate allows me to easily copy my user.properties file to new JMeter installations, giving me a more consistent installation.

Listing 7-2 shows my personal user.properties file with my favorite set of JMeter customizations that I recommend for all.

Listing 7-2. A few of my favorite JMeter properties in a user.properties file that overrides jmeter.properties; both files reside in JMETER_HOME/bin

```
#Add this to avoid truncated HTTP & other responses in View Results Tree
view.results.tree.max_size=0

#Add this so the Active Threads over Time Listener will
#render from your .jtl file
jmeter.save.saveservice.thread_counts=true

#Add this to use the csv format (instead of XML) for jtl output files.
#This lowers jtl size, lowers JMeter CPU consumption during test
jmeter.save.saveservice.output_format=csv

#These csv field names make it much easier to read/understand .jtl files.
jmeter.save.saveservice.print_field_names=true
```

When you share your .jmx files with your friends, you also might want to share properties like the ones above. But you might instead want to use the pom-load.xml file, above, to specify any properties you want your friends to use. Check out the above pom-load.xml file for the syntax in Listing 7-3, which does the same thing as setting summariser.interval=5 in JMeter's user.properties file.

Listing 7-3. A JMeter property that is specified in the jmeter-maven-plugin

```
<propertiesJMeter>
    <summariser.interval>5</summariser.interval>
</propertiesJMeter>
```

You can use the technique in Listing 7-3 to specify any JMeter property. Here is a reference to all of JMeter's properties:

http://jmeter.apache.org/usermanual/properties_reference.html

JMeter Introduction

When I was starting out with JMeter, I wish I'd had a screenshot like Figure 7-2. An upscale framed copy on your wall is a bit overkill, but how about a photocopy taped to the bottom edge of one of your massive 42 inch monitors? The text I added to the screenshots shows basic load generation functionality, and the arrows point to the JMeter Test Element you will need to implement it. The first screenshot in Figure 7-2 is the blank slate you get when you start JMeter. To set up JMeter as you see in the second screenshot, you right-click on Test Plan and start adding things.

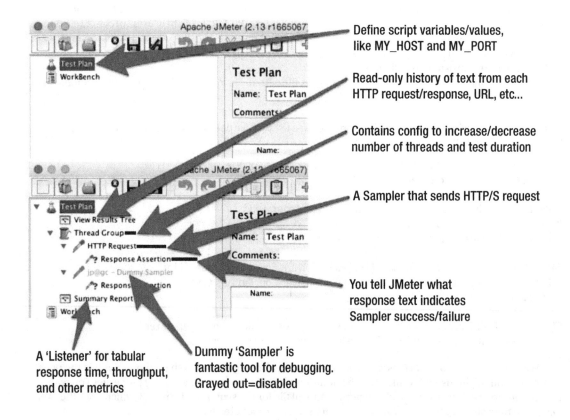

Figure 7-2. *How to get things done with JMeter Test Plan Tree. The First screenshot is a blank slate. Second screenshot is after right-clicking, adding many Test Plan Elements.*

I must concede that the JMeter load plan tree, that tree-like structure on the left side of the main window, is a tough usability hurdle for new users. Users generally know the end result they're after. For example, "apply 5 threads of load to two different SOA services over HTTP for 5 minutes, need response time and throughput times series graphs." But to accomplish this seemingly straightforward goal, JMeter forces the uninitiated into an ugly little trial-and-error game that I call "Right-Clicking Education." Intermediate users navigate this easily, but not beginners. In that left pane of the UI, you assemble a tree structure with funny named building blocks called Test Elements. (Thread Group, Dummy Sampler, View Results Tree, and so on). Each Test Element in the tree has a type, and it has to be precisely positioned according to a set of rules that a beginner knows nothing about. The Test Elements and the types (I work mostly with these types: Thread Group, Sampler, Listener, Assertion) and all of the individual Test Elements are documented here:

http://jmeter.apache.org/usermanual/component_reference.html#introduction

There is some nice high level documentation here:

http://jmeter.apache.org/usermanual/test_plan.html

Table 7-1. *Frequently Used Components in a JMeter Load Plan*

Name	Description	Example
Listener	Graphs and other ways to display results	
Thread Group	Configure how many threads of load are applied. Configure test duration.	Stepping Thread Group (https://jmeter-plugins.org/wiki/SteppingThreadGroup/) or the clunky default Thread Group (http://jmeter.apache.org/usermanual/component_reference.html#Thread_Group)
Sampler	The doer. Do an HTTP request. Do a JMS request. Execute java code.	
Controller	Controls the flow of your samplers, including "If" logic and looping logic	
Assertion	Allows you to configure how JMeter decides whether one run of a Sampler succeeded or failed.	

If you right-click on a particular Test Element, you'll see what kind of child Test Elements you can legally add from that spot. So if your right-clicker has enough gusto on that day, you can right-click every node on the tree (sometimes there are dozens or hundreds of blocks) and deduce and commit to memory the whole set of rules—which Test Element types can/should be the parents/children of other Test Element types. That's a lot of right-clicking fun. Or not.

My point here is not to dish out a black eye to "the one I love." Instead, it is to encourage you to avoid the pain of the Right-clicking Education. At first, start by relying on the help of others to structure your load plan tree. Specifically, you can use the screenshot in Figure 7-2 as a guide, or perhaps use the relatively new JMeter Template feature to start with a ready-made load plan tree, or just have a friend share their load plan (a .jmx[2] file of a proprietary .xml grammar). To use the Template feature, start JMeter with an empty load plan tree, and then choose File ➤ Templates. Even with a lot of experience, I still rely on the Record template to record a new HTTP load script, because the tree structure is a little unique. You will soon become comfortable with which Test Elements go where, and you can then branch out (ha) and get more creative with your load plan tree structure.

UI Features for Working Quickly

The quiverful of big red arrows in Figure 7-2 all point to individual items, the Test Elements. Navigating, nay surfing, around all of those Test Elements is a breeze by simply using the arrow keys on your keyboard. Each Test Element has a particular Test Element type. All graphs, for example, are of the Test Element type Listener. Test Elements for submitting HTTP requests are called Samplers. To make them easy to find, I stick all my graphs at the highest level (as children of Test Plan, the root). But let's say I have inadvertently placed some graphs further down into the tree. There are a number of features you could use to quickly relocate them, and do other things as well:

- Drag and drop. The drag and drop implementation is surprisingly easy to use. Try it out for yourself, dragging a test element to either change the order of siblings or to change parentage altogether.

- Cut/Copy/Paste. Bill Gates' familiar keyboard shortcuts (Ctrl+X, Ctrl+C, Ctrl+V) work very well. All three of these operate on both the selected node and on all its children.

- Multi-select. Shift+click (selecting adjacent Test Elements) and Ctrl+click (selecting non-adjacent Test Elements) work as you would expect.

- Duplicate the current Test Element. Need another test element just like the selected one? Ctrl+Shift+C adds a copy just below the current. This even works if you copy a parent test element that has many children.

- You can also quickly disable a single Test Element and all its children with the Enable/Disable/Toggle functionality, Ctrl+T.

- If you launch two completely different instances of the JMeter UI, you can effortlessly cut/copy/paste between the two trees.

All of this cut/copy/paste functionality is great for:

- Combining two load scripts. Start two instances of the JMeter GUI at the same time. Copy all the HTTP Request samplers from one instance to the other. I can't overestimate how important this technique is. Here are three examples:

  - The Load Generation overview in Chapter 4 showed a First Priority and Second Priority scripts. You can record First and Second Priority stuff in separate scripts, and then use this technique to append the HTTP Samplers (and other stuff) in the Second Priority to the script for the First.

---

[2]http://jmeter.apache.org/usermanual/get-started.html#template

- Every developer records their own business process, and this technique is later used to combine them all into a single script.

    - When make code changes to a web page (like adding new required data entry), that often makes the .jmx file out of date. To update the script, record the new version of the web page in a separate, stand-alone .jmx file. Then carefully delete the outdated portion of the old script, and use this technique to copy/paste the new script into the old script.

- Rearranging components in the Test Plan. So that they are easy to see/find, I like to put all my graphs at the highest level (as children of Test Plan). If graphs get scattered around, I can easily use the arrow keys to surf around the load test plan, Ctrl+Click to multi-select the ones I want to move, then Ctrl+V them to the new location.

- Easily duplicate the currently selected node. Let's say you have configured one Java Sampler and you want to create five others right long side it, as siblings. Just select your Java sampler, and hit Ctrl+Shift+C five times. Voila.

- I use the Toggle/Ctrl+T feature heavily. Let's say I want to compare the performance of the code at two different URLs. I will create an HTTP Request sampler for each, and then run them one at a time, using Ctrl+T to switch the one that is enabled. If you avoid clearing out the results between runs, you'll have a nice graph like this: (TODO: Need graph of two different samplers, run one at a time w/o clearing out results between runs).

Functional Validation During Load Test Using JMeter Assertions

The .jmx script for this example is in the jpt github.com repo in this location:

```
sampleJMeterScripts/jpt_ch07_functionalValidation.jmx
```

In Chapter 5, I mentioned a half dozen situations where you should bite the bullet and discard the results of a test and rerun the entire thing. One of those potential reasons was lots of SUT errors. You'll have to decide for yourself exactly what percentage of errors triggers a redo.

But if your SUT fails silently or important client data is quietly omitted from an SUT web page, you might end up basing all kinds of decisions on really faulty data. To avoid that situation, please take the time to tell JMeter what constitutes a successful HTML response by adding JMeter Assertions to check the HTML responses for key pieces of text, like the title of a web page, or perhaps HTML text labels for a few key fields. Figure 7-3 shows how to add an Assertion.

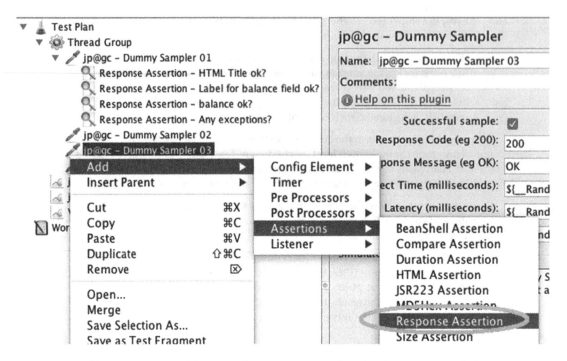

Figure 7-3. *Adding an Assertion. If the text in this Assertion is not found in the parent Sampler's response, then JMeter will tally an error in the "Summary Report" and/or "Synthesis Report".*

Figure 7-4 shows how to enter the text to be verified. Before entering the text, you'll need to first click the 'Add' button—bottom, center. If JMeter finds that the text you enter is missing from the corresponding HTTP response, it will tally an error. If your entire business process culminates in an "Order Submitted" message, this is your chance to validate that the system coughs up this all-important message. Don't miss this chance.

Response Assertion

Name: Response Assertion - Label for balance field ok?

Comments:

Apply to:
○ Main sample and sub-samples ◉ Main sample only ○ Sub-samples only ○ JMeter Variable

Field to Test
◉ Text Response   ○ Response Code   ○ Response Message   ○ Response Headers
○ Request Headers ○ URL Sampled   ○ Document (text)   ☐ Ignore Status

Pattern Matching Rules
○ Contains ○ Matches ○ Equals ◉ Substring ☐ Not ☐ Or

Patterns to Test

Patterns to Test
1 Account Balance is:
2 Ledger Balances is:

Figure 7-4. *A JMeter 'Response' Assertion. If you click 'Add' multiple times and add text on each line, JMeter will flag this sampler as having errored out if any of the lines of text are missing from the parent Sampler's response.*

It would be bittersweet, to say the least, if your application displayed "Order Submitted" immediately followed by "Fatal Exception / Your code failed." You can add a second Assertion as shown in Figure 7-5 that flips the logic. Just mark the 'Not' flag and JMeter will tally an error if the given text, like 'Fatal Exception' is present.

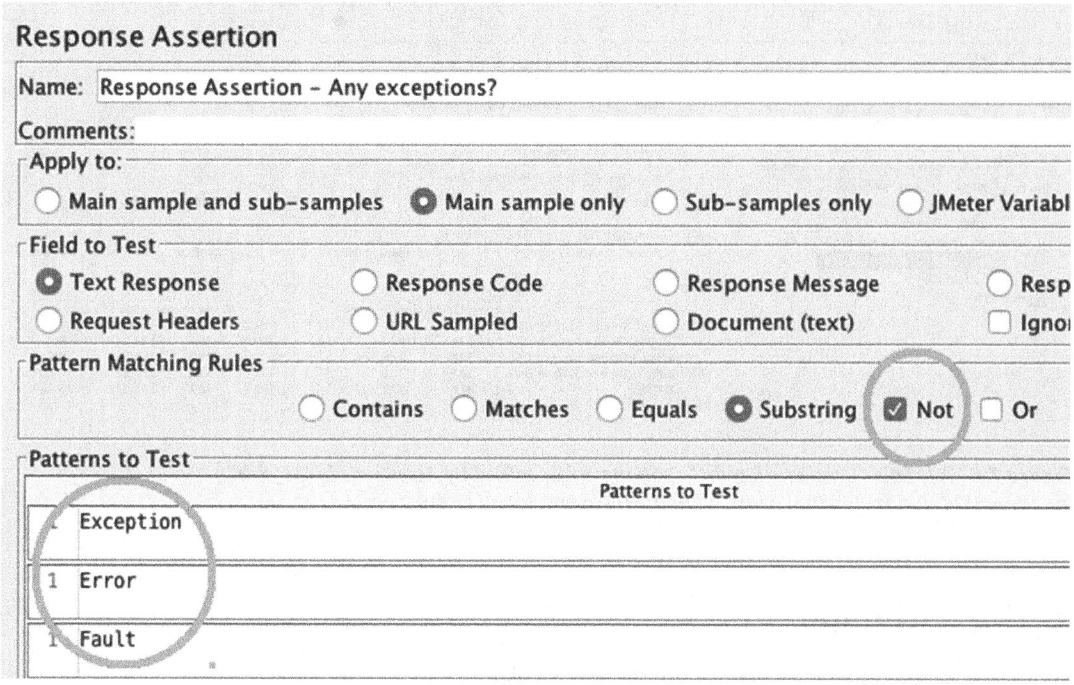

Figure 7-5. A JMeter Response Assertion like in the previous Figure, but with 'Not' checked. This tallies an error if the given text, like and error message, is found in the Sampler's response.

I have prematurely claimed performance victory before, only to later discover that 100% of the requests failed. Its pretty embarrassing; I don't recommend it.

Not only should you take the time to add Assertions, you also need to watch for error counts/percentages, where all Assertion failures and other errors (like HTTP errors) are recorded. Here are three components (there are probably others) that will help you track errors:

- jp@gc - Transactions per Second (from JMeter Plugins)
- Summary Report (Error % column)
- Synthesis Report (Error % column and from JMeter Plugins)

The Assertion discussed here (Figures 7-4 and 7-5) only checks for preordained list of strings. There are a number of other more sophisticated Assertions detailed here:

```
http://jmeter.apache.org/usermanual/component_reference.html#assertions
```

For example, the JSR223 Assertion lets you write code to validate any Sampler response.

Figure 7-6 shows a "Synthesis Report" with failed Assertions. The Synthesis Report from JMeter Plugins performs much better JMeter's "Summary Report", which lacks a few key columns like "like 90% response time." The Sumary Report has less functionality and worse performance.

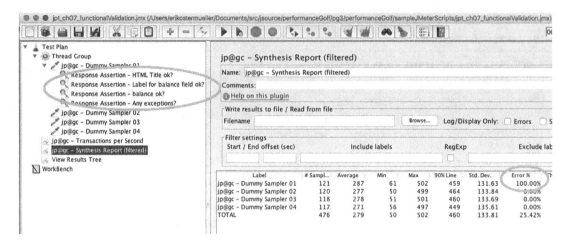

Figure 7-6. *A JMeter "Synthesis Report" showing errors tallied by Assertions in jpt_ch07_ functionalValidation.jmx that comes with the jpt examples on github.com*

Script Variables

Almost every script I create has a few script variables, making it easier to run the script in different hardware environments. The MY_DIR variable shown in Figure 7-7 will be used in the following examples to indicate where to store JMeter output files on the machine where JMeter is running.

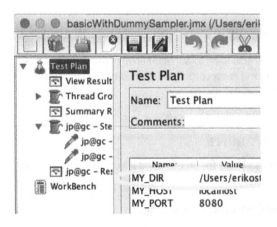

Figure 7-7. *Use a MY_DIR variable to store JMeter output files in the following examples*

Figure 7-8 shows how to reference a variable. Practically all input boxes in JMeter, for either numeric or text data, like the one displayed here, will correctly resolve the value of a script variable—just don't forget to wrap the variable name in the ${} syntax.

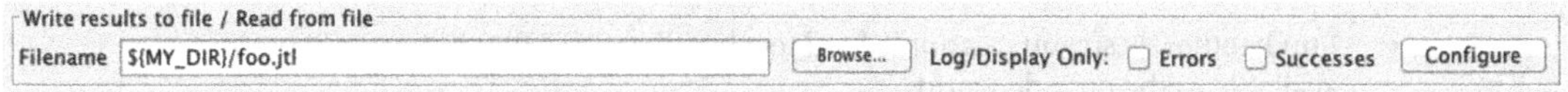

Figure 7-8. *When referencing a variable like MY_DIR, you must wrap the name in special syntax: ${MY_DIR}. You can reference variables in just about any place where you can enter text data*

Saving Performance Results to Disk

You can save/persist JMeter results (response time, throughput, and so on) to disk in a few different ways. You will need this for many reasons, like comparing current performance to that of the last release, documenting performance defects, or showing throughput process to your peeps.

- Copy screenshots from the UI, which is quick. Keep in mind that with just a .png image of a graph, you lose ability to add other metrics, reset sampling granularity, rescale to zoom in, change colors, and so on.

- Save raw results to a text file—by convention JMeter uses a .jtl file extension. This is a bit more complicated (see details below), but you get great flexibility to re-envision your graph on the raw data. This flexibility is especially helpful if you don't review your results until long after the tests have run. I often generate load on a headless machine. After the test, I'll just copy the raw .jtl files back to my desktop to render in the JMeter UI. From a headless machine, you can even generate .png files (https:// jmeter-plugins.org/wiki/GraphsGeneratorListener/).

- Save results to central database (http://jmeter.apache.org/usermanual/ realtime-results.html, or http://www.testautomationguru.com/jmeter-real- time-results-influxdb-grafana/). Great approach to allow multiple users to view metrics during a live test, or for comparing results for multiple SUT releases (to keep all results in one place), or perhaps for an enterprise repository of all results. This is a relatively new approach, and I do not have any experience with it.

- When running headlessly, JMeter displays to stdout (and perhaps to JMETER_HOME/ bin/jmeter.log) a small and rudimentary set of (non-configurable) performance metrics every 30 seconds—very helpful for short, quick tests. The Console Status Logger (https://jmeter-plugins.org/wiki/ConsoleStatusLogger/) JMeter-plugin is no longer needed, because more recent versions of JMeter (certainly 2.13 and higher) display this data without even asking for it. There are a number of reasons why you'd want to run JMeter headlessly:

  - Run headlessly because JMeter says so. When starting JMeter GUI, this message displays to the console window: "Don't use the GUI for load testing" (Figure 2-6). This is likely because GUI overhead might impact load test results. In my experience, load testing with the GUI and 10 requests per second or fewer has sufficiently low overhead.

- Run headlessly on the SUT so you can avoid network performance issues discussed in Chapter 2 on the Modest Tuning Environment. Avoid bandwidth limiters. Avoid multiple firewalls that might cause performance degradation. Avoid load balancers whose concurrency and other configuration has not yet been vetted for performance.

- Run headlessly so you can apply load to a headless SUT that has no TCP ports available to the outside world.

To save JMeter UI graphs to .png files, start by adding a graph to the test plan tree, as shown in Figure 7-9. For a nice "response time over time" graph, right-click on the root test plan and choose Add ➤ Listener ➤ jp@gc - Response Times Over Time. After you run the test, you can just right-click to copy the image of the graph to the Clipboard or to the file system.

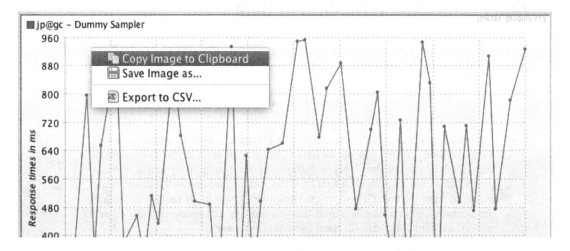

Figure 7-9. *Just right-click on a JMeter-Plugin graph to save the image to the Clipboard or to the disk*

The second way to save your test results is to have JMeter save the raw data to the disk. The .jtl file extension is a nice convention, although it is not enforced. For saving data to .jtl files, you can use the same graph as Figure 7-9 by specifying it as shown in Figure 7-10. All of the graphs are Test Elements with the type Listener, and they each have this panel.

Figure 7-10. *After restarting JMeter, if you want to reload metrics into a graph from a populated .jtl file, make sure the .jtl file name is specified, set UI focus in this text box, and press Enter*

Yes, the screenshots in Figures 7-8 and 7-10 are identical, but only because this is important functionality. Even though the UI plainly says, "Write results to file / Read from file," most people, including me, have trouble seeing that this box is used to render a graph from a .jtl file.

Note that Run ➤ Clear All (Ctrl+E) will clear out all the results in graphs and most Test Elements in the UI, but it will neither delete nor zero out the .jtl results file. It appends data. You have to manually delete the .jtl file to start from scratch. This can be a pain when you start what you thought was a new test, but you were really appending data to the test you ran yesterday at the same time of day. If you try to render the data in the .jtl to a graph, say a throughput graph, you will see throughput from yesterday's test on the left, a huge, vacuous 24 hour gap in the middle, followed by today's throughput on the right. Not what you expected. So, remember to clear out your .jtl files when restarting to avoid this huge gap.

To avoid playing "file system hide-and-seek" to find your output files, I strongly recommend specifying a full path with the Filename input box; Figure 7-7 shown earlier shows how to use a script variable to say which folder the file will land in.

That shows how to write the .jtl files. To read a .jtl file and display the graph, for example when you restart the JMeter UI, you need to load each Listener Test Element one at a time. There is an interesting usability quirk here to get JMeter to read the .jtl file: make sure the .jtl file name is in place. Then put or keep focus on the input box, and press the Enter key. That starts the process to paint the graph from text data in the .jtl file. Alternatively, using the Browse button to select the file will paint the graph based on the .jtl data.

How to Avoid Redundant Copies of Huge Files

The configuration in Figure 7-11 looks perfectly reasonable to me. It looks like we are trying to create one output file for response time data and one output file for throughput data.

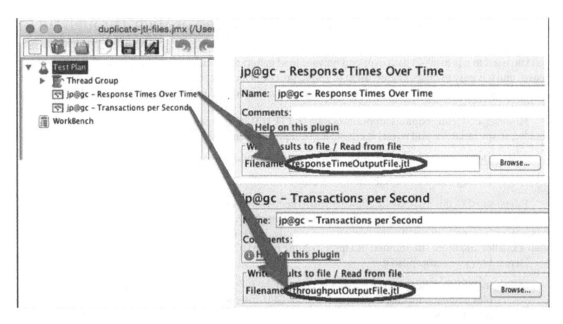

Figure 7-11. *Perfectly reasonable-looking configuration that has very unexpected consequences. On a separate note, the path to the .jtl files is not specified, leaving in question where these files will land on the file system.*

It looks like response time data will land in one file and throughput data will land in a separate file. But, JMeter does not work this way. Instead, it creates two identical output files. This wastes gigabytes of disk space with longer, high-throughput tests. So follow my lead with this: for each JMeter .jmx script, just pick a single one of your Listeners, arbitrarily, and specify the path/name of a .jtl file for just that one. As such, it seems like you could infer a rule that just one Listener (both of the components in Figure 7-1 are Listeners) for the entire .jmx file should be configured with an output file. I will call this the only-one-output-file-per-jmx rule. The rule holds true with other Listeners, ones that I call the "Basic Listeners," like Active Threads Over Time, Response Time Percentile, Summary Report and others, but there are two exceptions.

The first exception to the only-one-output-file-per-jmx rule is for the PerfMon Listener (which collects CPU consumption and other OS data) and JMXMon Listener (captures JMX data from a remote system). They are both from jmeter-plugins. Unlike all other Listeners, they each require their own output file. Neither PerfMon nor JMXMon will read data from other Listener's .jtl files. Likewise, other Listeners will not read data from PerfMon and JMXMon .jtl files.

Here is a summary of how to avoid this confusion of what-data-gets-written-to-where:

1. Choose any single Listener in your .jmx, one other than PerfMon and JMXMon, and specify a full path/file name to the .jtl to be written.

2. In addition, if you have PerfMon or JMXMon, each should have its own .jtl file.

3. If you are running JMeter from the command line (without the user interface), you may specify your .jtl file name with the -l command-line parameter. Keep in mind that any .jtl files specified in your .jmx file will also be written, even if -l is specified. See section 2.4.8 at `http://jmeter.apache.org/usermanual/get-started.html`) for documentation of all command-line parameters.

Right-Sizing Output Files for Heavy Debugging or High Throughput

Here is the second exception to the only-one-output-file-per-jmx rule, and it doubles as a fantastic feature that you need to use to avoid data overload on your load generator. Load generators are highly configurable beasts, and it is easy to misconfigure them to graph, process, calculate, and store so much data, that load generator performance suffers and test results reflect more of the load generator's problems and less of the SUT's performance.

However, collecting copious amounts of data (HTTP URL, response codes, input and output XML, cookies, script variables, and so on) is critical for troubleshooting in two different scenarios:

- Debugging a load script, for both errors and successful requests.

- During a load test, troubleshooting errors from the SUT.

JMeter satisfies this use case by allowing you to keep two Basic output files, one in the .csv format and the other in XML. The larger footprint of the XML file, along with its higher CPU consumption, is only used for sampler failures, which will only happen infrequently. In the separate csv-formatted .jtl file, JMeter will keep a smaller and more streamlined but high -volume record of all activity, success or failure.

Here is how you accomplish this:

1. In `JMETER_HOME/bin/user properties`, add the following property to default .jtl files to the csv format, instead of the more CPU-intensive, verbose, and larger XML format:

   `jmeter.save.saveservice.output_format=csv`

2. Add some other Listener, perhaps a nice `jp@gc - Synthesis Report (filtered)`, which is a more full featured version of the vanilla Summary Report. Specify

a .jtl file name (and do not forget to include the path to the .jtl, of course, as I recommended above to avoid protracted hide-and-seek).

3. Add a View Results Tree Listener to the load plan tree. Specify a different .jtl file name than the one used in step 2. For me, it is helpful to use the same path for all .jtl files.

4. For just this one Listener:

    i) Put a check in the Errors check box. Somewhat confusingly, this tells JMeter to only log errors and avoid the huge overhead of detailed logging for successful Sampler requests. Do not forget this check mark when applying load; we will discuss why in the next section.

    ii) Override the csv file format in the View Results Tree by clicking on the Configure button, as shown in Figure 7-12.

Figure 7-12. The "Configure" button that allows you to enable/disable XML format of the ouput file

    iii) To override the csv file format with the XML file format for just this one Listener, put checks in the boxes as shown in Figure 7-13.

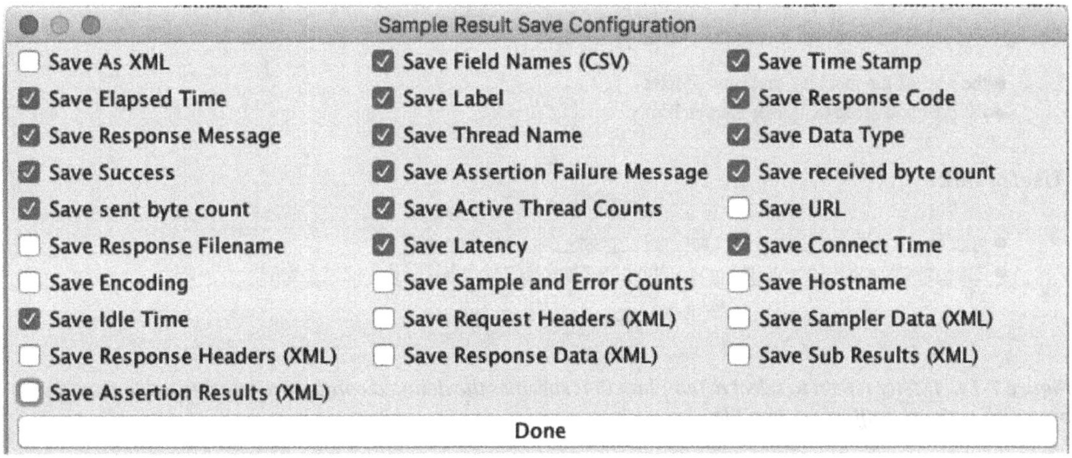

Figure 7-13. The checkboxes required to specify XML format for the output log file

Recording an HTTP Script

These instructions show how to record an HTTP script:

http://jmeter.apache.org/usermanual/jmeter_proxy_step_by_step.pdf

Rather than duplicate the instructions, I think it is important to highlight a few key steps in the recording process.

Configuring a .jmx file just right for recording used to be very difficult. Now, there is an easy way to create it: start with .jmx configuration from a JMeter Template.

Choose the File ➤ Templates menu option. Then choose the Recording template in the combo box at the top center. Finally, click Create, as shown in Figure 7-14.

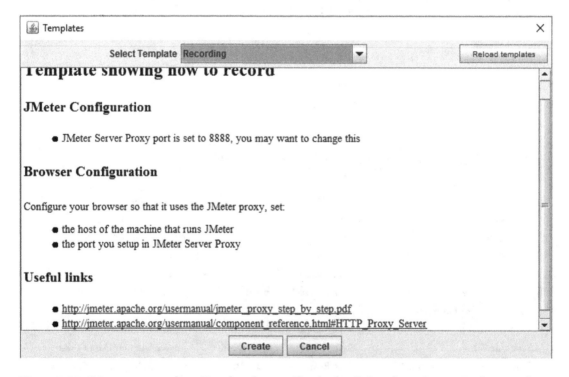

Figure 7-14. *JMeter screen to select a Template that specifies the detailed configuration required to record your browser's network traffic to a .jmx file.*

Once the Recording template is selected, the JMeter plan tree should look like Figure 7-15.

Figure 7-15. *The JMeter Plan Tree after the Recording template has been selected*

Figure 7-16 details a critical part of the process: your browser's HTTP proxy configuration. With no HTTP proxy configured, your browser makes requests directly to the Internet. With a proxy configured, all requests are forwarded to a specific host (labeled as Address) and port specified as shown.

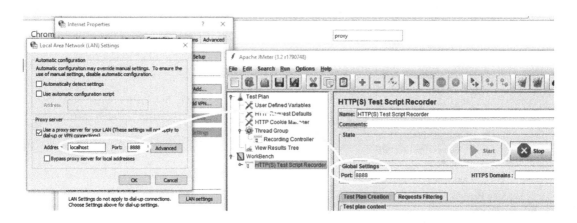

Figure 7-16. *Internet Explorer HTTP proxy configuration and the JMeter HTTP Proxy server. See how IE is configured to make all requests on port 8888 of localhost, and JMeter is configured to listen for all requests on this exact same port? Many JMeter users do not get this configuration correct.*

Note that the IE Address input box on the left must point to the local machine and the port number in IE (left) and the port number on the JMeter panel (right) must match. The value in Figure 7-16 is 8888. Also note the JMeter Start button is disabled, meaning that it has already been clicked to start the JMeter HTTP proxy program.

When the IE proxy is correctly configured and you click the big Start button on the HTTP(S) Test Script Recorder, all browser network traffic will be forwarded to the JMeter HTTP proxy, and JMeter proxy will immediately forward all traffic to the SUT. JMeter will record all traffic as you navigate the SUT.

Paste your SUT's URL into the browser and start navigating the business processes you want to record. When finished navigating, log out of the SUT and click Stop on the JMeter's HTTP(S) JMeter Test Script Recorder on the right of Figure 7-16.

JMeter will display all the recorded traffic in the Recording Controller, as shown in Figure 7-17.

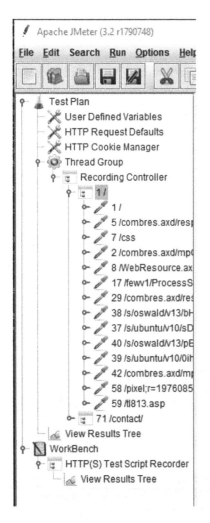

Figure 7-17. *JMeter's Recording Controller has captured network traffic as a user navigated the SUT in the browser*

Debugging an HTTP Recording

Working with XML Schema validators can be a pain. The validation errors are so cryptic, so not-quite-English. It reminds me of being on a technical support call with the dunce of the English-as-a-second-language (ESL) class.[3] But the only thing worse than working with a tightly governed XML Schema is a system without any schema at all, where there are no good rules for right/wrong input.

This is exactly like the load generator's task of properly assembling the HTTP GET to pass to a web application. What URL parameters are required on the HTTP GET? What kind of web authentication is used? Are CSRF tokens or JSESSIONID required? Any other cookies? What HTML "hidden" variables are pulled from the previous HTML response by the SUT's browser code and used to build the HTTP GET parameters for a subsequent page? All this uncertainty makes me pine for some kind of tightly governed schema that would plainly spell out the requirements. In fact, answering any of these questions wrong generally results in an incomplete HTML response and/or an exception on the server side, and getting this kind of an error is a likely sign that your .jmx load script is broken—perhaps out of sync with SUT requirements.

One way of dealing with this uncertainty is to keep a backup of the verbose HTTP log of the initial recording, along with the initially recorded load script itself. This creates a tidy little vault of all the required data items; it isn't a schema, but it is close enough. But then load script maintenance happens. Bugs are easily introduced later on when enhancing the script as detailed in Chapter 4. Remember? These are the changes required to make your load resemble the actual production load.

When a load script bug shows, you can find whether you have all the required data items by performing a detailed text file "diff" between the original verbose HTTP log and the one from the test run with the bug. The following JMeter instructions show how to capture those verbose HTTP logs.

When you look at the differences between those logs, you most often find that you did not fully understand the HTTP GET requirements (two paragraphs above). Alternatively, perhaps you have deployed a different version of the SUT with different requirements for an HTTP GET.

To repeat, the "diff" you will need to perform is between two different logs: one of the HTTP recording of the business process and the other from playing back the script. I use the JMeter View Results Tree to create these logs. The one for the recording must be under the Workbench (see Figure 7-18). The one for the playback must be configured to record in XML format like the first one, but instead it must be an immediate child of Test Plan, with a different output file name (obviously). You can use the JMeter copy/paste to copy the one created in the Workbench (as in the following instructions) to the Test Plan.

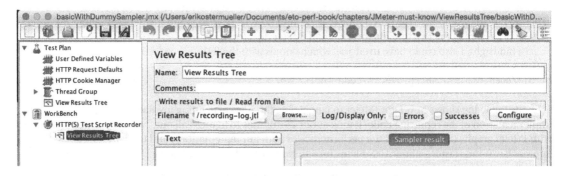

Figure 7-18. *The JMeter Recording template (File ➤ Templates ➤ Recording ➤ Create) used to record full request/response and other detail of the HTTP recording process*

---

[3]I was never the dunce of an ESL class myself, but I did flunk out of the Russian language program at the University of Kansas before going on to get my computer degree.

To capture that very detailed log of the HTTP recording, do the following:

1. Start a new test plan for recording: File ➤ Templates ➤ Recording ➤ Create.

2. Select the View Results Tree that is a grandchild of the WorkBench, as shown in Figure 7-18.

3. Specify the path/file for the log to be created.

4. Make sure there is no checkmark in the Errors checkbox. This will insure that everything gets recorded.

5. Click the Configure button and set the check marks as shown in Figure 7-13 earlier.

6. Start the recording, as shown in the JMeter doc: (`http://jmeter.apache.org/usermanual/jmeter_proxy_step_by_step.pdf`).

Load Testing Java Directly and Debugging

Once upon a time I was load-testing the reporting section of a loan system. When a user requested a small 1K report, it had to be extracted from specific byte offset into a single multi-megabyte file that was periodically downloaded from a back-end system. Response time under load for this component got as slow as 5 seconds; server-side concurrency was about five threads.

Unfortunately, the system was down for database maintenance, so the environment wasn't available for further investigation. I didn't have access to the source code, so I decompiled the source code (using jad.exe) to have a look. The code used `java.io.FileInputStream` to read() through the file one segment of bytes at a time, which provides no option to skip any bytes or jump to a particular location in the file. So if my 1K report was located at the end of the 10MB bundled report, the code would have to read through 9+ MB of data that was discarded. What a waste! By the way, this is an example of the Main Anti-Pattern 3—Overprocessing.

So I needed to test my new implementation of the code, which used the `java.io.RandomAccessFile` to "seek" directly to the specified offset and return the 1K report. When I ran my test 100 times in a row from a single thread, the new implementation was faster. But I had to convince my boss that response time at five threads of load would be better than the 5 seconds seen previously.

I knew how to launch my code five separate threads, but I thought collecting the results from those separate threads would take too much time to code, and then I'd have to graph the data somehow. So instead of launching the five threads myself, I had JMeter do it for me.

In hindsight, I also could have used jmh, which comes with the JDK:

`http://openjdk.java.net/projects/code-tools/jmh/`

The following shows how I got JMeter to launch five threads, all running my RandomAccessFile implementation of the reporting code; it took about 15 minutes to figure it all out. I actually ended up with JMeter graphs that compared the performance of both implementations, and the RandomAccessFile approach was tons faster—about 100-400ms for 5 threads of load, zero think time.

1. Put the code that you want to performance test into a new class that implements `org.apache.jmeter.protocol.java.sampler.JavaSamplerClient`. Extending one of these classes could be helpful too:
   `org.apache.jmeter.protocol.java.sampler.AbstractJavaSamplerClient`

   `org.apache.jmeter.protocol.java.test.JavaTest`

2. Create a new jar file with your class and dependent class files in it, although there is no need to package files in the JMeter package space.

3. Add your .jar file and any dependent third-party jar files in the `JMETER_HOME/lib/ext` folder.

4. Create a new JMeter .jmx plan. Add a Thread Group and configure the five threads of load.

5. As a child of that Thread Group, add a new Java Request Sampler:

   `http://jmeter.apache.org/usermanual/component_reference.html#Java_Request`.

6. Restart JMeter.

7. Select the Java Request Sampler. In the Classname combo box, select the class name you coded in step 1.

8. To enabled debugging, add the following environment variable before launching jmeter.sh or jmeter.cmd:

   `JVM_ARGS=-agentlib:jdwp=transport=dt_socket,server=y,address=8000`

9. In Eclipse, start a remote debugging session listening on port 8000. Set breakpoints in your source and then launch the JMeter script from the JMeter menu (Run ➤ Start) to trigger the breakpoint.

JMeter Sandbox

The JMeter .jmx file for this section and the next section is located in the jpt repo in this location:

`sampleJMeterScripts/jpt_ch07_sandbox.jmx`

Are you a little hesitant about mastering the art of load generation? You should be—it takes work. But fortunately, learning JMeter is easier than other load generators, because you can test just about every Test Element in its own little sandbox without the complexity of your SUT. So turn off the Wi-Fi (don't do that) and let's get started:

With this little sandbox technique, you can:

1. Create graphs with lots of live-looking squiggly lines, even ones with different metrics (like response time and throughput) on the same graph.

2. Process text, like creating an "output-input" script variable, that ever-so-important technique I mentioned in Chapter 4 on load scripting priorities.

3. Read data from a .csv file into JMeter script variables.

4. Control script flow using "If-then" logic or perhaps repeating a few steps with a Logic Controller.

5. …much, much more.

Once we cover items 1 and 2 from this list of sandbox tests, you will be primed and ready to play (yes play) with 3, 4, and 5 for homework. It is just plain fun. Here is how the sandbox works: close out any script you're working on and add a Thread Group and a child `jp@gc - Dummy Sampler` (https://jmeter-plugins.org/wiki/DummySampler/). Here are the steps:

1. Right-click on the Test Plan and choose Add ➤ Threads (Users) ➤ Thread Group.

2. Configure test duration.

91

3. Check Forever to keep the test running indefinitely (Run ➤ Shutdown, or Ctrl/Cmd+Comma to stop the test).

Thread Properties

Number of Threads (users): `1`

Ramp–Up Period (in seconds): `1`

Loop Count: ☑ Forever

4. Or leave Forever unchecked and put a 1 in the adjacent text box to run the Dummy Sampler just one time—used to run your script just one time, as when testing/debugging.

5. In the tree on the left side of the screen, right-click on the new Thread Group and select Add ➤ Sampler ➤ jp@gc - Dummy Sampler.

6. Select the newly added Dummy Sampler and duplicate it using the hotkey Ctrl+Shift+C.

7. See how I added - 01 and - 02 to the sampler names? The JMeter tree is on the left side of the screen. Look on the right side for the Name input box (above the word Comments). You can add the - 01 or - 02 to change the name here.

This will leave you with the screen shown in Figure 7-19.

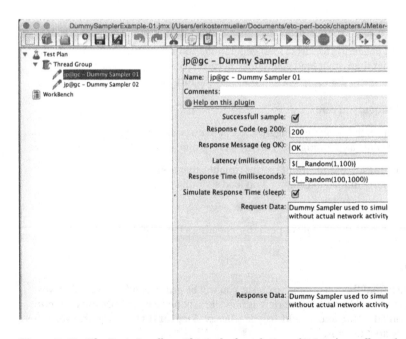

Figure 7-19. *The Basic Sandbox. This is the foundation of JMeter's sandbox play environment. Note the default values for Latency and Response Time. These variables that resolve to random numbers add a little interest when taking a graph for a test drive.*

JMeter Sandbox with One Graph

The JMeter .jmx file for this section is the same file used in the previous section:

```
sampleJMeterScripts/jpt_ch07_sandbox.jmx
```

With the sandbox foundation in place, just add one of the dozens of Test Elements you want to play with! In Figure 7-20, I added jp@gc Response Times Over Time (`https://jmeter-plugins.org/wiki/ResponseTimesOverTime/`)and started the test (Ctrl+R or Cmd+R) and voila, live-looking graphs. Use Ctrl+Comma or Cmd+Comma to stop.

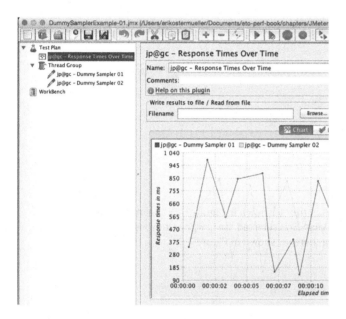

Figure 7-20. *Using the JMeter sandbox to get a quick demonstration of a graph*

JMeter Sandbox / Multiple Metrics on Same Graph

This section shows how to put two or more metrics on a single JMeterPlugins graph.
To see this in action yourself, look in the jpt repository for this .jmx file. Open it in JMeter:

```
sampleJMeterScripts/jpt_ch07_multipleMetricsOnOneGraph.jmx
```

Of course taking guesses, educated ones, is a key part of performance troubleshooting. But if a guess cannot be supported by data, we all need to be big enough to fall on our swords and verbally disown the unproven assertion. In fact, in Chapter 3 I called metrics the antidote to guesswork. So, I think developers need to hone their skills a little bit at finding, collecting and efficiently presenting performance data so we can substantiate more of our guesses or cleanly divorce them.

To see the impact of one metric on another, I think it's important to put two different metrics on the exact same graph. In Chapter 6, on the Scalability Yardstick, I showed you one example of that. Remember that we had to check to see how many thread of load were required to push the SUT CPU to 25%? The two metrics were CPU and count of JMeter threads of load. In this case, the increase in threads of load impacted two other metrics: both CPU and throughput were impacted—they both increased.

Actually, my favorite four metrics for a single start are CPU, response time, throughput, and load generator thread count.

To help you get up-to-speed on displaying graphs like this yourself, Figure 7-21 shows my test plan, still using the jp@gc - Dummy Sampler sandbox, to put two metrics on the same graph: jp@gc - Response Times Over Time and jp@gc - Transactions per Second.

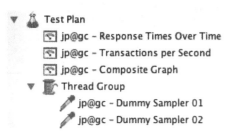

Figure 7-21. *The test plan required to get multiple lines of the same graph*

Once you have added them to your load plan tree as shown in Figure 7-21, you need to tell the new jp@gc - Composite Graph which metrics to display. So I selected the jp@gc - Composite Graph and clicked the Graphs tab. Whoops, but there was nothing there, as shown in Figure 7-22.

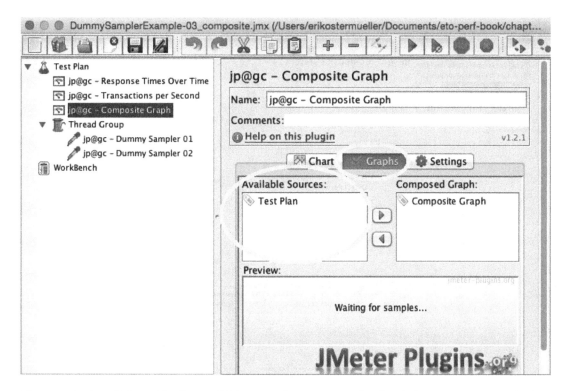

Figure 7-22. *A usability quirk: The Available Sources box is not populated with the metrics I want to display in the graph. See Figure 7-23 for a solution.*

To fix this little problem, you just need to run the test for a few seconds and stop the test. This will populate the Available Sources box so you can select the metrics you want to see (Figure 7-23).

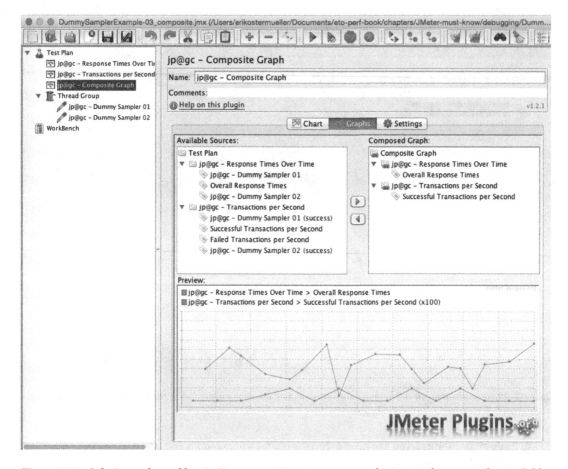

Figure 7-23. *Solution to the problem in Figure 7-22. To get your metric selections to show up in the Available Sources box, just run the test. Then stop the test and double-click your selections in Available Sources to move them into the Composite Graph section.*

Once the Available Sources box is populated, you can double-click the metrics you want to move to the Composed Graph box.

JMeter Sandbox for Testing Correlation Variables

The JMeter .jmx files for the next two examples are located in the jpt repo in this location:

sampleJMeterScripts/ folder for jpt_ch07_correlationVariables.jmx

In Chapter 4, I showed a number of circumstances where the load generator script has to step in and do small data movement chores that in a live situation are done by your SUT's JavaScript in the browser. But in that chapter, I tried to show everything in a load-generator–agnostic way. This section jumps into the JMeter specifics on how to implement this.

Sometimes with the right SUT functionality, a unique ID generated on the server SUT gets recorded into your load script. Adding the right script variable, one that I'm calling an "Output-Input" variable, will retrieve the freshly generated value, instead of relying on the single, static value that was initially recorded into the script. That way, the generated ID can be submitted somehow (you have to figure that part out) in a subsequent request, perhaps as a query parameter or somewhere in the body of an HTTP post.

But before sticking a generated ID like this into a script variable, your JMeter script first has to find that particular ID from its location embedded hopefully a predictable place in lots of text in the output HTML stream.

Fishing Expedition—Step One, Find the Data Item

Two popular ways of finding a data item in the output HTML are with a regular expression or an XPath expression. Choose whichever way you feel most comfortable with, but here is a regular expression example.

Step One is simply to perfect the regular expression to find your data item in the XML or HTML.

Using the JMeter sandbox approach, start by creating a little sandbox test plan like the one shown in Figure 7-24. The goal is to simply embed the HTML that you expect your SUT to return into the Dummy Sampler and then use JMeter to play around with various regular expressions to identify the one that will correctly identify the data.

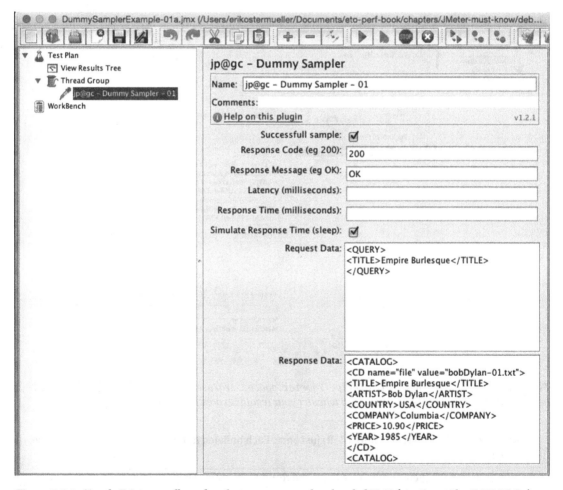

Figure 7-24. *Simple JMeter sandbox plan that returns some hard-coded XML (starting with <CATALOG>) that contains the text to be placed into the Output-Input variable.*

Here is our goal: to find the regular expression that will locate the following text:

The bobDylan-01.txt is the value we want to place in the Output-Input script variable.	`<CD name="file" value="bobDylan-01.txt">`
This regular expression used to identify bobDylan-01.txt	`name="file" value="(.+?)">`

Before running this test,

1. Make sure the Thread Group is configured to execute the Dummy Sampler one time (hint—make sure the Forever box is unchecked); you don't need 5235 executions to debug this—you need just one.

2. In the View Results Tree (Figure 7-25), make sure the Errors and Successes boxes are unchecked. (Learn more about these checkboxes here: `http://jmeter.apache.org/usermanual/component_reference.html#View_Results_Tree`.) This will make sure none of the results are hidden or filtered out.

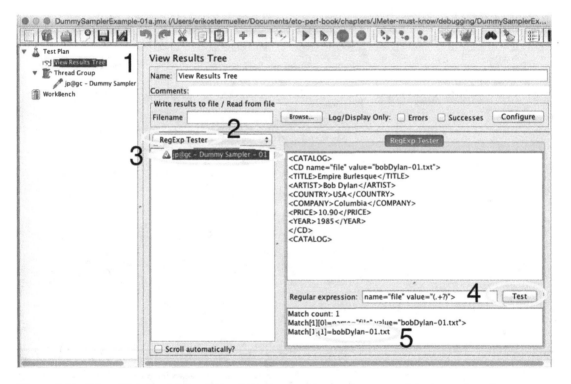

Figure 7-25. *JMeter View Results Tree (`http://jmeter.apache.org/usermanual/component_reference.html#View_Results_Tree`)—use this to test whether your regular expression works.*

Run the test (Run ➤ Start or Cmd/Ctrl+R) just once. Each bulleted number below corresponds to the number in Figure 7-25.

1. Click on the View Results Tree to see the result of the single Dummy Sampler execution.

2. Change the combo box to RegExp Tester from the default value of Text. This basically reconfigures the UI so we can test the hard coded XML result against the regular expression.

3. Do you see the green triangle with the check mark inside it, next to jp@gc - Dummy Sampler - 01 ? Select this—it is the result of the single run of the Dummy Sampler.

4. Finally, we get down to business. Type in the value of the regular expression you want to test, and then click the Test button.

5. This shows that our regular expression worked, because it isolated bobDylan-01.txt from the rest of the XML.

Fishing Expedition—Step Two

Now it is time to put your perfected XPath or RegEx expression into place. Right-click jp@gc - Dummy Sampler (or the real HTTP Request that will produce the HTML or XML responses that you are fishing through). Choose Add ➤ Post Processor ➤ RegEx Extractor (or XPath Extractor). The JMeter doc for the Extractor you're using will also show you how to specify the name of the JMeter script variable the fished out value should be stored in. Your JMeter test plan should look like Figure 7-26.

Figure 7-26. *When creating an Correlation variable in JMeter in the sandbox, the load plan tree should look like this*

When this runs, JMeter will attempt to find the value your looking for. It will then place that value into a script variable. To see whether JMeter has done this as you were expecting, you need to add a Debug Sampler as shown in Figure 7-27. The actual debug information will show up in the View Results Tree at the top of Figure 7-27.

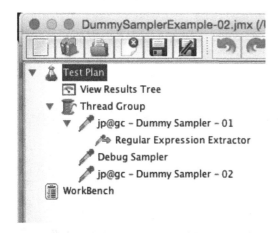

Figure 7-27. *The JMeter Debug Sampler and jp@gc—Dummy Samplers have very similar names. The Debug Sampler acts as a simple request to show all JMeter variables in the View Results Tree, as shown in Figure 7-29.*

Figure 7-28 shows how to specify exactly what you want to find from the HTTP response. It is helpful to choose a default value that will indicate when something has likely gone wrong.

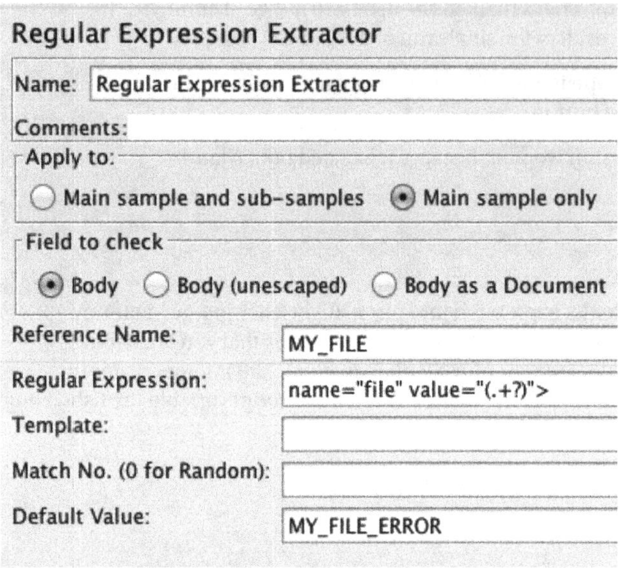

Regular Expression Extractor

Name: Regular Expression Extractor

Comments:

Apply to:
- ○ Main sample and sub-samples   ● Main sample only

Field to check
- ● Body   ○ Body (unescaped)   ○ Body as a Document

Reference Name: MY_FILE

Regular Expression: name="file" value="(.+?)">

Template:

Match No. (0 for Random):

Default Value: MY_FILE_ERROR

Figure 7-28. *The JMeter Regular Expression Extractor. The Regular Expression field is used to search the HTTP response for a string of text used in a Correlation Variable.*

To find the debug information to troubleshoot problems with the correlation variable, click on the View Results Tree on the test plan (left side of the screen) and select the Debug Sampler as shown in Figure 7-29.

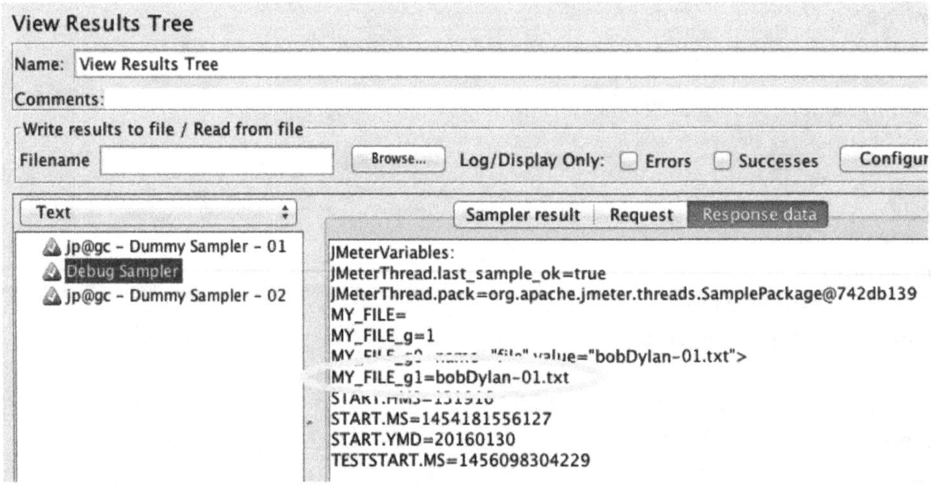

View Results Tree

Name: View Results Tree

Comments:

Write results to file / Read from file

Filename [   ] [Browse...]   Log/Display Only: ☐ Errors ☐ Successes   [Configur

| Text | Sampler result | Request | Response data |

- jp@gc – Dummy Sampler – 01
- Debug Sampler
- jp@gc – Dummy Sampler – 02

```
JMeterVariables:
JMeterThread.last_sample_ok=true
JMeterThread.pack=org.apache.jmeter.threads.SamplePackage@742db139
MY_FILE=
MY_FILE_g=1
MY_FILE_g0=... name="file" value="bobDylan-01.txt">
MY_FILE_g1=bobDylan-01.txt
START.HMS=151916
START.MS=1454181556127
START.YMD=20160130
TESTSTART.MS=1456098304229
```

Figure 7-29. *This View Results Tree output shows how the Debug Sampler has dumped the values of all JMeter variables for debugging purposes*

Finally, it is time to use the variable extracted from the response of the previous Sampler. Note in Figure 7-30 how the variable name (MY_FILE_g1) is wraped in curly braces. The "dollar curly" syntax is used to evaluate the variable.

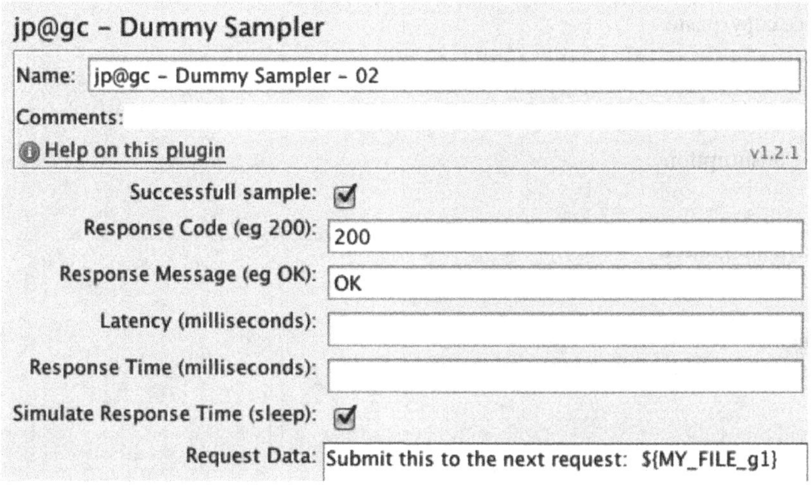

Figure 7-30. *The Request Data field at the bottom of this figure simulates POST data for an HTTP Requst. The ${MY_FILE_g1} variable is a Correlation Variable being passed back into the SUT.*

Prerequisites

To conclude this chapter, I'll present a to-do list of things you should know how to do:

- Record a JMeter load script. During the recording, save every last byte to a log file for future reference.

- Flag a logon script as "run once."

- Run JMeter headlessly.

- Debug JMeter load script.

- Configure load script to use data from a .csv data file. The file should contain a list of users to log on, lists of accounts and customers to query.

- Create assertions to validate that something actually happened, that your SUT is actually doing its job.

- Using a correlation variable, capture the output of one request and submit to the input of another.

- Create ramp up, ramp down load plans.

- Create a load plan that distributes load by the percentages of business processes see in production.

- Create and use JMeter variables, perhaps reading a variable from the command line.

Load gen features:

- Use multiple network protocols: HTTP/S, JMS, Sockets, JDBC.

- Run headless; also, run from the same machine as the SUT.

- Use JMeter's nice copy/paste.

Graphing features:

- Composite graphs

- CPU/Resource Consumption

- JMX

- Grafana/InfluxDB integration

Must know:

- Avoid heavy logging.

- .jtl files

  - Reading

  - Writing

  - How many output files? 1, 2 or 3

  - Merging

  - Clearing UI results does not clear data file.

- Use JDBC sampler for data creation.

- Save the initial Recording using View Results Tree.

- Managing colors.

- Maven, ANT, Jenkins integration.

- Thread groups: separate samplers (SOA), or combined (Web).

- Debugging tips:

  - Use a Dummy Sampler to specify sample HTML responses, before hooking your test plan up to a live HTTP system.BSF PostProcessor:

    ```
    var myVariable = vars.get("MY_VARIABLE");
    OUT.println('The value of MY_VARIABLE is [' + myVariable + ']' )
    ```

- Assertions. Configure an Assertion to raise a red flag when text from an error is present.

- Where to stick the Listeners.

Don't Forget

This chapter provided a tour of some JMeter functionality that is rarely if ever documented, and other functionality that is documented but still causes trouble for the many technicians that I have taught JMeter to.

Don't forget that if you can't figure out how to get some JMeter feature to work, create a little "Hello World" sandbox-like .jmx script to experiment with the feature. Copy and paste a snippet of HTML (or json or XML or whatever) into the Dummy Sampler so that your test plan can operate on it. Just about every single JMeter Test Element can be tested like this. You can experiment with logging, load plans, Correlation Variables, JMeter Assertions, Composite Graphs (multiple metrics on the same graph), you name it.

What's Next

The next chapter provides an overview of the two sample applications that come with this book. These applications reproduce the write-once-run-anywhere (WORA) performance defects that are detectable in both large environments and small ones. These examples will give you hands-on experiences hooking up plug-it-in-now performance and observability tools, where available, that will help you find and fix performance defects quickly.

PART III

■ ■ ■

The P.A.t.h. Checklist and Performance Troubleshooting

CHAPTER 8

■ ■ ■

Introduction to the P.A.t.h. Checklist

In the Introduction, I asked how close you could come to the root cause of a performance problem in just 30 minutes. That is about how long it should take to capture and review data from the four items in the P.A.t.h. Checklist.

But before getting into the technical details of the Checklist, this chapter provides a quick review of previous chapters. Then it describes how to use the Checklist when troubleshooting, and finally it provides a brief introduction to the two sets of code examples.

The objectives of this chapter are:

- Understand the basic principles of using the P.A.t.h. Checklist to identify and fix performance problems.

- Understand how to run the javaPerformanceTroubleshooting and littleMock code examples.

- Understand the architecture of the javaPerformanceTroubleshooting and littleMock code examples.

The first two items in the P.A.t.h. Checklist, database persistence (P) and network connections to other (Alien=A) systems, are common integration points that historically have caused performance problems. JDBC is the focus of the Persistence work, but the concepts apply to almost any database. The last two, t. and h., examine the threads (t) that execute code and memory consumption (h., the heap), along with its memory recycling process—the Garbage Collector. So, the P.A.t.h. checklist takes a closer look at the performance health of a few key integration points and the thread and memory management that underpins all processing. Yes, the focus of this book is the most common problems, but the toolset is capable of finding virtually any problem.

With real-world systems, you look at the data from all four of the items in the P.A.t.h. checklist. You decide which one looks the least healthy and then focus on tuning that part. But in the four P.A.t.h. chapters, I will make it easier on you by telling you straight up which Checklist item (hint: look at the chapter title) is causing the main, single performance problem that is dragging down the performance.

Quick Review

The first three chapters set the stage for what to expect when performance tuning.

- Chapter 1: I presented the Main Performance Anti-Patterns early on so you have a rough idea what to look for when hunting for performance defects. Start with the first anti-pattern, and ask whether it matches the problem that you're seeing. If you find a match, generally you can stop; otherwise check out the second, third, and fourth ones in order.

© Erik Ostermueller 2017
E. Ostermueller, *Troubleshooting Java Performance*, DOI 10.1007/978-1-4842-2979-8_8

1. Unnecessary Initialization: Small processing challenges that mostly happen prior to and during the initialization for the main (larger) processing event in your request, they often have a small amount of I/O but are repeated many times.

2. Strategy / Algorithm Inefficiency: A misconfigured or poorly chosen algorithm or coding strategy is causing performance problems. A strategy is a technique used throughout a code base, and an algorithm is a plan used to implement a single component.

3. Overprocessing: The system is doing unnecessary work. Removing that work provides measurable performance benefit. One example is retrieving too much data, where most of the data is discarded. Another example is including in your load test the wrong resource-hungry use case—one that is seldom used in production.

4. Large Processing Challenge: Attempting to process and conquer a massive amount of data. Very few applications legitimately have such a need, but these do exist. Other examples would be querying 4 billion rows of data, transferring 10MB of data repeatedly over a slow network, and the like.

-   Chapter 2: A Modest Tuning Environment: This chapter showed how most performance defects can be found in both large and small environments. It showed a few techniques (stub servers, graphing CPU by PID) that are very helpful for tuning in a smaller environment, where tuning can be especially productive, with as many as 10 fix-test cycles in a single day.

-   Chapter 3 on metrics is a life preserver to keep you from drowning in a vast sea of confusion deciding which performance metrics to use:

    -   Load generator metrics, for the most part, assess whether performance requirements have been met. Enough throughput? Fast enough response time?

    -   Resource consumption metrics show when you have run out of hardware, CPU or RAM, meaning you'll either need more hardware or you need to tune the system to consume less.

    -   Lastly, "Blame metrics" point to which component in the SUT is causing the slowdown or high CPU consumption; this is the part we are about to get to. The P.A.t.h. Checklist in the next four chapters provides these 'blame' metrics.

But before you can reproduce and solve performance troubleshooting problems, you must first master the basics of load generation, as I have detailed in the load generation Chapters 4, 5, 6 and 7. Let's cement those basics in your head with a quick overview before moving on to the part where we cast blame upon slow or otherwise problematic SUT components.

-   Chapter 4 on load scripting priorities discussed how load scripts must be recorded and enhanced to produce a realistic load. Don't forget how we broke down the various script enhancements into First Priority and Second Priority. The First Priority script enhancements are enough to stress out the SUT's basic architecture, where fixing a single performance defect can improve performance for many business processes across the entire architecture. The Second Priority script enhancements aim for that added touch of "system realism" on individual business processes. Fixing these kinds of defects might be critical, but their impact is limited to individual business process.

- Chapter 5 on Invalid Load Tests details a few circumstances (seen all too frequently) that make a given load test so unlike production that the results should be discarded. This is your chance to learn from the many mistakes that I and others have made. Don't generate load over a WAN. Raise resource caps before tuning and lower them before deploying into production. Triple check that the business processes (and the data) in your load script pretty much match those used in production. Enhance your load script to make sure there are no errors and the right data is getting returned. Be vigilant in using Brendan Gregg's USE method:

  `http://www.brendangregg.com/usemethod.html` to always watch resource consumption. Don't waste time tuning edge cases.

- Chapter 6 on the Scalability Yardstick provides marching orders for what tests to run and how much load to apply on a day-to-day basis. A doctor will assess the health of your sprained ankle by manipulating it and increasing pressure on it until you show signs of pain. Likewise, the Scalability Yardstick load test directs you to increase the load until the SUT shows signs, from load generator metrics, of "bad performance." Remember the clean, squared, leaps of throughput? You start by putting your SUT (and its performance problem) under the microscope. You do this by reproducing the performance problems using the Scalability Yardstick load test. Do you remember how this works? You run an incremental load test with four steps of load, the first of which pushes the app server CPU to 25%. Then you see at which of the four steps the nice, squared steps of throughput disintegrate into jagged and jumpy chaos—and you have reproduced the problem.

- Chapter 7 showed how anything in JMeter can be tested out in a small sandbox environment before live HTTP requests are sent across the wire. It showed the high-level tree structure of a load test, as well as how to capture and display extra metrics like CPU consumption from your SUT. Calibrating the Scalability Yardstick test was a lot easier because we saw on a single JMeter graph exactly how many threads it took to push the app server CPU to 25%.

Working the P.A.t.h. Checklist

With all of this slightly mundane groundwork behind us, the stage is set, and let the drum roll begin. The next four chapters finally show how to identify and blame and ultimately fix specific components of the SUT for performance problems.

To give yourself time to inspect the problem using the four different lenses, you need to manually reconfigure your load plan from four steps of incremental load to be a single steady-state test at the first level *after* the clean, squared throughput step disappeared. Perhaps set the duration to 20-30 minutes, knowing that you'll stop the test as soon as these performance lenses show you some actionable intelligence.

For example, say your Scalability Yardstick test ran with two threads at each level of load, and each level lasted for 2 minutes. If you got clean, chiseled steps at about 25% CPU (two threads) and 50% CPU (four threads) but no chiseled leaps after that, then the steady state "let's reproduce the bug" test needs to run at six threads for the duration (20-30 minutes).

While the load test with the performance problems is running at steady state, you will look at the SUT using each of the four items in the checklist. The problem (or problems) you are experiencing will show up in one or more of the lenses. So what does this mean, to look through a lens?

As you will see in the coming chapters, each of the four checklist items has its own set of monitoring and tracing tools (freely available), and I will describe how to capture and interpret the data from each, giving a "problem" or "no problem" assessment for each checklist item. The goal, of course is blame. To blame one particular component of the system for the performance problem(s) and then dream up a fix.

As the chapters ahead will show you, the four checklist items will point out a few problems. Somewhat subjectively, you need to pick one of these issues to attack first—whichever issue provides the most bang for the buck. In other words, you generally want to attack the defect that provides the biggest performance boost with the smallest effort, which may be a code change, configuration change, data change, or even a load script change.

Here are the four items in the P.A.t.h. checklist:

- P   Persistence: slow JDBC invocations and calling any one SQL too much.

- A   Alien systems (network calls to a system outside your main JVM)

- t   Threads (CPU overconsumption and blocked threads)

- h   Heap (garbage collection inefficiencies and memory leaks)

But what is so special about these four particular areas? For starters, this is simply a convenient way to categorize the locations of today's most common server side performance problems, but also to pair up those locations with their own set of observability tools. But more practically, the P for persistence represents the database, and there is wide agreement that database has more performance problems than any other area. We will focus on JDBC systems, but the same issues with JDBC performance in the P chapter also apply to NoSQL databases, as well; all this is covered in Chapter 9. I made up the term "Alien systems"— it is kind of a placeholder for performance issues with any system our JVMs talks to over a network. That is Chapter 10.

So the P and the A are systems we integrate with. The t and the h are different. Every bit of our Java code is run in by an operating system thread, so the t for Threads explores thread efficiency. Are there blocked threads? (More on this later.) Are there small processing challenges that are unnecessarily eating a lot of CPU? Lastly, the h in PATH stands for the health of the Heap. Poor garbage collection efficiency can really hurt performance, as well as stability. I was always hesitant to wade into the complex waters of understanding GC algorithms. Among other things, this h chapter goes out of its way to show how surprisingly little you have to know about GC to improve performance. The t and the h are in Chapters 11 and 12, respectively.

I mentioned earlier that the P and the A in P.A.t.h. are spelled out with capital letters because they are special: most of the time, you can detect problems in those areas with just a single user's traffic. One of the reasons this is true is because a single, lonely query to a large, unindexed table is often real slow, like slower than 1 second. Likewise, executing 100 SQL/NoSQL requests will likely be slow (more than 1 second) with any number of users, including just one.

Since no load required is required and it's easier to capture a one-time sample of P and A activity, you get the great benefit of being able to detect and fix performance problems without a load script (like a JMeter one) and without a load environment—any environment will suffice with P and A. An unindexed query to a large table is a good example of this, where lowering response time will yield higher throughput.

Unfortunately, the same thing does not work with the t. and the h. in P.A.t.h. Why? Because it takes more than one thread to cause a performance problem with the synchronized keyword. Likewise, it takes a good deal of traffic to exacerbate a memory leak or misconfigured Garbage Collection.

While you are running a Scalability Yardstick test to reproduce a performance problem, the four items in the checklist will show you what components are to blame for the performance problems. Of course, you might find problems in more than one of the checklist items while you are running a single test. If so, you will have to triage the problems and decide which one(s) to fix first.

In this triage process, you will have to make decisions like, "Which should we tune first, the slowest query in the system that is taking 1.5 seconds, or repeated BLOCKED threads in our XML processing?"

Remember the P.A.t.h. acronym. Persistence, Alien systems, Threads, and Heap. I mentioned this first in the chapter on load scripting priorities, but keep in mind that the first two checklist items, persistence and alien systems, highlight many tuning opportunities without load generation—in other words, when a single user traverses the system. If your performance environment is not yet built or if your load scripts are not yet created, you can still get started on improving performance.

Running the Examples

Because performance can go wrong in so many ways, the P.A.t.h system breaks problems down into four easier-to-understand categories. Its organization helps to grasp this large universe of performance problems. Most of the online examples that come with this book highlight just one performance problem in one of the four areas. The simplicity of looking at just a single problem at a time is really helpful to zero in and focus on performance problems that regularly go undetected, and the tools used to detect them.

There are two different github.com projects that come with this book. The first one I'll refer to as jpt, which stands for Java Performance Troubleshooting. It comes with about 12 pairs of examples. In each pair, one of the two has a performance problem, and the other one does not—I've already fixed it for you. The two tests are labeled as the *a* test and the *b* test. Table 2-1 in Chapter 2 has a full listing of the 12 pairs of tests.

However, the fact that I'm fixing these problems for you, and that I am training your eyes on just a single problem at a time—this is a bit unrealistic. It is even more unrealistic that I tell you in advance whether the problem is a P., A., t. or h. problem. If I tell you that a particular test is a P problem, then you know to hook up the monitoring/observability tools I have prescribed for P-like problems. This is very straightforward, but it is unrealistic. In the real world, problems generally just start out as bad/slow, and it's your burden to discover in which of the four areas the problem lurks.

This means that you generally must use the tools from all four items in the P.A.t.h. Checklist to fully understand the situation, a situation I have tried to model in the test 09a. This is an example of many problems all mixed together. There is no test 09b.

Java Performance Troubleshooting (jpt) Sample App

There are small scripts to launch various parts of the application. As a convention, any time I mention a Bash script that ends in .sh, you will find a corresponding MS-Windows script (in the same folder) that ends in .cmd.

Figure 8-1 shows the rough architecture of the jpt application.

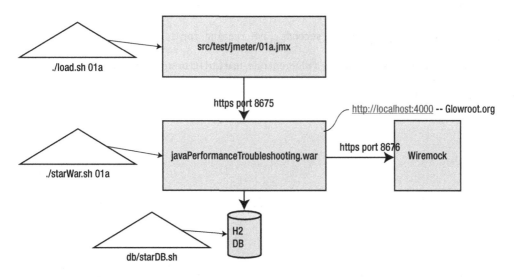

Figure 8-1. *Architecture of the jpt examples. The triangles indicate the three scripts that must be launched from three separate terminal windows. The parameters after the first two scripts indicate that this is test 01a.*

The download and instructions are available here:

https://github.com/eostermueller/javaPerformanceTroubleshooting

An overview of the installation and running of the examples is included below. If you run into any issues, be sure to consult the online version of the doc.

Table 8-1 shows that it takes three scripts to run one of the jpt tests. Prior to running any of the tests, the init.sh script must be executed. It creates and populates an H2 database with more than 2 million rows of data. On my 2012 MacBook, the init.sh script takes 10 to 15 minutes to run. You can re-run the init.sh script and it will recreate the db from scratch.

Table 8-1. *Three Terminal Windows (Aka Command Prompts) Are Required to Run Each Jpt Example.*

1	`# cd db` `# db/startDb.sh`	Launches the H2 Database
2	`# ./startWar.sh 01a`	Launches the web application. Note the 01a parameter to run web server configuration for test 01a. Note that both glowroot and wiremock, depicted above, launch with this script.
3	`# ./load.sh 01a`	Launches JMeter from the command line. Note the 01a parameter to run the load test 01a.

This table shows the commands required to run example 01a. The commands must be launched in the specified order. Ctrl+C should be used to stop each of these. Prior to running any of these, the init.sh script must be run just once.

Here are a few notes for launching the tests.

Note that after running .startWar.sh, you should wait to start ./load.sh until you see this startWar.sh message:

Started PerformanceSandboxApp in 11.692 seconds (JVM running for 19.683)

To stop running one test and start running a different one, use Ctrl+C to stop both the ./startWar.sh and the load.sh scripts. Then restart the same scripts with the desired test ID. The startDb.sh script can stay running for as long as you like.

You will use the port numbers in Table 8-2 to help with your performance troubleshooting in the jpt examples.

Table 8-2. TCP ports Used by the jpt Examples

Description	Value
Using JMeter, HTTPS load is applied on this TCP port	8675
`javaPerformanceTroubleshooting.war` runs under Spring Boot (`https://projects.spring.io/spring-boot/`). It connects over HTTP to a backend system that listens on this TCP port.	8676
glowroot (`https://glowroot.org/`) Monitoring	`http://localhost:4000`
h2 (`http://h2database.com/html/main.html`) TCP Server	`tcp://localhost:9092` (only local connections)
h2 PGServer	`pg://localhost:5435` (only local connections)
h2 Web/Console Server. You can execute ad-hoc SQL on this web page.	`http://localhost:8082` (only local connections). There is no username and no password.

littleMock Sample Application

For the jpt github.com project above, to decide what kind of test you want to run, you need to pass the test ID (01a, 01b, 02a, 02b, and so on) into both the startWar.sh and the load.sh scripts. If you pass in a different test ID, you get different behavior, based on Table 2-1 in Chapter 2.

The littleMock github.com project is different. There are no parameters for the startup scripts to determine configuration. Instead, the configuration is done via a small web page that is available via `http://localhost:8080/ui`. If you're ever in the mood stir up a little trouble, littleMock's web page is just for you. Would you like to overrun the heap with large RAM allocations, just to see GC response time suffer? Perhaps you'd like to iterate endlessly (almost) through meanlingless loops? With littleMock, you can even grind the system to a halt with pathetically slow (but very commnly used) XPath and XSLT idoms. The littleMock web page puts the power in your hands.

Just click a few buttons and the performance change is implemented immediately. Toggle the change off, if you'd like. No, don't do that. Instead, brew up a perfect storm by configuring half a dozen nightmares simultaneously using a "Performance Key", a comma-separated list of multiple configurations that can be applied at the same time. Athena and Ares, look out.

Just enter a Performance Key as shown in Figure 8-2 and click 'Update.' Subsequent chapters will provide various Performance Keys so you can learn how to troubleshoot certain performance problems. Alternatively, you can click on the individual settings below the Key (not shown) to see how they impact performance. Every individual change you make is immediately reflected in the Performance Key, and vice versa.

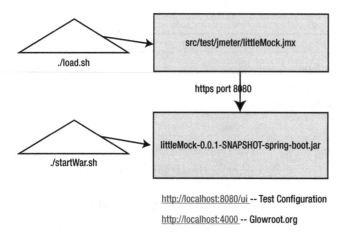

Figure 8-2. *littleMock's web page and the command-separate Performance Key that enables you to dial in multiple performance settings at a single time. Individual settings (between the commas) are described further down the page, below the Key.*

The littleMock web page lets you make on-the-fly tuning changes whose impact can be immediately seen in the glowroot monitoring, which is available at http://localhost:4000, just as it is in jpt. Figure 8-3 shows the architecture.

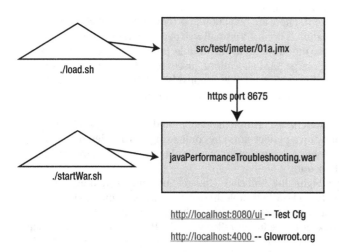

Figure 8-3. *Architecture of the littleMock application. Note that the load.sh and the startWar.sh do not accept any parameters. To alter performance of littleMock, use the small UI web page:* `http:/localhost:8080/ui`

Don't Forget

Running the jpt and littleMock applications on your own machines will provide a hands-on-experience that you can't get from just reading along, so I encourage you to download the applications now. Here are the URLs, one more time:

```
https://github.com/eostermueller/javaPerformanceTroubleshooting
https://github.com/eostermueller/littleMock
```

Once these examples are up and running, you will be able to demonstrate write-once-run-anywhere performance defects that can be reproduced in small and large environments, alike.

What's Next

After you run the init.sh script with the jpt project, you will have a database on your machine with more than 2 million rows—and it takes just 10-15 minutes to create all that data. The next chapter on P for Persistence, will help you diagnose garden-variety problems with individual queries, but also it will show how to detect inefficient strategies around multiple queries that execute as part of a single server-side request.

CHAPTER 9

■ ■ ■

Persistence, the "P" in P.A.t.h.

This chapter covers the first item in the P.A.t.h. checklist, "P" for Persistence, and it shows how to assess performance health and how to interpret the resulting data to improve system performance.

The objectives of this chapter are:

- Know the biggest performance problem in Java server-side software and the two most common anti-patterns that cause it.

- Learn how to diagnose application performance problems caused by:

  - Individual JDBC SQL queries

  - Multiple JDBC SQL queries, regardless of how fast the individual queries run

- Learn how a small development database can lead to a false sense of performance security.

I believe there is wide agreement among a variety of performance experts that "too many database calls" is the worst performance defect in Java server-side software, but we continue to see systems with this problem, one that is almost prohibitively costly to fix (refactor all the SQL).

To help cement this opinion, I keep the following blog post up-to-date with various opinions on the matter:

`http://ostermueller.blogspot.com/2014/11/the-worst-server-side-performance.html`

This chapter shows how to detect the "too many database calls" problem in a running system—a system you can run on your own machine. It also shows how to find the problem just by looking at the source code, by looking for a few different performance anti-patterns. Finally, it quantifies the great performance boost you can get by fixing the problem.

The previous chapter described the two sets of run-on-your-own-machine performance examples that come with this book. The littleMock examples do not use a database, so this chapter's examples come from the other set—jpt—which come with an H2 database (h2database.com). The jpt init.sh/init.cmd script populates the database with more than 2 million rows of data for a more realistic look at these issues.

Test 05: Performance Issues with One SQL

Test Results, captured from Glowroot:

Test 05a: **3,500** requests per minute; **50ms** response time.

Test 05b: **14** requests per minute; **13,500ms** response time

Metrics that you will need:

Response time and throughput for all SQL statements executed

A few tools that provide this data: Glowroot, JavaMelody, JDBC Performance Logger

© Erik Ostermueller 2017
E. Ostermueller, *Troubleshooting Java Performance*, DOI 10.1007/978-1-4842-2979-8_9

With response time of more than 13 seconds, Test 05b is horribly slow, and throughput is very low. In fact, throughput is 250 times less than 05a, but why?

In the real world you will also need to check for issues in the other P.A.t.h. items as well, but since this is the Persistence chapter, let's jump right into the SQL metrics to see what's causing this 13.5 second response time. The first task is to identify the queries with the slowest response time, especially ones that get executed a lot. Then, we will see whether any obvious improvements can be made.

Figure 9-1 shows the one query whose performance is much slower than the other two:

```
SELECT hid from history WHERE aid = ?
```

All Web Transactions

Response time	Slow traces (30)	Queries	Service calls	Continuous profiling

	Total time ▾ (ms)	Execution count	Time per execution (ms)	Rows per execution
SELECT hid from history WHERE aid = ?	200,755.8	560	358.5	10.0
SELECT tid, hid, bid, aid, delta, mtime, …	147,473.8	5,600	26.3	1.0
SELECT aid, bid, abalance, filler, filler…	24,735.1	560	44.2	1.0

Figure 9-1. *For test 05a, throughput and response time for all SQL, provided by glowroot.org. The slowest query on the top row (358.5ms average) also happens to be the one with the most Total Time.*

Because we're trying to remedy 13.5 second response time, and because this query's response time (358.5ms average, top row below) is more than 10 times slower than the other two queries, it is worth some time to investigate this query further. Even being just a few times slower would merit some investigation.

In this query, there are no JOINS to other tables, the list of fields selected is very short (just the Hid column), and the WHERE criteria of WHERE aid = ? is trivial. The entire query is very basic. In fact, the other queries are pretty basic as well, and even for the same reasons. So why does the performance of these "basic" queries vary so greatly?

In many development shops, SQL tuning falls mainly on the (hopefully) capable shoulders of the DBA, and that's an OK thing. But even if this is the case, and developers have little or no responsibility for performance of individual queries, I think developers need at least some rudimentary understanding of what's required to make basic queries perform well, including basic queries in this example. More specifically, developers need to:

- Notify the DBA when all changes to SQL are made, so the DBA can review it for performance in general, but specifically to assess whether any indexes must be added, changed, or removed to get your query to perform well.

- Know how to find out whether a SQL statement is using indexes. This is done by asking the database for the "execution plan" for the query. If the plan shows a "table scan," then it's likely your query isn't using the right indexes and will have performance problems.

Of course, there are other problems that can cause performance issues, but all developers should know these basics. And as you might have guessed, Test 05b is so incredibly slow because that one slow query identified by Glowroot is querying a column in the HISTORY table that doesn't have an index. Ouch. The 05a test (Figure 9-2) fixes that. This test uses a different version of the same database that includes the right index. Query response time improved from 358.5ms without the index

All Web Transactions

	Response time	Slow traces (0)	Queries	Service calls	Continuous profiling	

	Total time ▾ (ms)	Execution count	Time per execution (ms)	Rows per execution
SELECT tid, hid, bid, aid, delta, mtime, …	107,492.6	1,074,600	0.10	1.0
SELECT aid, bid, abalance, filler, filler…	48,699.8	107,460	0.45	1.0
SELECT hid from history WHERE aid = ?	20,196.6	107,460	0.19	10.0

Figure 9-2. *With all db indexes now in place, response time for all queries is faster than 1ms*

This blog page shows all the steps necessary for troubleshooting and fixing a performance problem with a missing H2 database index:

`http://ostermueller.blogspot.com/2017/05/is-my-h2-query-slow-because-of-missing.html`

Retrieving and analyzing the execution plan is a similar process for other databases, but you'll need to get help from your DBA or from the DB doc on the specifics. Is your DBA responsible for detecting problems, or does the DBA rely on dev to set tuning priorities? These are important things to decide, and good JDBC performance like those from glowroot.org are great for setting priorities for the dba.

Query response time is really composed of two parts that we don't discuss often enough when troubleshooting: execution and optionally, result-set iteration. Indexing issues like the problem in Figure 9-2 cause slowdowns in the first part—execution.

I just glanced back at the list of jpt performance results, Table 2-1 in Chapter 2. It shows that jpt test 04a includes an example of slow result-set iteration. If you run this example and capture some thread dumps, you will see the `java.sql.ResultSet#next()` method show up repeatedly, but it won't show up repeatedly in other tests. This is how you detect problems with the second part of query performance—result-set iteration.

Thus far, we have focused on how the performance of individual queries can cause problems. The rest of this chapter is dedicated to the performance problems caused by multiple SQL statements acting in concert (bad acting in concert?), as part of a single database strategy.

Performance Issues with Multiple SQL Statements

Near the beginning of *Java Performance: The Definitive Guide* (O'Reilly, 2104), Scott Oaks has a peculiar little section that is aptly named "Look Elsewhere: The Database Is Always the Bottleneck." It is really just a page or two that cautions against blaming Java for all your performance woes, because database performance issues, regardless of the programming language, will very likely eclipse any vanilla Java performance issues. I generally agree; this is why most of the 12 jpt load tests that come with this book include database activity.

From the developer's perspective, I see database performance as an effort to tame a two headed sea serpent:

- First head of the serpent: performance of individual queries, as shown by our missing index example.

- Second head of serpent: cumulative performance overhead of executing a group of SQL statements, like all SQL executed for one business process.

Many teams struggle to find and retain DBAs (or perhaps other staff) who can, in concert with the development team, keep the performance of individual queries under control. This is the first head of the serpent.

The second head is managing the performance of groups of queries from a single component, more simply described as the problem of "too many database calls." This problem has gone largely unchecked by development teams, but a small, vocal group have warned about this problem for more than a decade. It still inflicts much pain, today. The blog post URL at the beginning of this chapter shows how long we have been living with this problem.

There are two main anti-patterns behind this "too many database calls" problem. Let's look at the first, which is called the *SELECT N+1* issue; it could easily have been called "SELECTs in a loop."

The First Issue: SELECT N+1

Recognizing the SELECT N+1 in code is pretty straightforward. Just look for any SELECT executed in a loop, especially when the loop iterates through the result set of a different SELECT. In the example shown in Listing 9-1, for each iteration through the outer result set, one SELECT is executed.

Listing 9-1. Partial source code example of SELECT N+1 anti-pattern. For each row in the set of N items in the outer result set, an additional 1 query is executed. One way to refactor this is to join the outer and the inner table. Yes, the join is faster than the chatty behavior.

```
ps = con.prepareStatement(
    "SELECT hid from history "
    +"WHERE aid = " + accountId);      // outer SELECT

rs = ps.executeQuery();

while(rs.next()) {                     // start of loop

    long hID = rs.getLong(1)
    ps = connection.prepareStatement(
        "SELECT tid, hid tid, hid, "
        +"bid, aid, mtime from"        // SELECT executed
        +"HISTORY WHERE hid = ?");     // inside loop

    ps.setLong(1, hID);
    histRs = ps.executeQuery();
    short count = 0;
```

In this example, both the outer and the inner query hit the HISTORY table, but most times the outer and inner SELECTs hit different tables that should probably be joined together.

But what does SELECT N+1 mean? Jeremy Bentch, a software architect from Portland, OR, described it to me this way: given a collection of N rows in a result set, do 1 additional query for each. N+1.

Here is another angle, aside from "Look for SELECTs in a loop." Martin Fowler has written two books on the "Most Influential Book Every Programmer Should Read" list on stackoverflow.com; he is certainly an important voice. Way back in 2003, he wrote

"Try to pull back multiple rows at once. In particular, never do repeated queries on the same table to get multiple rows."

http://www.informit.com/articles/article.aspx?p=30661

This is a great, succinct way to address this problem. But unfortunately, it still doesn't quantify how bad the performance problem is.

Five Variations of SELECT N+1 Load Tests

So to quantify the performance problem, I coded up five different variants of a SELECT N+1 issue and found that there was a dramatic performance difference between the five strategies, as shown in Figure 9-3.

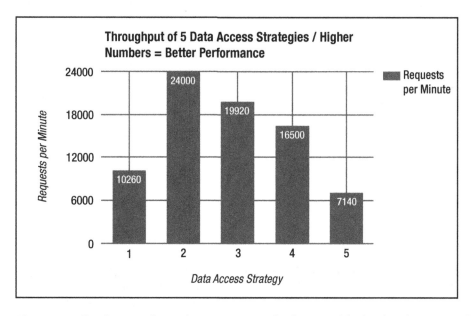

Figure 9-3. *Chunky outperforms chatty. Strategy 5, the chattiest of the five, has the worst performance in this test. All the queries were very fast (~20ms or less). Slower queries would certainly exaggerate this problem.*

In Figure 9-3, strategy 2 had the best performance and strategy 5 had the worst—it has the most SQL executions. The fastest test, strategy 2, had the fewest SQL executions, with the exception of strategy 1, which I will come back to in a minute. Each strategy provides a different implementation of the exact same SOA service with this use case:

> Given 10 bank account numbers, return transaction history and balance info for all accounts. All five strategies must build the response data using exactly the same POJOs and the same XML serialization code.

The RDBMS schema in the H2 database is based on the performance-testing schema from Postgres:

https://www.postgresql.org/docs/9.6/static/pgbench.html

There is a simple one-to-many relationship utilized, in which each row in ACCOUNTS has a list of many records in the HISTORY table.

To make it easier to understand the strategies, I created a visualization that I call a "SQL Sequence Diagram." As an introduction, Figure 9-4 shows just part of one of the strategies. The S in the top row represents the first SELECT statement executed. It p ulls data from one table—the ACCOU NTS table. The row below it represents the second SELECT statement which pulls data from the HISTORY table. Actually, each row just shows FROM clause tables. The SELECT list (of column names) is not represented at all.

Figure 9-4 shows the FROM clauses from the first two SELECTs for strategy 4. There is a SELECT to the ACCOUNTS table, then a SELECT to the HISTORY table.

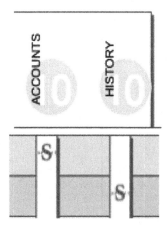

Figure 9-4. *A SQL Sequence diagram that helps understand whether the code has repeatedly queried the same table. Per Martin Fowler, a single request should access each table no more than once.*

When I ran the code, I submitted 10 accounts for inquiry, and sure enough, the same two SELECT statements in this little diagram are executed 10 times each.

Figure 9-5 shows the full list (where possible—strategy 5 didn't fit) of SELECT statements for each strategy. Note that we can easily see how many times each strategy has gone back to the same table; data represents all SQL executed during a single round trip to the server.

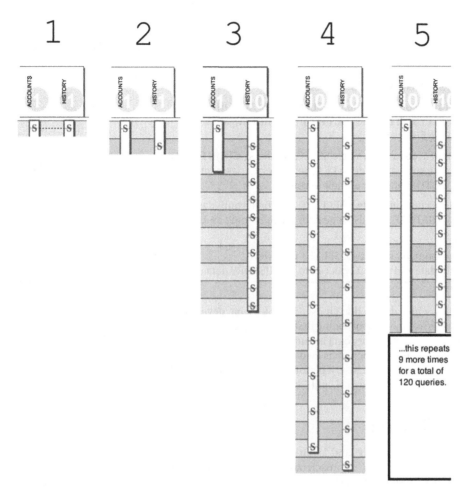

Figure 9-5. *A single SQL sequence diagram for each of the five database strategies. Strategy 5 is the chattiest and performs the worst, per data in Figure 9-3. Per the same data, strategy 2 performs the best. Strategy 1 is the chunkiest, but doesn't perform well because the join results in more rows/results than necessary.*

Strategies 1 and 2 abide by Fowler's direction—they never do repeated queries on the same table—they access each table just one time. Strategy 3, on the other hand, follows Fowler's advice for the ACCCOUNTS table, but not for the HISTORY table. Strategies 4 and 5 are super chatty, revisiting both tables multiple times—Fowler is unhappy.

Table 9-1 shows my rough characterization of each strategy. See if you can match each characterization in the table with each strategy's depiction in Figure 9-5. Also think about which strategy most resembles your coding style.

Table 9-1. *The Five Database Strategies*

Strategy	Characterization	Count of SELECT statements
1	With a single execution of a query, SELECT all rows from ACCOUNTS, joined to the HISTORY table.	1
2	SELECT all 10 accounts in a single SELECT to the ACCOUNTS table and SELECT all 200 HISTORY records from a single SELECT to the history table.	2
3	SELECT all 10 accounts in a single SELECT to the ACCOUNTS table, just as in strategy 2. But make 10 separate queries, each gathering HISTORY data for a single account.	11
4	For a single account, make two SELECTs: one for account data, and one for HISTORY records. Repeat for the remaining nine accounts.	20
5	For each account, make a single SELECT to retrieve ACCOUNTS data and make 11 queries to get HISTORY data.	120

Of all five strategies, which do you think most resembles what developers use most? My personal bet is strategy 4, because that is just the style of coding that I have been around, where one account component retrieves all data for that account, history data included. When data for multiple accounts is required, a "reuse" victory is tallied, and the component is invoked an additional time for each subsequent account. Well, the reuse victory is bittersweet, at best, if performance suffers because of an increased number of database calls, as is the case of strategies 3, 4, and 5 in Figure 9-4.

Chunky Outperforms Chatty

Ultimately, the two extremes are "chatty" and "chunky." Chatty has many executions and small result sets—often just a single record. The "Chunky" approach has fewer executions and bigger result sets. But just to be clear, this thing about "large results sets are OK" does not mean you can cavalierly pull back more data than necessary and discard the rest (anti-pattern #3 from Chapter 1 , Overprocessing). For example, it would be really inefficient to retrieve 1000 rows and return only the first (or second or fifth) page of 100 to the end user and discard the rest. So, craft your WHERE clause to retrieve just what you need.

If you would like a more detailed look at the code to better understand the strategies, see the com.github.eostermueller.perfSandbox.dataaccess packages here:

https://github.com/eostermueller/javaPerformanceTroubleshooting

Remember, chunky outperforms chatty, and not just with executing SQL statements. Chatty anti-patterns often cause problems with NoSQL databases, flat file reads, and even with HTTP or other network requests to backend systems.

Chunky Doesn't Always Perform Well

When I first coded these examples, strategy 1 had the best throughput, not strategy 2. But then I wondered whether adding a handful of columns to the ACCOUNTS table to model a more fully fleshed out master ACCOUNTS record would hurt performance. It did. The low throughput of strategy 1 was caused when I added 20 columns, 84 bytes each to the ACCOUNTS table. Don't forget that because the tables are joined, all SELECTed ACCOUNTS columns will get repeated (bad → big inefficiency) for each row in the HISTORY table.

Detecting SELECT N+1

Test results:

> Test 07a: ~18,000 requests per minute (strategy 4).
>
> Test 07b: ~26,000 requests per minute (strategy 2)

HINT: To explore how the other three strategies (1, 3 and 5) perform, open `src/test/jmeter/07a.jmx` in JMeter, change the `SCENARIO_NUM` JMeter variable to 1, 2, 3, 4 or 5, and then re-run test 07a.
Metrics that you will need:

> Total Time and Execution count for each SQL statement
>
> A few tools that provide this data: Glowroot, JavaMelody, JDBC Performance Logger

When troubleshooting the missing index at the beginning of this chapter, we saw that the problem query's response time was more than 10 times slower than the other queries that were of similar complexity. That "10 times slower" is a bit of a smoking gun. If not a smoking gun, it was at least "lowest hanging fruit" that directs and motivates your research.

Take a look at the Glowroot Queries data for load test 07a in Figure 9-6. Do you see any smoking gun? This screenshot shows two minutes of data after the throughput had leveled out—my version of warmup.

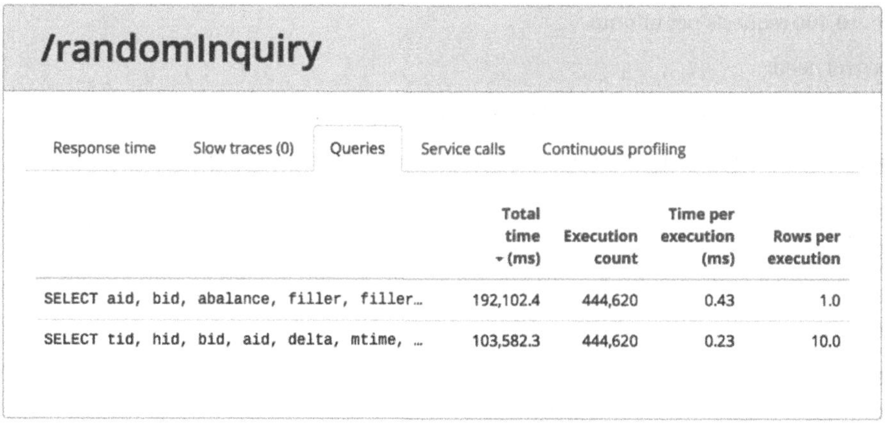

/randomInquiry

| Response time | Slow traces (0) | Queries | Service calls | Continuous profiling |

	Total time ▾ (ms)	Execution count	Time per execution (ms)	Rows per execution
`SELECT aid, bid, abalance, filler, filler…`	192,102.4	444,620	0.43	1.0
`SELECT tid, hid, bid, aid, delta, mtime, …`	103,582.3	444,620	0.23	10.0

Figure 9-6. *Glowroot Queries tab for test 07a. Individual executions seems fast. Execution count seems high, but how high is a problem?*

Average time per execution is very fast—less than 1ms for both queries (0.43 and 0.23), so no obvious problem there.

The Execution Count and the Total Time values seem high, but how high is too high for these values? If you run the 07b test (strategy 2) and look at the same screen, the execution count and the Total time are lower, but there is still no guidance on what measurements/thresholds indicate a problem. The Total Time (ms) metric is roughly the "average time per SQL" multiplied by the count of invocations—it's how long the JVM has spent executing this query.

As such, I recommend the following:

1. Take a close look at the 2–3 queries with the highest total time and the highest execution count.

2. Find out what code executes these queries and look for the SELECT N+1 issue as well as the other performance issue with multiple SQL statements that we'll cover in the next section.

3. It is also helpful to compare the Glowroot Execution Count in Figure 9-6 to the load generator throughput for the same time period. This is a much more meaningful comparison when you disable all business processes in your load script except the one with questionable SQL performance. Use Fowler's rule as a guide.

4. Fix and retest.

The Second Issue: Uncached SELECTS to Static Data

Test results:

Test 03a: **14,000** requests per minute

Test 07b: **10,400** requests per minute

Metrics that you will need:

Total Time and Execution count for each SQL statement.

A few tools that provide this data: Glowroot, JavaMelody, JDBC Performance Logger

Load test 03b is a lot slower than load test 03a, but why? To find out more, look at the Glowroot Queries page for 03b in Figure 9-7.

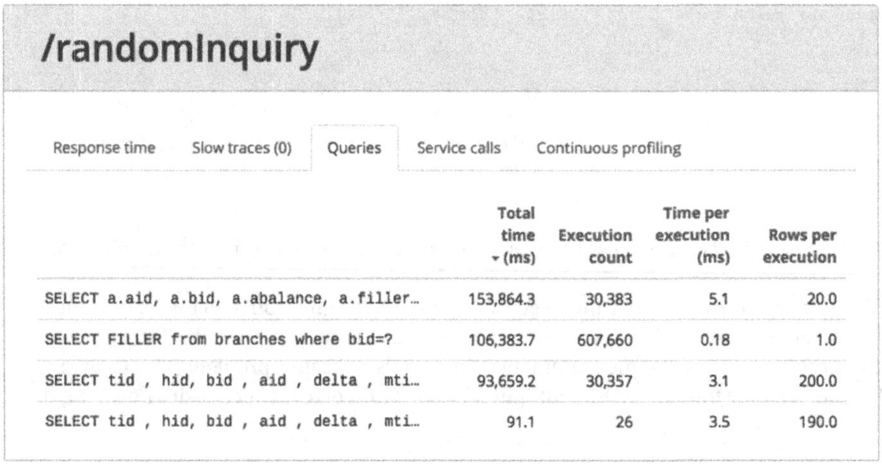

/randomInquiry

Response time   Slow traces (0)   Queries   Service calls   Continuous profiling

	Total time ▾ (ms)	Execution count	Time per execution (ms)	Rows per execution
SELECT a.aid, a.bid, a.abalance, a.filler…	153,864.3	30,383	5.1	20.0
SELECT FILLER from branches where bid=?	106,383.7	607,660	0.18	1.0
SELECT tid , hid, bid , aid , delta , mti…	93,659.2	30,357	3.1	200.0
SELECT tid , hid, bid , aid , delta , mti…	91.1	26	3.5	190.0

Figure 9-7. *Glowroot query panel for test 03b*

Just as with the SELECT N+1 issue in test 07, there are no obvious slowdowns in the Time per Execution column, as there were in test 05 with the missing index. The response times of 5.1, 0.18, and 3.1ms are all very quick compared to the 358.5ms for the unindexed query. So this means the DBAs did their job and there are no issues with individual queries—the first head of the serpent.

On the surface, this looks very similar to the SELECT N+1, but there is one key difference—the ACCOUNTS and HISTORY tables from previous examples hold live data that could change at any second, and the BRANCHES table does not. Theoretically, that data holds static data that changes less than once a day—probably less than once a week. Here are the types of things that a branch table might hold: Branch Name and Street address, City, State, Postal Code, and so on. Since this data changes so rarely, caching it in RAM could really boost performance.

I can imagine good reasons to be hesitant about using a cache, because operating on slightly stale data from a cache might cause problems. Say that a disgruntled employee needs to be immediately locked out of your system. You don't want an out-of-date cache of user permissions to mistakenly allow entry. But we can have our cake and eat it too. We can use caches to make these user permissions perform better and we can also evict those caches on demand when it is critical that they are up-to-date. This link shows one example:

http://blog.trifork.com/2015/02/09/active-cache-eviction-with-ehcache-and-spring-framework/

To avoid so many executions, the branch lookup code in the fast test (the *a* test) only occasionally incurs the overhead of the round trip to the database—just occasionally. The rest of the time, it pulls the results from an in-memory, hash table-like singleton—a cache—provided by http://www.ehcache.org/.

In the jpt repository at https://github.com/eostermueller/javaPerformanceTroubleshooting, look for this configuration file:

warProject/src/main/resources/ehcache.xml.

This controls how frequently the cache is emptied (aka, evicted), thus occasionally forcing your code to get fresh results using a full database round trip. By contrast, the code in the slow test incurs the overhead of the round trip for every single request. Take a minute to look at the slow and fast versions of the code in this package in the jpt repository:

com.github.eostermueller.perfSandbox.cache

Figure 9-8, from the 03a test, shows the proof in the pudding. Now that the cache is in place, see how few queries there are to the BRANCHES table, as compared to the other three queries? There are just 25 in 2 minutes, compared to 35k-ish invocations of the other queries.

/randomInquiry

| Response time | Slow traces (0) | Queries | Service calls | Continuous profiling |

	Total time ▾ (ms)	Execution count	Time per execution (ms)	Rows per execution
SELECT a.aid, a.bid, a.abalance, a.filler…	188,419.6	35,987	5.2	20.0
SELECT tid , hid, bid , aid , delta , mti…	113,677.1	35,952	3.2	200.0
SELECT tid , hid, bid , aid , delta , mti…	106.3	35	3.0	190.0
SELECT FILLER from branches where bid=?	17.0	25	0.68	1.0

Figure 9-8. EHCache has minimized the count of queries to the BRANCH table. See, just 25 in 2 minutes!

I can understand why you might think the throughput is so high in some of these examples that any lessons learned would not apply to smaller loads. That is almost a fair criticism; I think that the artificially fast query response times in my examples make up for that. With more realistic, slower DB queries seen in production environments, all the problems I've highlighted in this chapter are significantly worse.

JPA and Hibernate

JPA, the Java Persistence API standard, and widely used implementations like Hibernate (hibernate.org) and MyBatis (mybatis.org) are in common use today. JDBC still executes under the covers, but the minutiae of JDBC and the drudgery of moving ResultSet data into Java objects is much easier.

JPA is out of scope for this small book. If you'd like to learn more about JPA performance, consider the 2016 book *High Performance Java Persistence* by Vlad Mihalcea (self-published).

But a brief suggestion can be helpful:

> Spend the time to make sure your JPA code abides by Martin Fowler's rule:
> "never do repeated queries on the same table" for a single server-side request.

JPA provides a very helpful way to apply common approaches to JDBC access across a large code base. That is a good thing. However, I generally find the developers using JPA are so abstracted from knowing this size, shape, and count of SQL queries that execute under the covers, that performance is suffers. Hibernate is very capable of proliferating the SELECT N+1 anti-pattern; be sure to flag it as a problem at your next code review—perhaps using glowroot.org.

The following post will help you do that, especially the part about avoiding Hibernate's "Batch-size=N" fetching strategy.

https://www.mkyong.com/hibernate/hibernate-fetching-strategies-examples/

Don't Forget

From a high level, it seems that the lack of good, freely available SQL performance tools like Glowroot has kept this "too many database calls" problem from being addressed—that's why this is the second head of the nasty persistence dragon, which Java developers always seem to miss. Even super-fast queries can drag down performance if your code executes them enough times.

There are other promising open source tools available, like Glowroot.org, that provide similar JDBC metrics:

```
https://github.com/sylvainlaurent/JDBC-Performance-Logger
https://github.com/javamelody/javamelody/wiki
http://www.stagemonitor.org/
```

We have been writing chatty code for more than a decade. Perhaps the new visibility provided by these more mature monitoring options will make it easier to implement chunky database access strategies that perform significantly better. When an application has a long history of too many db calls, it's really tough to change the culture. Setting good standards early on in a project seems like a promising start. Trying to keep SQL counts low without good metrics seems impossible. Work towards getting team-wide adoption of a good tool for SQL metrics.

It is worth mentioning one more time that the results of the chunky vs. chatty tests are skewed because of my smoking fast database. In the real world, chatty strategies coupled with poor individual query response time are a perfect storm waiting to happen.

What's Next

This chapter covered the first item in the P.A.t.h. checklist. Chapter 10 looks at troubleshooting the performance of all the back-end systems that your JVM connects to, referred to as *Alien Systems*. There is one important optimization discussed that almost every system needs—the chapter has a nice test on how much benefit it can provide, but it also highlights important security concerns that are frequently overlooked when implementing this optimization: data compression.

CHAPTER 10

■ ■ ■

Alien Systems, the "A" in P.A.t.h.

I generally start performance troubleshooting by walking through the P.A.t.h. Checklist for a single JVM. If there are no obvious issues, then I will move on to an "Alien" system—one connected to the first JVM. With a more sophisticated toolset, like an Application Performance Monitoring solution, data from multiple systems collects in a single location and application, making the process a lot easier, although licensing can get pretty expensive.

The objectives for this chapter are:

- Learn how to use a thread dump to detect slow network transmissions and which Java code invokes them.

- Understand how compression dramatically speeds up transmissions over 'slow' network connections, but must be carefully implemented to avoid creating some very specific security vulnerabilities.

- Learn how to use Wireshark to inspect the payload of a transmission to see whether it is "clear text", which is one indicator that compression will help.

With the exception of glowroot.org, the basic tools in this book (jstack, jstat, jcmd, and so on) provide visibility into slow or inefficient activity in a single JVM. The easiest way to use these tools is to sign on to the machine running the JVM you want to observer. The RMI server jstatd (https://docs.oracle.com/javase/8/docs/technotes/tools/unix/jstatd.html) can be used to enable remote access for many of these tools.

The point of this small chapter is to remind you to assess performance of all the components in a system, whether they are strung together serially, one calling the next, or lined up behind a load balancer as identical, parallel nodes in a cluster.

Lowering Response Time over Long Distances

One of the first things I do when assessing a system I'm not familiar with is to check to see whether compression is enabled for connections between data centers or over a leased line or the Internet. I have run some tests with and without compression to make this advice a little more compelling.

Compression Makes Things Go Faster

Tests 10a and 10b were both run with the configuration shown in Figure 10-1. Note that there is about 1700 miles between the JMeter load generator in Little Rock, AR and the jpt example application deployed in Portland, OR. Both tests contain six different HTTP requests with different response sizes: 20K, 60K, 100K, 200K, 600K, and 1MB. By default, the jpt server returns a compressed response, but only if the HTTP request specifies the "Accept-Encoding: gzip" HTTP Header parameter. I configured the 10a test to include this header, but the 10b test did not. My goal was to see the speed benefit in the 10a test using compression.

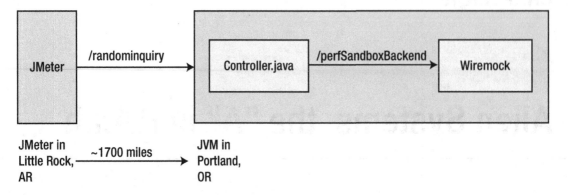

Figure 10-1. *JMeter and the littleMock application were separated by about 1700 miles. The tests compared results of compressed and uncompressed payloads returning from the littleMock server which was running Tomcat under Spring Boot.*

To see exactly how much of a benefit you are passing up by not using compression, I installed the Java Performance Troubleshooting (JPT) examples on an Amazon Lightsail Linux box located in the far Northwest corner of the United States: in the state of Oregon. I ran the JPT init.sh to install and then reconfigured the app (in the application.properties) to take traffic from the outside world on port 443, instead of the default 8675. I then used Lightsail to expose that port over the Internet and started test 01a like this:

```
db/startDb.sh
```

in one window and

```
./startWar.sh 01a
```

in a separate terminal window. Then, from roughly 1,700 miles away in Little Rock, Arkansas, I changed both src/test/jmeter/10a.jmx and 10b.jmx to point to the IP address of the AWS Lightsail machine. I did this by changing the value of the HOST JMeter script variable. I then ran JMeter with 10a.jmx for several minutes. I stopped the test and then ran 10b.jmx for about the same time. The response time results of these two tests are graphed in Figure 10-2, with 10a in red and 10b in blue. The 10a/red test had compression enabled.

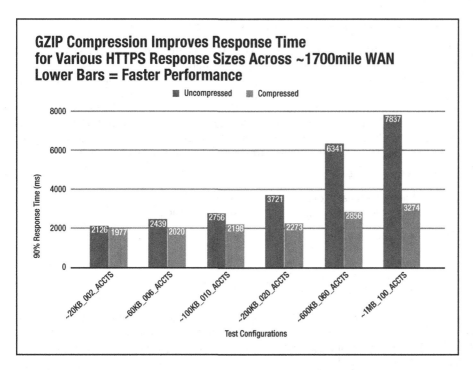

Figure 10-2. The red bars (Test 10a) are dramatically lower than the blue bars (Test 10b), showing how much faster network requests are when compressed. The larger the payload (right most bars), the bigger the benefit. The sizes on the horizontal axis lables (like ~20KB_002_ACCTS) are the blue/uncompressed sizes.

When HTTPS responses are about 200K, compressing that response speeds up the request by 1500ms (2273ms in red is almost 1500ms faster than 3721 in blue). That's a serious improvement. I used the following URL parameter (values 2, 6, 10, 20, 60, 100) to increase the size of the HTTP response for the tests with and without compression.

```
https://my_aws_server.com/randomInquiry?numAccounts=100
```

It was a lucky coincidence that each account produced about 10K of response data (uncompressed), making it easier to remember the sizes For example, with two accounts: 2x10k=20k of data, 100 accounts, 100x10k=1mb of response data.

Here are the required Spring changes to enable compression in application.properties:

```
server.compression.mime-types=application/xml
server.compression.enabled=true
```

Additionally, your HTTP request must have the header Accept-Encoding: gzip, and only JMeter script 10a.jmx included this HTTP header.

Security Warning for Compression with HTTPS

But before you get all excited about these results (as I did), you must acquaint yourself with the security concerns of using HTTPS and compression together (my exact configuration).

Without the right implementation, combining HTTPS and compression can enable hackers to view private data (like credit card numbers) that your users type into your web page.

I am not a security expert, so you will have to educate yourself on the risks, with the two types of vulnerabilities called Crime and Breach. Here are a few links to get your research started. It pains me to actually type these words, but security is probably a bit more important than performance. But don't fear, security folks have recommended ways of getting around these attacks so we can keep our compression! Read on.

```
http://breachattack.com/#mitigations
```

```
http://www.infoworld.com/article/2611658/data-security/
how-to-defend-your-web-apps-against-the-new-breach-attack.html
```

```
https://blog.qualys.com/ssllabs/2013/08/07/defending-against-
the-breach-attack
```

Message Size

I grin every time I zip a text file. It just blows my mind that you can regularly get 80% reduction of the original file. Well, the same thing is true for compression of an HTTP stream. But the performance improvement is not a direct result of the sophisticated zipping algorithms—it is simply a matter of message size. Smaller messages are faster, especially as distances increase.

I say this so you will not limit yourself to using a single tool (compression) for optimization. There are all kinds of strategies for decreasing message size.

I worked with one group where a simple change in the XML format brought a 250K transmission down to 10K. You could also make sure you only send data that gets used, and consider adding a caching solution as well.

Figure 10-3 shows exactly how much size reduction (in bytes) was required for each improvement in Figure 10-2.

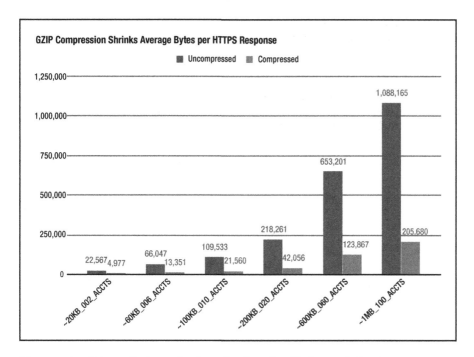

Figure 10-3. *This graph shows the sizes of each payload before and after GZIP compression. The count of bytes for the same HTTP response message, both compressed (red) and uncompressed (blue).*

Using Thread Dumps to Detect Network Requests

To find out whether a network request is slowing down your system, I put together examples 01a and 01b in the JPT examples. Both of these examples share the same architecture, as shown in Figure 10-4.

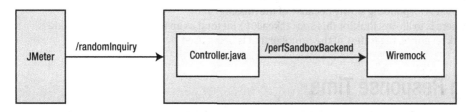

Figure 10-4. *Flow java JPT example 01a and 01b. Both /randomInquiry and /perfSandboxBackend are both HTTP requests and both JMeter and the server (Spring Boot) are deployed on localhost of the same machine.*

Note that Wiremock runs in the same JVM as the Controller.java, which is slightly artificial.

Tests 01a and test 01b are configured to "sleep" in Wiremock for two different times. Which test is slower, 01a or 01b?

Once you have these examples up and going, take a thread dump of the war process, as follows.

Start by finding the process ID of the war file:

```
# jcmd
15893 warProject/target/performanceGolf.war
```

I trimmed out a bit of the output for brevity—be sure to look for the war file.

Then pass that PID (15893 from above) to stack like this, redirecting the output to a text file:

```
# jstack 15893 > myThreadDump.txt
```

In both test plans 01a.jmx and 01b.jmx, you will find that JMeter is configured to apply 3t0tt load, which is three threads of load with zero think time. Likewise, when you look at the thread dump, you find three threads that are nearly identical to the stack trace shown in Figure 10-5.

```
"qtp614185476-122" #122 prio=5 os_prio=31 tid=0x00007fa5611f9000 nid=0x7807 runnable [0x0000700008a74000]
   java.lang.Thread.State: RUNNABLE
        at java.net.SocketInputStream.socketRead0(Native Method)
        at java.net.SocketInputStream.socketRead(SocketInputStream.java:116)
        at java.net.SocketInputStream.read(SocketInputStream.java:170)
        at java.net.SocketInputStream.read(SocketInputStream.java:141)
        at java.io.BufferedInputStream.fill(BufferedInputStream.java:246)
        at java.io.BufferedInputStream.read1(BufferedInputStream.java:286)
        at java.io.BufferedInputStream.read(BufferedInputStream.java:345)
        - locked <0x00000007b195efd8> (a java.io.BufferedInputStream)
        at sun.net.www.http.HttpClient.parseHTTPHeader(HttpClient.java:704)
        at sun.net.www.http.HttpClient.parseHTTP(HttpClient.java:647)
        at sun.net.www.protocol.http.HttpURLConnection.getInputStream0(HttpURLConnection.java:1536)
        - locked <0x00000007b195d2b8> (a sun.net.www.protocol.http.HttpURLConnection)
        at sun.net.www.protocol.http.HttpURLConnection.getInputStream(HttpURLConnection.java:1441)
        - locked <0x00000007b195d2b8> (a sun.net.www.protocol.http.HttpURLConnection)
        at java.net.HttpURLConnection.getResponseCode(HttpURLConnection.java:480)
        at com.github.eostermueller.perfSandbox.HttpServer.getHttpResponse(HttpServer.java:104)
```

Figure 10-5. stack trace from one of three threads in a thread dump for test 01a. Test 01b will look identical.

The method you see at the top is one that you will see for all kinds of network request, not just HTTP:

```
at java.net.SocketInputStream.socketRead0(Native Method)
```

If you capture thread dumps from the slow database index example in the previous chapter, you will find this exact same socketRead0() method, but used by the H2 database driver to wait for a response from the H2 database, which is responding slowly because of the missing index.

The takeaway here is to always look for this socketRead0() method as an indicator that your code is waiting for a network response, regardless of the protocol that is being used.

Quantifying Response Time

The thread dump approach just shown frequently helps me figure out whether response time from an Alien system is one of the largest performance issues—the beloved "lowest hanging fruit." This is a very useful technique, but unfortunately, it would be much more helpful to quantify exactly how much time is being spent in the back-end system.

To find out the exact response time, I have configured Glowroot to run with both the JPT and the littleMock examples. Just point a browser to http://localhost:4000 (Figure 10-6).

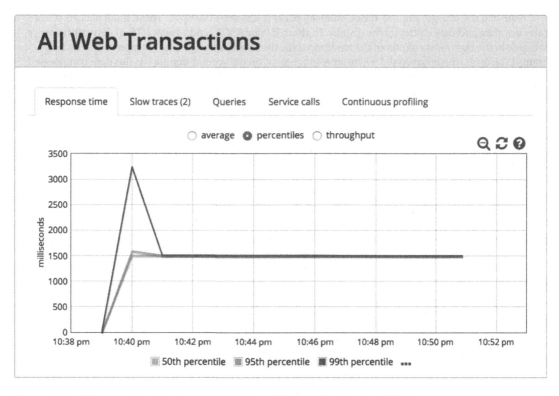

Figure 10-6. *Glowroot data showing response time of the /randomInquiry URL for test 01a.*

So jstack provides us with a plug-it-in-now indication that we are waiting for a network request. But unfortunately, thread dumps for 01a and 01b will look nearly identical. Glowroot installation requires that you add a javaagent parameter pointing to the Glowroot jar file, and it requires a restart—this is not plug-it-in-now, in my book, but it is nice to quantify the response time for these tests. If you look at the same Glowroot metrics for test 01b, you'll find that response time is 500ms.

Identifying Clear Text Payloads That Could Benefit from Compression

Figure 10-2 showed that compressing a 1MB file yields a 200K or smaller zipped file. 80% reduction in data size is impressive, and this is why compression over a WAN (Wide Area Network) provides such a great performance boost. The lingering question here is whether the systems you work with actually leverage this optimization and compress their data over the slow wire (aka WAN).

To find out, you need to eyeball the data in the actual message going over the wire. tcpdump, windump, and wireshark are great network observability tools, but they have no easy way to aggregate or summarize response time data on a very busy system. For laying your eyes on the actually message, these tools are the way to go, and I will try to help with some common frustrations that come with them.

You can run the following command on either the machine sending or the one receiving the data. Find the port that the server is listening on. For jpt, you will find "server.port = 8675" in warProject/src/main/resources/application.properties. Note that 01a.jmx and 01b.jmx specify this port number, was well. While JMeter is applying load to jpt, start a separate terminal window and capture a trace using tcpdump as shown here.

```
tcpdump -X -i any -s 0 "port 8675 and greater 100"
```

Note that the text 'greater 100' hides small tcp packets less then 100 bytes. These small packets don't carry any data and they clutter up the display. In short, if your ASCII (and I guess UTF-8) network message is visible in the rightmost column of the tcpdump data, then your message is not compressed. The first example below is uncompressed. I will reserve judgement on the second sample—is this data compressed, or is it merely encrypted? Somewhat surprisingly, not all encrypted data is compressed (`https://www.belshe.com/2010/11/18/ssl-compression-and-you/`), as shown here:

```
0x0090: 3a20 4a65 7474 7928 392e 322e 7a2d 534e   :.Jetty(9.2.z-SN
0x00a0: 4150 5348 4f54 290d 0a0d 0a33 4537 0d0a   APSHOT)....3E7..
0x00b0: 4865 6c6c 6f57 6f72 6c64 4672 6f6d 5065   HelloWorldFromPe
0x00c0: 7266 6f72 6d61 6e63 6553 616e 6442 6f78   rformanceSandBox
0x00d0: 4261 636b 656e 6453 6572 7665 7220 4845   BackendServer.HE
0x00e0: 4c4c 4f20 4845 4c4c 4f20 4845 4c4c 4f20   LLO.HELLO.HELLO.
0x00f0: 4845 4c4c 4f20 4845 4c4c 4f20 4845 4c4c   HELLO.HELLO.HELL
0x0100: 4f20 4845 4c4c 4f20 4845 4c4c 4f20 4845   O.HELLO.HELLO.HE
0x0110: 4c4c 4f20 4845 4c4c 4f20 4845 4c4c 4f20   LLO.HELLO.HELLO.
```

The rightmost column of data above shows "HELLO" ASCII representation of hex data. Conclusion: this data is not compressed.

```
0x0410: b64c 3fa1 386c a9cf 0f67 ca5b 803c d06b   .L?.8l...g.[.<.k
0x0420: 58c1 9c74 83f2 d5b3 9074 17d6 d49c edfd   X..t.....t......
0x0430: db8f 0e5c c312 afb7 9b0c 0001 4903 0017   ...\........I...
0x0440: 4104 609c b859 1283 4746 de7b d3c9 d3dc   A.`..Y..GF.{....
0x0450: eb18 2ef0 2287 c68f fdcb fd17 df46 c959   ...."........F.Y
0x0460: 8e19 8731 91d2 48f2 3336 6237 f402 8fca   ...1..H.36b7....
0x0470: dd0e 4048 2fda e4a5 6948 6b8a 036b f351   ..@H/...iHk..k.Q
0x0480: 0cf4 0601 0100 287b c742 a426 3332 d192   ......({.B.&32..
0x0490: 8e39 8edd 271a d0e0 2e67 2eba 37aa e3fb   .9..'....g..7...
0x04a0: 7311 075e 31d6 bd3f 7767 468c 0476 445a   s..^1..?wgF..vDZ
```

I was expecting to see an XML message in this text, but HTTPS was used to send the data. Conclusion: Not enough info to know whether data is compressed.

Don't Forget

`jstack` is a great plug-it-in-now tool that can tell you quickly whether your system is waiting for response from "Alien" systems. Just look for the following method call in your thread dump:

```
java.net.SocketInputStream.socketRead0()
```

Whether your system is making HTTP or HTTPS requests, JDBC requests, or talking over any other protocol, this is the method you will see. Furthermore, regardless of the protocol that is use, smaller messages travel significantly faster of long distances, and compression is a great way to make your payload smaller. But keep in mind, there are many ways to shrink a payload. One way is to refactor the client code so less data is needed. A second way is to change the message format—like by shrinking the size of XML tags. If the data is static and doesn't change much, consider caching the request instead of repeatedly sending it over the wire.

Don't forget, as mentioned in Chapter 9, chunky outperforms chatty. This applies to network requests to Alien systems, not just to JDBC.

The most important issue, though, is that compressing HTTPS carries some risk. This chapter briefly mentioned some security vulnerabilities that can be caused by HTTPS compression—these would be very foolish to ignore.

What's Next

You can find many books and blogs that show you how to diagnose BLOCKED threads in a thread dump. The same goes for finding a single runaway thread in a thread dump that uses a lot of CPU like an application server startup thread gone crazy. Unfortunately, these two use cases happen pretty infrequently. Guidance for using thread dumps to find garden-variety slow threads and garden variety over-consumption is altogether absent. Chapter 11 aims precisely in this space, to use thread dumps to provide Java-profiler like diagnostics that point to the exact code executing in slow threads. This novel technique is essential for shedding light on the dark environments where so many performance defects breed.

■ ■ ■

Threads, the "t" in P.A.t.h.

Knowing how much load to apply in a load test has long been a question without a well-defined answer. The Scalability Yardstick (Chapter 6) finally answers that question with an easy-to-follow test formula, which also provides an uncommonly convenient way to assess scalability. The test itself is just a small, evolutionary improvement to the very commonly used incremental load test.

So, the Scalability Yardstick claims to make small improvements on existing techniques. That's nice. This chapter intends to go way beyond that, with the claim that radically more performance visibility is possible with extremely low overhead using simple tools that have long been a trusted, but severely underused part of the JDK.

The objectives for this chapter are:

- Understand that thread dumps are currently used in a very limited role; they solve a very small set of problems.

- Learn novel techniques that greatly expand the role of thread dumps into a general-purpose, low-overhead, plug-it-in-now diagnostic tool.

- Learn how to use thread dumps to identify the class and method name(s) causing performance problems in any environment.

To be clear, my purpose in writing this chapter is not to share and review a commonly used performance technique. Instead, I am trying to take a powerful technique used by a pitifully small fraction of performance-minded engineers and document it clearly so that it can be widely adopted to address longstanding gaps in visibility—the gaps I've referred to as Dark Environments.

I am ready to sit down and visit with those who are skeptical about this. Anything that gets wide adoption needs a good vetting. I understand that. I just want to make sure the reader gives a little more than a passing, ho-hum look at this proposal.

Current use of Thread Dumps

Today, thread dumps are mostly used for investigating BLOCKED threads and related multi-threaded problems. A quick Internet search for "thread dump Java" will confirm that. Because the topic has such great coverage on the Internet, I chose not to waste the space on it in this book. A lot of smart people have shown how to use thread dumps to diagnose and fix these problems.

But before moving on to using thread dumps in other areas besides multi-threaded problem detection, I do have a few quick comments about multithread coding. Firstly, any time the synchronized keyword is used in Java, a simple load test with three threads of load should applied with zero think time, and four or more thread dumps should be taken.

© Erik Ostermueller 2017
E. Ostermueller, *Troubleshooting Java Performance*, DOI 10.1007/978-1-4842-2979-8_11

In the thread dumps from the previous test, you should verify that BLOCKED threads show up infrequently, perhaps in 1 out of 20 stack traces you see. BLOCKED threads show up when synchronization methods or blocks wrap slow code, and every kind of I/O—disk, network and display—must be considered slow. I will grant exemptions to the expert writers of specialized libraries (like logging or caching frameworks) who regularly load test their code. My comments are for us application developers. Remember, don't put any I/O in a sync block—and that means no JDBC or other database calls inside a sync block.

There is nothing wrong with having the synchronization in your code. The problem is when multiple threads try to access the block at the same time, and the JVM has to make other threads wait while the owner of the lock executes. This is when the BLOCKED thread shows up, and when it happens it is called a *contended sync block*.

Also, I have yet to mention there are a number of GUI tools designed to visualize and highlight multi-threading problems. Jack Shirazi wrote the first great Java performance book, *Java Performance Tuning* (O'Reilly,), and this link to his website contains a list to a number of programs the help you visualize thread dumps. Personally, I like the IBM Thread Dump Analyzer and ThreadLogic, which lets you configure the tool with patterns of text that should raise red flags or concern. You'll find it at

```
http://www.fasterj.com/tools/threadanalysers.shtml
```

To repeat myself a little bit, this little section has some helpful but still garden-variety thoughts on synchronization. The next section starts with some basics—it shows how threads created in some simple code actually look inside a thread dump. Then, I talk about navigating thread dumps. This doesn't sound earth-shattering, but it is really key to understanding what code is running and who called it and why.

After that, we will get into the more controversial part, where we use thread dumps very much like we use a Java profiler. To fully understand what's going on here, you really need to run the examples on your own machine; just reading this chapter is not enough. Be sure to start up the littleMock application for the section "Interactive Thread Dump Reading Exercise." The littleMock sample application will be used, and it just takes a few minutes to download, install and launch.

Threads and Thread Dumps

Listing 11-1 is a very simple program that launches three threads that each sleep for 1 minute, before quitting. Let's run it and capture a thread dump so we can see one stack trace for each thread.

Note that at start-up time, this program calls `java.lang.Thead#setName()`, thereby giving each thread a name used to identify each thread in the actual thread dump. The names here start with the prefix jpt-. We will talk about why this name is so important in a little bit.

Listing 11-1. A Java Program That Starts Three Named Threads, Which We Will Look for in a Thread Dump

```
package com.jpt;
public class MyThreadStarter {
  public static void main( String[] args ) {
    new MyThread("jpt-first" ).start();
    new MyThread("jpt-second" ).start();
    new MyThread("jpt-third" ).start();
  }
}
class MyThread extends Thread {
    public MyThread(String name) {
        setName(name);
    }
    private void mySleep() {
        try { Thread.sleep(60000); } catch(Exception e) {}
    }
```

```
public void run() {
    mySleep();
}
}
```

Place this text into MyThreadStarter.java located in one folder. From a prompt in that same folder, run the commands in Listing 11-2 to compile and run the program.

Listing 11-2. Compiling an running MyThreadStarter.java, a little program that ties stack trace activity in a thread dump (from jstack) back to line numbers in source code

```
# mkdir classes
# javac -d classes MyThreadStarter.java
# java -cp classes com.jpt.MyThreadStarter
```

Now that the program is running, the terminal window will appear to be hung.

Navigating Thread Dumps

After the 60 second Thread.sleep() calls, the "hung" program will return control back to the prompt, so you have 60 seconds to open another prompt, find the process id (PID) using the JDK's jcmd utility, and capture a thread dump using the JDK's jstack.

In the new prompt that you open, get the PID using the JDK's jcmd program (8341 in Listing 11-3), which is passed to jstack, and then the jstack output (the text of the thread dump) is redirected into the file myThreadDump.txt. Note that the JDK's jps command could also be used, but it requires a few extra command-line parameters (which I'm too lazy to type) to display the name of the Java class running. The 60 second sleep time in the program means the program will finish after 60 seconds, so don't waste any time. The last line shows that the PID we care about is 8341.

Listing 11-3. Using the JDK's jcmd to find the PID of the program launched in Listing 11-2

```
#~/jpt_threads: jcmd
6817 org.h2.tools.Server -tcp -web -baseDir ./data
8342 sun.tools.jcmd.JCmd
6839 warProject/target/performanceGolf.war
8341 com.jpt.MyThreadStarter <<<< 8341 is the PID we just started
```

Now that we know the PID of the process that of the program launched in Listing 11-2, the JDK comes with a number of plug-it-in-now tools we could use to learn more about the process: jstat, jmap, jinfo, and jdb. Listing 11-4 shows how we'll pass the PID to jstack to capture a thread dump. The syntax > myThreadDump.txt is used to redirect the thread dump text to the .txt file instead of displaying it in the command-line window.

Listing 11-4. Using the JDK's jstack to Take a Thread Dump of the PID We Found in Listing 11-3

```
#~/jpt_threads: jstack 8341 > myThreadDump.txt
```

Key Landmarks in a Stack Trace

For each java.lang.Thread#start() in myThreadDump.txt captured in Listing 11-4, you can see one thread with the jpt- prefix (lines 01, 07 and 13) that I set in the code. Listing 11-5 shows three stack traces from the thread dump.

Listing 11-5. Displaying Selected Lines from myThreadDump.txt in an Editor

```
01 "jpt-third" #12 prio=5 os_prio=31 tid=0x00007fd8b605b800 nid=0x5803 waiting on condition
   [0x0000700005031000]
02  java.lang.Thread.State: TIMED_WAITING (sleeping)
03     at java.lang.Thread.sleep(Native Method)
04     at com.jpt.MyThread.mySleep(MyThreadStarter.java:18)
05     at com.jpt.MyThread.run(MyThreadStarter.java:21)
06
07 "jpt-second" #11 prio=5 os_prio=31 tid=0x00007fd8b5840800 nid=0x5603 waiting on condition
   [0x0000700004f2e000]
08  java.lang.Thread.State: TIMED_WAITING (sleeping)
09     at java.lang.Thread.sleep(Native Method)
10     at com.jpt.MyThread.mySleep(MyThreadStarter.java:18)
11     at com.jpt.MyThread.run(MyThreadStarter.java:21)
12
13 "jpt-first" #10 prio=5 os_prio=31 tid=0x00007fd8b6853000 nid=0x5403 waiting on condition
   [0x0000700004e2b000]
14  java.lang.Thread.State: TIMED_WAITING (sleeping)
15     at java.lang.Thread.sleep(Native Method)
16     at com.jpt.MyThread.mySleep(MyThreadStarter.java:18)
17     at com.jpt.MyThread.run(MyThreadStarter.java:21)
```

When looking at a map of say, a large city, finding the "you are here" landmark to get your bearings is critical. Working with stack traces is no different. To find my bearings in a single thread's stack trace, Table 11-1 defines a few "landmarks" used to answer certain key performance questions.

Table 11-1. Landmarks of a Stack Trace, Using Listing 11-5 as an Example

Landmark Name	Question	Code from Listing 11-5	Lines of Code from Listing 11-5
Current	What line of code in this thread was executing when jstack was invoked? This is the "You are here" mark.	Thread.sleep()	3,9,15
Trigger	What code of mine triggered the Current line to execute?	MyThread.mySleep()	4,10,16
Entry	What started this thread?	MyThread.run()	5,11,17

So when you take a thread dump of a busy HTTP web container (like Tomcat) under load, each thread of traffic from the web looks like this:

1. The Entry mark is where Tomcat got an HTTP request and gave it to one of its threads to process. This is the first line at the bottom of each thread (aka stack trace).

2. Tomcat code calls your servlet code in your Java package. The "trigger" is one specific line of code in your package space—the last call your code makes that leads up to the currently executing code is the trigger. For example, if the current mark was in the JDBC driver package space waiting for a JDBC response, then the trigger would be the line of application code that executed the query. That line triggered the code to execute a query and wait for a response.

3. The Current mark is the topmost line of the stack trace—it's the line that was executing when jstack captured the dump.

This "entry-trigger-current", in that order, is the time sequence, kind of like an assembly line. The rest of this chapter relies on understanding "entry-trigger-current", so be sure to know which name points to which part of a stack trace. Each web container thread in a thread dump might be at any point in the assembly line at a given moment. In a way, it seems there might be equal probability that any single line of code executed in the system was positioned at the Current mark. That's pretty much what I thought before I ever did any performance tuning.

Thread Names are Helpful

Did you notice that in the MyThreadStarter example, we added a prefix (jpt) to the name of each thread? That is my naming scheme for my test program. Web/app servers have their own naming schemes for naming the threads that process incoming HTTP traffic and other traffic as well. Table 11-2 shows some examples for HTTP/S. Understanding how these containers name their threads helps understand which threads are under load.

Table 11-2. *Examples of How Popular Containers Name Their Threads*

Container	Example of thread name
WebSphere	WebContainer : 5
Spring Boot / Tomcat	http-nio-8080-exec-7
Spring Boot / Jetty	qtp266500815-40
Wildfly Servlet 11.0	default task-127

Focus on the Threads under Load

Java developers sometimes shy away from thread dumps because of the dizzying amount of thread activity. It is dizzying for me, too, and I saved you from all that detail. Specifically, I saved you by keeping my program very short, and in the thread dump, I showed you just the three threads started by my program, not all the other threads (beyond the scope of this book) started by the JVM.

So to make sense of thread dumps, you need strategies to weed out all threads that don't matter, so you can focus on the ones most likely to be causing the problem. Here is your first tip:

The threads under load are the ones causing the performance problem.

This sounds a bit evasive, unhelpful, and questionable at best. So it is not an absolute rule, but it should at least be one of your first lines of performance inquiry. You should ask whether there are there any obvious problems in the threads that are under load. Determining which threads are the ones under load is actually pretty straightforward.

First ask yourself what load is being applied. Are there production users coming over HTTP/S, or did you just kick off a test load script (like JMeter) that is also using HTTP/S? Is a batch job reading "work" from a file or database and then processing (that is, applying load)? Or perhaps this is a back-end JMS (Java Messaging Server) taking traffic from some unknown message producer?

Then, you find the threads in the thread dump that:

*   Have an Entry mark roughly looks like it's coming from the load that is being applied.

*   Have a thread name that also matches the load being applied.

*   Show Java method calls/activity from your package space.

*   Have a Thread status that is neither WAITING nor TIME_WAITING.

Let's look at these four, one at a time.

Listing 11-6 is a snippet from a thread dump from a Tomcat HTTP SOA app running under Spring Boot. Let's see if the thread in Listing 11-7, shortly, is consistent with all of that. Probably all Entry marks start with Thread.run()—or the run() method of some subclass of Thread; the examples in Listing 11-5 earlier and Listing 11-6 are no exception. Thread.run() on line 87 is essentially the emblem of the Entry mark. Three of the lines above that include classes in the tomcat package, so it sounds like we're still in the right place. Lastly, on Line 78, the text "http11.Http11Processor" shows that this is HTTP activity. So the first bullet point suggests we are on the right track. The rightmost portion of Listing 11-6 is truncated for readability.

Listing 11-6. A Stack Trace That Shows (Line 78) That It Was Launched by Tomcat's HTTP Engine

```
78     at org.apache.coyote.http11.Http11Processor.service
79     at org.apache.coyote.AbstractProcessorLight.process
80     at org.apache.coyote.AbstractProtocol$ConnectionHan
81     at org.apache.tomcat.util.net.NioEndpoint$SocketPro
82     at org.apache.tomcat.util.net.SocketProcessorBase.r
83     - locked <0x0000000747d9f320> (a org.apache.tomcat.
84     at java.util.concurrent.ThreadPoolExecutor.runWorke
85     at java.util.concurrent.ThreadPoolExecutor$Worker.r
86     at org.apache.tomcat.util.threads.TaskThread$Wrappi
87     at java.lang.Thread.run(Thread.java:745)
```

The second bullet point says that the thread name has to match the load being applied. My Tomcat thread name is http-nio-8080-exec-9 and that is consistent with Table 11-2. The thread name is in the first line of 11-7, below.

The third bullet point is just a reminder that normally you are looking for code from your own package space. In this book, that will mostly be com.github.eostermueller—and we'll have plenty examples of this later.

The fourth bullet point says that threads under load are in a thread state other than WAITING and other than TIMED_WAITING. Well, that is normally the case, but in a few of my examples, my use of java.lang.Thread.sleep() in sample code to simulate a slow piece of code are an exception to the rule—they'll show up as TIME_WAITING, even though load is applied.

The second line in Listing 11-7 shows a thread under load, with thread state of RUNNABLE.

Listing 11-7. Thread Under Load with thread state RUNNABLE

```
"http-nio-8080-exec-9" #56 daemon prio=5 os_prio=31
 java.lang.Thread.State: RUNNABLE
    at java.io.FileInputStream.readBytes(Native
    at java.io.FileInputStream.read(FileInputStr
    at sun.security.provider.NativePRNG$RandomIO
    at sun.security.provider.NativePRNG$RandomIO
```

So once you have verified these four things, you will be able to wade through all the threads in a thread dump and figure out which ones are currently under load. As one last sanity check, you could also check the CPU consumption on the machine. For sure, zero CPU consumption with occasional spikes will not suffice for load (even by this chapter's loose definition).

Manual Thread Dump Profiling (MTDP)

Now that you can identify threads under load in a thread dump, you are finally ready to use MTDP to find performance issues in any environment.

Here are the instructions:

1. Take four or so thread dumps as load is applied with a few seconds between each dump.

2. If something that you could fix shows up in the dumps for two or more threads that are under load, it is worth fixing.

Although these instructions are adjusted to work with Java, Mike Dunlavey was the first to document this technique (for C programs) in his book *Building Better Applications* (Van Nostrand Reinhold, 1994).

Example 1

This example shows how thread dumps point you to a performance defect, even one without Java synchronization issues. Start by following the instructions at `https://github.com/eostermueller/littleMock` to download and start a Spring Boot server, and then apply three threads of load. If Maven and Java 8 (or greater) are already installed, this should take five minutes or so. The general idea is to download the zip file or do a git clone. In one terminal window, launch `./startWar.sh`. In a separate window, launch `./load.sh`. Then do the following:

1. Open `http://localhost:8080/ui` in a browser.

2. We want the Sleep Time parameter to 50ms. In the browser at the above URL, clear out all the text in the Performance Key text box. Then enter L50 and click Update. If you open Glowroot at `http://localhost:4000`, the added sleep time will show up as shown in Figure 11-1.

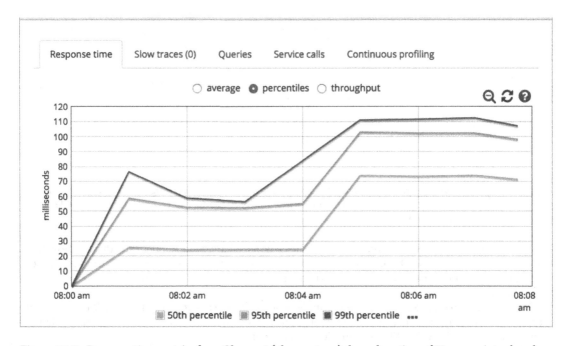

Figure 11-1. *Response time metrics from Glowroot (glowroot.org) show sleep time of 50ms was introduced halfway through the littleMock Spring Boot test*

The red line shows that 99% of all requests finished in about 58 ms or faster, until we added 50 additional ms at 8:04am, where response time jumped to about 110ms for the same 99% metric. This is a nice result—we added 50ms of sleep, and response time increased by just about the same amount (110–50 = ~58ms). But the question is this: If your client complains that response time more than doubled (like this), how would you find the root cause? If you explore the Glowroot interface, there is a good chance it will point to the Thread.sleep(), which is great. But finding the bug in any environment is the goal here, so we will use jstack, which comes with every JDK.

I invoked jstack four times (Figure 11-2) to get four text files, each with a thread dump. Then, I used the techniques in the previous section to find which threads in the dump were under load: each thread dump text file had exactly three threads with code in the com.github.eostermueller package space, and each of those had a Tomcat HTTP-looking entry mark, along with an HTTP-like thread name, such as http-nio-8080-exec-10.

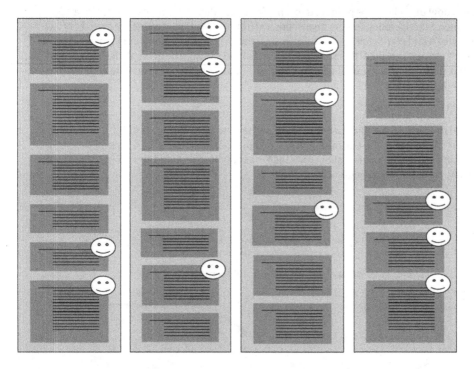

Figure 11-2. *Depiction of the four thread dumps taken earlier, one tall blue rectangle per thread dump. Each gray box is a single stack trace, aka thread. The smiley faces point to the only stack traces executing code in the com.github.eostermueller package space.*

This finding is critical, so I will repeat it: Three threads of load are being applied, and there are exactly that number of threads (three) from my com.github.eostermueller package space in each one of the four thread dumps captured. This is what happens when there is zero load gen think time and load is generated locally, not from across a network.

I mentioned earlier that to be considered "under load," a thread state much be running. Well, this is one exception, because my scenario uses Thread.sleep() to slow down the code, and that means the RUNNING state changes to TIMED_WAITING while inside Thread.sleep().

It is no coincidence that each thread dump had three threads under load, because the JMeter load script in use (load.sh invokes src/test/jmeter/littleMock.jmx) has three threads of load configured in it. If you launch the JMeter GUI with loadGui.sh (it is in same folder as load.sh) and point to the aforementioned .jmx file, you can confirm this number three in the JMeter Thread Group.

Had I added think time to the .jmx or ran JMeter from a slow network (over the Internet, or from a different data center) instead of running it locally on the same box, the number of threads under load in each dump (aka "JVM concurrency") would vary between zero and three.

So we have four threads dumps, each with three threads under load, for a total of 3x4=12 "sample" threads. Thus, we have 12 smiley faces in Figure 11-2. Let's get back to finding the code that caused this slowdown. The instructions for Manual Thread Dump Profiling (MTDP) say this:

> "If something that you could fix shows up in the dumps for two or more threads
> that are under load, it is worth fixing."

Of the twelve threads in the sample (the ones under load), eight of them were sitting on the Thread. sleep() that we introduced using the Sleep Time parameter on http://localhost:8080/ui. Listing 11-8 shows one of them.

Listing 11-8. Stacktrace of Thread.sleep()

```
29  "http-nio-8080-exec-10" #54 daemon prio=5 os_prio=31 tid=0x00007f90611d3800 nid=0x8603
     waiting
30   java.lang.Thread.State: TIMED_WAITING (sleeping)
31     at java.lang.Thread.sleep(Native Method)
32     at com.github.eostermueller.littlemock.Controller.simulateSlowCode(Controller.
       java:73)
33     at com.github.eostermueller.littlemock.Controller.home(Controller.java:60)
34     at sun.reflect.GeneratedMethodAccessor58.invoke(Unknown Source)
```

Furthermore, the instructions earlier tell us that seeing the same code show up just twice in 12 thread dumps is enough to cause concern. My test yielded four times that many—eight.

Sample Size and Healthy Skepticism

In the preceding example, we found that 8 out of 12 threads sampled were in Thread.sleep(), and we felt confident enough to claim we had found the culprit. Is 12 really a large enough sample to base real development/tuning changes on? What if I captured a new set four additional thread dumps and Thread. sleep() only showed in one or none of them? This is a fair point, one that I asked myself for many months when I first started using this technique.

The short answer is that it is extremely rare for relatively fast methods to show up as the Current mark in a thread dump. For instance, trivial getters and setters never show up. If one ever did, it would be years before you saw it again. The slower the execution time, the more a method will show up in the stack trace. Think of MTDP as an exclusive club for the slow, which is completely different than having equal probability that any single line of code executed will be positioned at the Current mark. This equal probability situation never happens.

For a slightly longer answer, I ran one test for almost 20 minutes and took one thread dump every second (1151 thread dumps to be precise). The average number of times that my Controller.simulateSlowCode() showed up in a single thread dump file? 1.94787 times out of three possible threads. So my measurement of 8/12 (2/3) only fractionally overstated the average captured from a more robust sample size.

If you are looking for a more complete justification for why it is safe to make development changes based on such small sample sizes, here are two math-based opinions on that matter. For full disclosure, one of the justifications is written by Mike Dunlavey, the guy who first published this technique:

http://ostermueller.blogspot.com/2017/04/the-math-behind-manual-thread-dump.html

Personally, I use this technique not because the math is convincing, but because it works. The next section shows the results from one such tuning success story, and you can have a close look at all the optimizations discovered by this technique, a technique you can finally take into any environment in the enterprise.

The example above showed how MTDP can detect a 50ms response time increase, where the response time was doubled. Regardless of whether you think that is a large or a small slowdown, the next section shows how MTDP is capable of detecting response time problems much smaller than 50ms.

MTDP Demonstration

I am expecting, almost hoping, that you will be skeptical that performance defects can accurately be identified with the small number of samples discussed in the preceding section. I'm not really seeking out disagreement; instead I just want to say "welcome." The world of performance assessment needs the skeptics.

This section provides an overview of a small tuning effort, with basic before-and-after performance results. To give you a rough idea of how littleMock works, there is no detailed review of thread dumps in this first example—just an overview. All the defects on this adventure were discovered using the Manual Thread Dump Profiling (MTDP) technique described earlier. But instead of just replacing slow code with the fast as in a normal tuning effort, we will use the littleMock web page that allows us to live-toggle between the slow and the fast code. You just click a button to toggle between slow and fast, and the Glowroot (point your browser to `http://localhost:4000`) throughput measurement leaps, like resuscitating a dead patient. You should try it.

Since this is a run-on-your-own-machine demo, when a "slow" option is enabled, you get to see each defect rear its ugly little head in the thread dumps (the exclusive club for the slow). When you click to toggle on the "fast" option, you can take more thread dumps to insure that same defect vanishes and that there is a corresponding boost in performance.

The application is the same one used earlier, but the Sleep Time option is not used. Here is the link again for the install:

`https://github.com/eostermueller/littleMock`

I ran the littleMock UI with the some slower options for almost 10 minutes. Then, just before 5pm in Figure 11-3, I used the GUI to apply some more efficient settings, where you can see a dramatic spike.

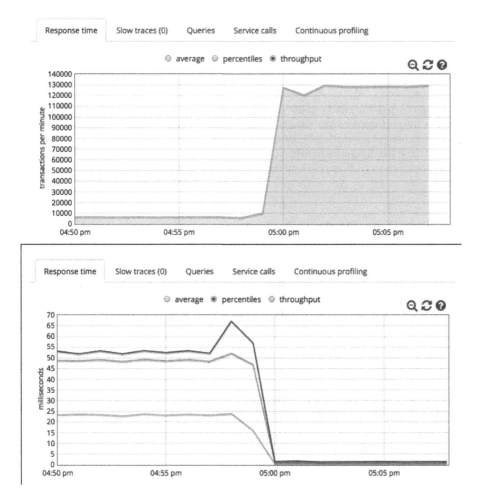

Figure 11-3. *The big boost in performance right around 5pm happened when I applied a different performance key. The load.sh script was running for the duration of the test.*

As you can read from Figure 11-3, the tuning fixes boosted throughput by a factor of 13; throughput started out at fewer than 10K requests per minute and ended up at more than 130K per minute. For response time, 99% of all responses started out around about 53ms or faster, and ended up faster than 2ms.

Here are the performance keys to the slow and fast tests shown above in Figure 11-3.

Slow: X0,J100,K100,Q0,R0,S0

Fast: X2,J25,K25,Q1,R1,S1

But what code is making such dratic changes between these two different performance keys? The littleMock web page, below the performance key, details all the options. It even provides web links to github source code that shows what changes are made when you choose a slightly different option.

For example, to understand the difference between the X0 and the X2 settings, look for the [X0] text as you scroll down the littleMock web page. If you click on the 'Source Link' to the right of [X0], it will take you to the github.com code.

Navigating Unfamiliar Code

Finding the entry, trigger, and current marks is the first step to getting your bearings when looking at a stack trace. Unfamiliar code is everywhere, because our applications now rely on so many different libraries. It took a while, as a performance engineer, to get comfortable making assessments of code I'd never seen before. It is just part of the job I had to get used to.

My first reaction to looking at a stack trace from unfamiliar code used to be one of these:

1. Fear.

2. I can only tune something I've got the source code to, and if it's not in one of our company's package spaces, forget it.

I still feel like this on a bad day, but there is one simple question that disarms all of this fear for me: When in the logical timeline of the request was this stack trace taken?

1. Was it in the beginning, when the code is reading the input from the caller and figuring out what processing to tackle?

2. Or was it in the middle, when the beef of the main process is well underway, like an INSERT into a massive database table of orders?

3. Or was the code toward the end of the request, closing resources and preparing the result (like marshaling a result to json or HTML rendering) for the caller?

The easiest way for me pinpoint the location on the timeline is this: the stack trace includes the line number of the trigger mark—this is the last method called in your package space before the current mark executes. Open the source code to the line number specified in the trigger mark. If you don't have the source code, consider getting the .class file and using an open-source Java decompiler to get the source. I have had good luck with JD-GUI (http://jd.benow.ca/) and jad.exe (https://sourceforge.net/projects/originaljavadecompiler/).

Once you have the source code in front of you, assess whether the trigger code executes before, during, or after the "main" processing for this request—you'll have to be the judge of this "main" event. Is it a request to a back-end system? Calculation of some result? You make the call. I'll refer to this timeline exercise as "plotting the request's timeline."

When I look at unfamiliar class names on the current landmark in a stack trace that repeatedly shows up in MTDP analysis, I'm inclined to say "not my problem." But if I instead ask "Where in the stack trace do I have any control?" or "At what point in the stack trace could I have done anything different?" there is hope, because normally a trigger landmark exists, one that my code executed, and that is where I need to reevaluate.

Leveraging the Four Anti-Patterns

The performance anti-patterns discussed in Chapter 1, admittedly, are a bit over-generalized. But that all changes, now that we have the Entry, Trigger, and Current vocabulary in hand; we can get a little more specific.

The answer to the question about where in the timeline of a request was a particular stack trace captured, makes all the difference in painting a story around how this defect came to be. Let's do a quick review:

1. Unnecessary Initialization

2. Strategy/Algorithm Inefficiency

3. Overprocessing

4. Large Processing Challenge

If the trigger mark comes before the "main" processing, check to see whether this is an Unnecessary Initialization problem—number 1. An unsettling number of performance defects happen here. If there is a lot of data to initialize (like 500MB of product descriptions loading from a database), then consider processing the data once at start-up (or when the first request comes thru) and then cache the result for quick access later.

If the process doesn't have 500MB of product description loading or other similar large data tasks, then you should ask yourself why it's taking so long (remember, the MTDP is the exclusive club for the slow) to process just a small amount of data. If the amount of data is small, then perhaps the path the trigger code takes to get to the current mark needs to be rethought. Most APIs have multiple usage idioms, and perhaps the one your code took is not optimal. When the trigger code makes its first call that leads to the current mark, it is broadcasting to you which idiom (or at least part of the idiom) was selected by the trigger.

If the stack trace is part of the main process, then check to see whether you're looking at number 2—Strategy/Algorithm inefficiency. A slow individual database query falls into this category, as well as a chatty database strategy caused by a SELECT N+1 issue, or perhaps just too many database calls in general. That said, these culprits can be more easily recognized using the toolset and approach in the P for Persistent part of the P.A.t.h. checklist.

The third anti-pattern is pretty easy to check for. Judging by the class and method names and even the entry mark, determine whether this is a business process that belongs in the load test. For example, perhaps sample data in the JMeter load test use that one special test customer from QA with a hundred times as many accounts as a regular customer (it was QA's fault!). If so, fix the load script to call less off this business process.

For anti-pattern 4, the Large Processing Challenge, just as with anti-pattern 3, check the calls leading up to the trigger to assess which business process is executing. Large Processing Challenges are so large that you should know about them and start planning for them (installing extra disk space, scripting a large data load and backup, and so on) during development.

Interactive Thread Dump Reading Exercise

This is where the examples get detailed and you will really want to run this on your own desktop.

One of the first hurdles to get over when you start tuning is to decide on one particular stack trace to target for improvement. This example provides a walkthrough of one such example.

Use the following performance key as the starting point for this example.

X0,J25,K25,Q1,R1,S1

Once the load.sh/cmd was up and running, I ran jcmd to find the PID of littleMock and captured four thread dumps using jstack. I used the criteria discussed earlier to find which threads were under load. As we saw before, there were three threads under load in each thread dump, times four dumps, or 12 stack traces total.

Listing 11-9 shows key parts from the 12 threads under load. The first two threads showed up in five threads each, and the last two threads show up one time each. 5+5+1+1 = 12. I encourage you to try this example yourself on your own machine to see whether you get stack traces in similar proportions; I think you will.

Listing 11-9. The four unique stack traces under load in the four thread dumps

```
at com.sun.org.apache.xpath.internal.jaxp.XpathImpl.getResultAsType(XPathImpl.java:317)
at com.sun.org.apache.xpath.internal.jaxp.XpathImpl.evaluate(XPathImpl.java:274)
at com.github.eostermueller.littlemock.XPathWrapper.matches(XPathWrapper.java:25)
at com.github.eostermueller.littlemock.PlaybackRepository.getConfigByXPath(PlaybackRepository.
java:144)
at com.github.eostermueller.littlemock.PlaybackRepository.locateConfig_noCaching
(PlaybackRepository.java:96)

at com.sun.org.apache.xerces.internal.parsers.XMLParser.parse(XMLParser.java:141)
at com.sun.org.apache.xerces.internal.parsers.DOMParser.parse(DOMParser.java:243)
at com.sun.org.apache.xerces.internal.jaxp.DocumentBuilderImpl.parse(DocumentBuilderImpl.
java:339)
at com.github.eostermueller.littlemock.PlaybackRepository.getConfigByXPath(PlaybackRepository.
java:143)
at com.github.eostermueller.littlemock.PlaybackRepository.locateConfig_
noCaching(PlaybackRepository.java:96)

at javax.xml.xpath.XPathFactoryFinder.newFactory(XPathFactoryFinder.java:138)
at javax.xml.xpath.XPathFactory.newInstance(XPathFactory.java:190)
at javax.xml.xpath.XPathFactory.newInstance(XPathFactory.java:96)
at com.github.eostermueller.littlemock.XPathWrapper.matches(XPathWrapper.java:22)
at com.github.eostermueller.littlemock.PlaybackRepository.getConfigByXPath(PlaybackRepository.
java:144)

at java.security.AccessController.doPrivileged(Native Method)
at javax.xml.parsers.FactoryFinder.findServiceProvider(FactoryFinder.java:289)
at javax.xml.parsers.FactoryFinder.find(FactoryFinder.java:267)
at javax.xml.parsers.DocumentBuilderFactory.newInstance(DocumentBuilderFactory.java:120)
at com.github.eostermueller.littlemock.PlaybackRepository.getDocBuilder(PlaybackRepository.
java:167)
```

The application under load that we've been using since the beginning of this chapter is littleMock. It is a tiny little HTTP stub server that I modeled after wiremock.org. A stub server is basically a test double, used in a test environment as a stand-in for some other system that was too expensive or too troublesome to install. If the XML-over-HTTP input (from load.sh/JMeter) matches one of five XPath expressions configured in littleMock's application.properties, it returns a preconfigured response XML that mimics a response from the stubbed-out system.

As such, XPath evaluation and XML parsing (of the HTTP input requests) are the main processing of this application, and this is our first task—to assess whether these four stack traces occurred before, during, or after the main processing.

The trigger in the first stack trace calls XpathImpl.evaluate(); the second calls DocumentBuilderImpl. parse(). Obviously, the bulk of the processing is happening in these 5+5 threads doing XPath evaluation and XML parsing, but there are no obvious optimizations, here—no low-hanging fruit.

But the third stack trace, which showed up just once out of 12 threads, is certainly suspect, and I will show you exactly why.

Listing 11-10 shows that the trigger is on line 22 of XPathWrapper.java. The stack trace shows that line 22 should be a call to XPathFactory.newInstance().

Listing 11-10. A small excerpt from the third stack trace in Listing 11-9

```
at javax.xml.xpath.XPathFactory.newInstance(XPathFactory.java:96)
at com.github.eostermueller.littlemock.XPathWrapper.matches(XPathWrapper.java:22)
```

...and sure enough, when we look at the source code, line 22 contains exactly what we expected, a call to newInstance():

```
19 boolean matches(Document document) throws XPathExpressionException {
20
21     XPath xpath = null;
22     XPathFactory factory = XPathFactory.newInstance();
23     xpath = factory.newXPath();
24
25     Object xpathResult = xpath.evaluate(this.getXPath(),
                   document, XPathConstants.BOOLEAN);
26
28     Boolean b = (Boolean)xpathResult;
28     return b.booleanValue();
29 }
```

This code was taken from the following link:

```
https://github.com/eostermueller/littleMock/blob/1206673fc57b09effd2152c0c4e1414fd1911508/
src/main/java/com/github/eostermueller/littlemock/XPathWrapper.java#L19-L29
```

Furthermore, the third stack trace's trigger (line 22) clearly comes before the main processing of this request, right there in the same method in Listing 11-10, line 25.

The very important point is this:

Slow initialization code begs for optimization.

We know this code is slow because it shows up in the "exclusive club for the slow"—MTDP.

We know that the slow code, the call to XPathFactory.newInstance() on line 22, is initialization code because it comes before the main processing—the XpathImpl.evaluate() on line 25.

Why does slow code beg for optimization? I went over this in the "Leveraging the Four Anti-Patterns" section earlier, but the general idea is this: it takes a lot of work to get large processing challenges to perform well, but initialization tasks often have static data that can be processed and cached one time at start-up, or there isn't that much data to process at all—processing small amounts of data is generally fast.

How to Make Code Faster

Once you have found some slow code to focus on, unless you have some bright ideas on how to optimize, it's time put this in the good hands of the Internet. If you factor out environment-specific factors like "processing too much data," "misconfigured virtual machine," or "faulty network cable," your answer lies on the Internet. I'm telling you, you are not the first one to run into a performance problem with a commonly used API. My search for "XPathFactory.newInstance() performance," for example, yielded a handful of discussions that led me to the fix in Listing 11-11. Actually, both the third thread and the fourth thread (the two that showed up in a single stack trace each) have similar problems, and both of them are addressed with the change shown here.

Listing 11-11. In pom.xml (same folder as startWar.sh/cmd), Make Sure This Text Is Commented In, for a Performance Improvement.

```
<argument>-Dcom.sun.org.apache.xml.internal.dtm.DTMManager=
com.sun.org.apache.xml.internal.dtm.ref.DTMManagerDefault</argument>

<argument>-Djavax.xml.parsers.DocumentBuilderFactory=
com.sun.org.apache.xerces.internal.jaxp.DocumentBuilderFactoryImpl</argument>

<argument>-Djavax.xml.xpath.XPathFactory:http://java.sun.com/jaxp/xpath/dom=
com.sun.org.apache.xpath.internal.jaxp.XPathFactoryImpl</argument>
```

You should probably beat me up a bit because I broke my own rule. Earlier, I said this about MTDP:

> If you see a particular something that you could fix that shows up in the dumps on two or more threads that are under load, it is worth fixing.

and the thread dumps didn't meet this criteria, yet I plodded ahead with the optimization and got roughly a 20% throughput boost. Early in this chapter, we added the Thread.sleep() to littleMock UI and easily found the Thread.sleep() in the thread dumps. That was an obvious problem, but this one, not so much. The thread dumps showed the problem in both cases (Figure 11-4).

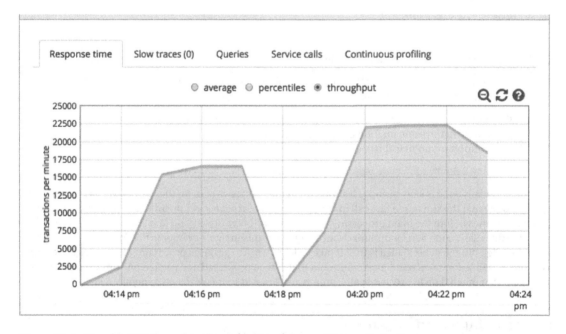

Figure 11-4. Roughly 20% throughput boost (right test) from adding optimizations.

Limitations

There is a reason why MTDP isn't in a book by itself—because there are a number of blind spots, when you use it alone; other tools are required to fill in the gaps. For example, the garbage collector only runs while jstack is not running. That means jstack can't see or diagnose GC performance problems.

Likewise, the Chatty SELECT N+1 issues are part of a strategy unto themselves, and it really helps to visualize them in a SQL Sequence Diagram to fully understand the problem.

There are other blind spots, as well. Consider a container's Web Container Max setting—the setting the limits the number of threads processing HTTP requests. If that number gets maxed out, then thread dumps will do very little to show the problem. To get around this, it might just be helpful to follow the "Raise caps before production and lower them before production" idea.

How Much Load?

I mentioned elsewhere that the P and the A in P.A.t.h. are spelled out with capital letters because they are special: most of the time, you have the luxury of being able to detect problems in those areas with just a single user's traffic, and thus avoid the hassle of creating a load script and finding a performance environment. Well, here we are in the "t" part of the checklist and load is required here. The sampling techniques only make sense when constant load is applied, and understanding cumulative impact of all the processing is key.

But how much load should be applied? Frankly, I am undecided on which of these to recommend to you:

- The Scalability Yardstick: "Run an incremental load test with four equal steps of load, the first of which pushes the app server CPU to about 25%."

- 3t0tt, which means "Run three threads of load with zero think time."

…but since the second idea is easier, perhaps that is the best place to start.

In fact, I think all components as big as an SOA service should undergo the torment of three threads of load with zero think time, and thread dumps should be captured during this test.

Distinguishing High Throughput and Slow Stack Traces

Much of the time when I use MTDP, I am looking for the cause of some really slow processing. In the thread dumps I would expect to see the same stack trace show up in perhaps more than 50% of the stack traces. Let's say 6 out of 12 traces from 4 thread dumps have the exact same method.

An alternate reading of this same data is that instead of slow response time, this particular business process shows up more frequently simply because has higher throughput—it's executed more frequently so it shows up more frequently. That sounds like a possibility, but there is an easy way to check it.

Earlier, we said that thread dumps are taken at a point at time, and any give one was captured either before, during, or after the main processing event. Have a closer look at the method that showed up in 6 of the 12 thread dumps. If the "current" mark fluctuates in these 6 stack traces is sometimes before, sometimes in the middle, or sometimes after the main processing event, I concede that high throughput is the cause of frequent occurrences.

On the other hand, if the stack trace in question has the exact same current, trigger, and entry, then this is a slow request.

MTDP and Other Examples

Dial this performance key into littleMock:

X2,J25,K25,L0,Q1,R1,S1,T1

If you take some thread dumps, you will find both of these methods showing up:

javax.xml.transform.TransformerFactory.newInstance ()
com.sun.org.apache.xalan.internal.xsltc.trax.TransformerFactoryImpl.newTransformer()

Now, take the above key and change T1 to T2 and apply the new key. Performance improves dramatically. How does T2 process so much more throughput? Search the litteMock web page for T2 and click the 'source link.' to find the answer.

Let's shift gears back to the other set of examples—jpt. MTDP can diagnose a number of problems with the jpt tests. Here is the URL again for your convenience:

```
https://github.com/eostermueller/javaPerformanceTroubleshooting
```

Consider these examples:

- jpt test 01a has really slow requests to a back-end. Run jpt test 01a, capture some thread dumps, and look for SocketInputStream.socketread0().

- jpt test 02a has many reads to a 1MB data file. The thread dumps will show a number of thread that include this method:

  ```
  com.github.eostermueller.perfSandbox.filesystem.FileSystemReader.
  readFile()
  ```

- jpt test 04a. This test uses a questionable table join and ends up with slow result set iteration. I had to take 5 or 6 thread dumps, but the result set iteration really shows up here:

  ```
  org.h2.result.ResultRemote.next(ResultRemote.java:133)
  org.h2.jdbc.JdbcResultSet.nextRow(JdbcResultSet.java:3240)
  org.h2.jdbc.JdbcResultSet.next(JdbcResultSet.java:123)
  com.zaxxer.hikari.pool.HikariProxyResultSet.next(HikariProxyResultSet.java)
  com.github.eostermueller.perfSandbox.dataaccess_1.AccountMgr1.
  getAccounts(AccountMgr1.java:76)
  ```

- jpt test 05b. Thread dumps show two interesting things here:

  - As stated earlier, network activity will show up in a thread dump under this method: java.net.SocketInputStream.socketRead0()
    In this example, it's here because of a very slow query that is missing a database index.

  - See the executeQuery() call below? If you find the method that calls executeQuery(), you can find the SQL statement. I've highlighted the method that calls executeQuery(), and that's where you'll find the text of the SQL statement:

```
com.zaxxer.hikari.pool.HikariProxyPreparedStatement.executeQuery()
com.github.eostermueller.perfSandbox.dataaccess_1.AccountMgr1.getAccounts(AccountMgr1.
java:73)
com.github.eostermueller.perfSandbox.Controller.internalInquiry2(Controller.java:353)
```

So you can see from these examples the thread dumps are very powerful, shedding light on all of these problems, none of which have anything to do with BLOCKED threads.

Java Profilers can obviously find all these same problems that MTDP can find, and then some. So when should each tool be used and when? In short, use MTDP when you don't have access to a Java profiler or APM tool. In summary, use either, use both, just use them, whatever works best/fastest for you.

Don't Forget

We have covered a lot of ground in this chapter. We saw how to take thread dumps and identify the Entry, Trigger, and Current landmarks, and we also learned how to detect whether load is being applied to a particular thread or not. We also went over instructions for Manual Thread Dump Profiling (MTDP), and mentioned that the threads under load in thread dumps are rarely ever class/methods that are fast—instead, MTDP is an basically the exclusive club for the slow.

Then, we discussed how to plot the timeline of user activity, and determine whether the stack trace was captured before, during or after the main processing. Knowing this is essential, because if a stack trace appears slow and showed up prior to the main processing, then congratulations, you have found Main Anti-Pattern 1—Unnecessary Initialization.

Also, for one example, we inserted a 50ms `Thread.sleep()` and were easily able to detect that in thread dumps. MTDP is pretty impressive that it's capable of finding an issue so small. But the example with the XML optimizations was even more impressive. I didn't show the response time metrics, but the response time improvement for that example was less than 5ms. This shows that MTDP is not only effective, but it is very sensitive and can find issues both large and small.

So you see, there is much, much more to thread dumps than looking at blocked threads. You can actually use MTDP like it was a mini Java profiler. With such a powerful, low-overhead tool, there are all kinds of problems that you can discover in the Dark environments of this world.

Like any measurements, there will be variability, especially if you are operating in a medium to low throughput environment. Any tool you stick into an environment with low throughput will end up with variable results. That is a concern with any measurement. But just like most other profilers, MTDP does not show whether there are Garbage Collection slowdowns in your environment.

What's Next

Since MTDP and Java profilers in general don't have metrics for Garbage Collection, the next chapter provides a very quick way to assess GC health. There is also a great section on detecting the cause of memory leaks, so stay tuned for that.

CHAPTER 12

■ ■ ■

Heap, the "h" in P.A.t.h.

This is the last of the four P.A.t.h. Checklist chapters. Remember that until the root of the problem is found, you need to check all four parts of the Checklist. This chapter starts out with a very basic Garbage Collection health check—it should take just a few minutes to capture the data and make a healthy/not-healthy assessment.

But by the end of the chapter, I will have you doing more involved tasks, like rummaging through heap dumps to find the root cause of memory leaks that come with this book's sample applications.

The objectives for this chapter are:

- Learn how to quickly assess GC Health in any JVM. No extra configuration is required, no need to restart the JVM.

- Understand the high-level approach to troubleshooting performance issues with the heap.

- Fix the most common GC inefficiencies by first understanding which heap space is causing your problem, the old space or the new space.

- Pinpoint the cause of a memory leak by discovering the names of classes with high memory consumption, but also understand how consumption for individual classes trends over time.

- Take a first look at using a heap analysis tool to discover the root cause of a memory leak.

The Quick GC Health Check in this chapter boils down GC performance into two easy-to-capture metrics that are available from tools right there in the JDK. There are no extra JVM parameters to configure, no JVM restart is required. These are plug-it-in-now metrics, available right when you want them. I'll provide my own thresholds on what numbers translate into "healthy" or not; you can adjust them based on your own experience.

Along with this health check, this chapter provides a review of a number of other GC/heap analysis techniques. Ultimately I will roll them up into a nice little set of steps that will guide you through fixing the majority of all the GC/heap performance problems you encounter.

One of my goals for this chapter this to show that a great amount of GC/heap tuning can be done without knowing much at all about GC algorithms.

Quick GC Health Check

Understanding how much improvement can be made on a particular slow-looking GC metric, or any slow-looking metric actually, is a bit challenging. So when it comes to assessing GC health, I make it easy on myself with a simple RED-YELLOW-GREEN approach.

It starts with a simple "GC overhead" metric, which is the amount of time spent garbage collecting measured over an elapsed time. So if 150ms (0.150 seconds) of the last 1000ms have been spent in GC, then that's 15% GC overhead. 20ms (0.02 seconds) out of 1000ms is 2% overhead.

© Erik Ostermueller 2017

E. Ostermueller, *Troubleshooting Java Performance*, DOI 10.1007/978-1-4842-2979-8_12

Here is how I use the GC overhead metric to triage performance problems with the heap:

- RED: If sustained GC overhead is greater than 8%, then high priority should be given to improving GC performance.

- YELLOW: If sustained GC overhead is greater than 2% (but less than 8%), then start researching improvements, but there is no rush to implement a GC change. Moving from GREEN to YELLOW will often be an early warning sign of a memory leak.

- GREEN: when sustained GC overhead less than 2% GC performance is considered healthy, and no GC tuning is required. However, systems that require faster response times (perhaps less than 25ms) will still see benefit if GC is tuned more, perhaps down to 0.5%.

The phrase "sustained GC overhead" roughly means sustained for 5 minutes or more. If you don't like the percentages I've assigned to RED-YELLOW-GREEN, I promise I won't be offended if you alter them to accommodate your experience. The point is that development and operations teams need a consistent approach for determining when corrective action should be taken.

Even if aggregate overhead is low, occasional spikes can be worrisome. Consider using a similar grading scale, like this:

- RED: More than five 3-second pauses an hour

- YELLOW: Between two and five 3-second pauses an hour

- GREEN: one or fewer 3-second pauses an hour

Keep in mind that the G1 garbage collector algorithm was designed to minimize these spikes.

We will discuss the tools you can use to capture this GC overhead metric, but first let's look at the traditional approach/tooling to capturing GC metrics.

The Traditional Approach to GC Metrics

To use the latest and greatest GC performance analysis programs, you need to enable your JVM to capture a verbose GC file and then analyze the file. First add a few parameters to your JVM start up:

```
-Xloggc:gc.log
-verbose:gc
```

Then restart the JVM and reproduce the problem. Then you transfer the gc.log file back to your desktop, and download and install an analysis program that graphs the GC data.

That is a lot of work, but often, additional JVM settings like the following are required to get the full picture of the problem:

```
-XX:+PrintGCDetails
-XX:+PrintGCDateStamps
-XX:+PrintGCTimeStamps
-XX:+PrintTenuringDistribution
-XX:+PrintClassHistogram
-XX:+PrintGCApplicationStoppedTime
-XX:+PrintPromotionFailure
-verbose:sizes
```

I'm often unsure whether I know the current, full list of parameters to fully vet GC performance or whether the full list even exists. Furthermore, for operational harmony and to avoid filling the hard disk with great performance data, these parameters are essential:

```
-XX:+UseGCLogFileRotation
-XX:NumberOfGCLogFiles=5
-XX:GCLogFileSize=10m
```

It takes an unusually patient snake charmer to collect verbose GC metrics, with the many and varied JVM parameters and the requisite JVM restarts. Making sure all the right parameters stay in place across all environments seems difficult at best, even though real performance analysis stalls until the JVM snake charmers have done their work. When performance analysis stalls during a crisis, angst and frustration rise.

To the good people who run the OpenJdk project, I think it is reasonable to ask that all out-of-the-box JVMs capture these low-overhead metrics by default, with parameters to tweak or turn them off as necessary. How about as a default, we could have a modest 10MB max footprint for the data files?

New open source and freely available graphing and analysis tools show up every year that provide better understanding of verbose GC data. This is a nice, open and growing tool ecosystem, even if snake charming is required to capture data. It would be nice if the graphing tools displayed a live view of the data, instead of the current batched approach, processing from a file.

Live GC data, graphed, can be retrieved from a different toolset: the Visual GC and gcViewer plug-ins for JVisualVM that comes with the JDK. JConsole provides metrics, too. But these facilities lack a number of important metrics, they are less mature, and enhancements are infrequent.

Here are four main facilities for capturing GC performance data:

- Verbose GC

- `JAVA_HOME/bin/jvisualvm` and `JAVA_HOME/bin/jconsole`

- `JAVA_HOME/bin/jstat`

- Third-party tools like Application Performance Management (APM) tools, Dynatrace, AppDynamics, and so on

Ultimately, this third option, `jstat`, will be the tool we use to capture metrics for the RED-YELLOW-GREEN approach. But before we jump into that, let's quickly review a few high-level things in the next section about the GC.

Garbage Collector Overview

Of all the many JVM heap parameters, the `-Xmx` parameter plays the main role in heap performance. For example, `-Xmx2048m` defines a fixed 2GB of RAM, called the heap, that is at your Java program's disposal. Note that unlike many GC parameters, this one uses no equal sign (=)—it's a bit of an oddball that way. Never set this value higher than your available RAM. OutOfMemory errors show up when your program allocates more than your `-Xmx` heap max value. Additional RAM outside of the heap can also be used, as it is by implementers of JSR-107:

```
https://www.jcp.org/en/jsr/detail?id=107
```

However, that is out of scope for this small book.

The JVM's garbage collector (GC) is really just a recycler. Once your Java program is finished using a variable, the GC discards it by making the underlying memory available for subsequent variable declarations. It takes work for the GC to identify variables (and memory) still in-use by your application to ensure that they are not discarded. When I say "work," I mean it's going to eat CPU and it will cause some processing slowdowns.

GC algorithms, which are heavily configurable, rely on various carefully sized compartments of memory to pull off this recycling process efficiently. When certain of these compartments aren't sized right, end-user slowdowns ensue.

There are a number of different GC algorithms that can be used, and JVM start-up parameters decide which one is in use for a given Java process. Even though descriptions for the GC algorithms are available everywhere, somehow that doesn't translate into being able to quickly assess whether GC performance is healthy or not, and whether an inefficiency lies in the "old" or the "new" generation, which are two of the main heap compartments that I mentioned earlier. All modern GC algorithms split the heap into old and new generations and have different approaches to managing each one.

This document from Oracle provides detail on all the GC algorithms:

```
http://www.oracle.com/technetwork/java/javase/tech/index-jsp-140228.html
```

Plug-It-in-Now GC Metrics with jstat

I have mentioned elsewhere that if metrics aren't easy to capture, then performance problems often go unfixed. That's why I rely on JAVA_HOME/bin/jstat -gc to capture metrics from any running JVM—no need to add JVM GC parameters, no need to restart the JVM and reproduce the problem. Just pass in the PID of the Java process and review the data. The tool summarizes all its metrics for the time interval you give it. I told jstat to use an interval of 1 second (1s), like this:

```
# jstat -gc <myPid> 1s
```

Yes, this data is more convenient to retrieve, but there is nothing attractive about the presentation of Listing 12-1, and there are very few tools that create graphs from this format. Looks like a lot of data already, but there is more! I trimmed five columns out of the left side of this image.

Listing 12-1. Data from JAVA_HOME/bin/jstat, one new line of data every 1 second

```
YGCT    FGCT
-----   -----
1.719   1.028
1.721   1.028
1.724   1.028
1.728   1.028
1.734   1.028
1.738   1.028
1.744   1.028
1.748   1.028
```

Ultimately, we need to somehow get the GC overhead metric out of this data for the RED-YELLOW-GREEN scale discussed earlier, and we'll need it for both the young gen and the new gen. Fortunately, there is one column each for young and new gen: these are YGCT and FGCT, and they are documented here:

```
https://docs.oracle.com/javase/8/docs/technotes/tools/unix/jstat.html
```

But there is one last headache to deal with: each row in these two columns shows the accumulated GC time since you started jstat. Instead, we need GC time that happened in each 1 second interval, and that will allow us to easily calculate an average.

I created a four-line awk script to get around these headaches. The script selects only the two columns we care about (the ones highlighted in Listing 12-1), and it also calculates the differences between each row.

The readme.txt at this link has all the details on the gctime script:

```
https://github.com/eostermueller/littleMock/tree/master/gctime
```

As a point of interest, let's say that all you have is stdout from jstat with a 1-second interval, as you might get from an operations team. You can get the right gctime output by post-processing the stdout file with the (almost trivial) awk script at the link.

Let's do some tuning using gctime. Both of the following examples started out with the GC parameters in Listing 12-2, which means that the heap is split right down the center: 512MB old gen, 512MB young gen. For brevity, I have not shown the <argument> XML tags that surround each parameter in the pom.xml file. Results for this configuration are in Listing 12-3, following.

Listing 12-2. GC parameters dialed into littleMock's pom.xml for this example

```
-Xmx1g -XX:NewSize=512m -XX:MaxNewSize=512m -XX:+UseConcMarkSweepGC -XX:ConcGCThreads=4
```

These parameters are kept toward the end of littleMock's pom.xml (and they're all wrapped in XML <argument> tags).

Configuring littleMock Performance with Test Keys

We have two sets of performance examples, right? jpt and littleMock. With jpt, when you launch ./startWar.sh 05b and ./load.sh 05b, you see performance of a really slow query without an index. When you instead run with 05a, you get the same test but with the index in place (and better performance). The test ID passed into startWar.sh and tload.sh determines performance.

The littleMock startWar.sh and load.sh are different—they don't take any parameters. To "dial in" a particular performance problem or optimization, you instead change the 'performance key' or other options on the littleMock web page:

```
http://localhost:8080/ui
```

With jpt, we are limited to 12 pairs of tests. littleMock performance keys enable countless permutations of performance test scenarios that can be shared and explored together so we can discuss the best tools and performance remedies to use for very specific performance scenarios.

Don't forget that Glowroot is enabled—just browse to http://localhost:4000. When the ./load.sh script is running, you can see interactively how performance changes as you click options in the littleMock web page.

Optimizing Young Gen GC

Listings 12-3 and 12-4 show gctime GC metrics before and after tuning. Before tuning, the young gen GC health is YELLOW because dYGCT (the left column) has 4%-5% overhead. After tuning, the young GC health is GREEN; about 1% GC overhead. (Output from gctime.sh.)

Listing 12-3. Data from gctime.sh. GC Metrics Before Tuning

```
dYGCT  dFGCT
-----  -----
0.047  0.000
0.052  0.000
0.054  0.000
0.047  0.000
0.052  0.000
0.042  0.000
```

```
0.043  0.000
0.054  0.000
0.07   0.000
0.048  0.000
```

Listing 12-4. Data from `gctime.sh`. GC Metrics after Tuning

```
dYGCT  dFGCT
-----  -----
0.010  0.000
0.005  0.000
0.011  0.000
0.006  0.000
0.010  0.000
0.012  0.000
0.005  0.000
0.012  0.000
0.005  0.000
0.009  0.000
```

Listing 12-3, with New GC Health = YELLOW, was captured using a littleMock test key that simulates mostly stateless activity with little or no long-term cache. The scenario is basically an SOA system with no session management. Note that the B65535 means that there are 64K allocations during each request, which are then discarded after each request—definitely work for the young gen collection process. Here is the performance key that was used:

`X2,J25,K25,L0,Q,R,S,A10,B65535,C0,D10`

The `NewSize` and `MaxNewSize` values both started out at 512MB. Bumping them both to 750MB brought this 4%–5% down to 3.5% (not shown). After further increases to 1.5GB of new space, I got just below 2% new GC overhead and GC Health was officially GREEN (also not shown). But just for grins, I increased the new space all the way to 3GB (Listing 12-5) to lower overhead to 1%, as shown in Listing 12-4. All of these configurations had 512MB of old gen space.

Listing 12-5. GC Settings That Produced the Improved Results in Listing 12-4

`-Xmx3g -XX:NewSize=2500m -XX:MaxNewSize=2500m -XX:+UseConcMarkSweepGC -XX:ConcGCThreads=4`

Optimizing Old Gen GC

This next scenario starts with old gen GC health of RED. It simulates a large, ~500 MB cache that was not designed to expire—like sticking 500MB into a singleton, but inadvertently not allocating enough old gen in the JVM parameters for it. A scenario with a similar memory configuration is a very slow memory leak. Notice in Listing 12-6 that dFGCT (the right column) has greater than 100% overhead. `jstat`, how is this possible? Then, in Listing 12-7, the off-the-charts dFGCT metrics from Listing 12-6 came down to zeroes, with just 256MB added to the old gen.

Listing 12-6. Data from `gctime.sh`. Before: Old Gen GC Health Is RED

```
dYGCT   dFGCT
-----   -----
0.000   0.000
0.000   1.413
0.000   0.000
0.000   1.932
0.000   0.000
0.004   1.604
0.014   0.034
0.050   0.034
0.000   1.758
0.000   0.000
```

Listing 12-7. Data from `gctime.sh`. After: Health Is GREEN

```
dYGCT   dFGCT
-----   -----
0.010   0.000
0.008   0.000
0.010   0.000
0.009   0.000
0.010   0.000
0.009   0.000
0.010   0.000
0.008   0.000
0.010   0.000
0.008   0.000
```

The data in Listing 12-6 was captured by first running with one test key that added garbage that would not expire for a long time—an hour, past the duration of my little test. The C and D parameters set the duration of how long to keep the objects around—and I set it to be more than an hour (3600 seconds in an hour, and tack on three zeros to convert to milliseconds to get C3600000 and D3600001).

To fill up 512MB of old gen space as described earlier, it took littleMock a few minutes of runtime with this performance key:

```
X2,J25,K25,L0,Q,R,S,A4096,B100,C3600000,D3600001
```

As I was running this key, I closely watched Glowroot's JVM Gauge feature (Figure 12-1) to determine when the old gen part of the heap filled up.

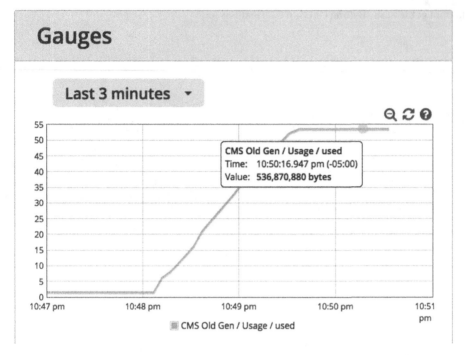

Figure 12-1. *The Gauges part of Glowroot displays CMS old gen bytes used. Here we create ~500 MB to simulate an in-memory cache of something and its effects on GC. This graph shows that my old gen is larger than 512MB. It isn't very germane, but I still wonder how that happened.*

When the old gen got to about 500MB (between 10:49pm and 10:50pm in Figure 12-1), I applied the A0 setting (Figure 12-2), probably right before poor littleMock started throwing out-of-memory errors.

Figure 12-2. *littleMock's A0=0 setting that turns off Extra Garbage Collection*

Once A0=0 was applied and the rising GC immediately and abruptly leveled out, I captured the overhead metrics in Listing 12-6, which are off the charts, with overhead that is over 100%. Dear jstat, how can one second duration (specified on the command line) contain more than a second of old gen activity, like the 1.x numbers in the dFGCT column of Listing 12-6? I suppose it's enough to know that the numbers are bad and need improvement.

Ultimately, in littleMock's pom.xml I added 256MB to the old gen, restarted littleMock, carefully put the roughly 500MB cache back in place, and used A0 to turn off Extra Garbage Collection to bring the heap to steady state. The off-the-chart metrics from gctime.sh came down to zeroes, so we got GREEN GC health for the old gen; see Listing 12-7 for details.

One moral of the story here is to triple check that your old gen has enough space to handle your big allocations, like this 500MB cache. Wouldn't you be a little embarrassed if you were the last one in the room to find out there was a huge elephant sitting in the seat right behind you? This is the same thing. Also keep in mind that performance degrades when available heap space shrinks.

Heap Trending

Having immediate access to GC performance with `jstat` is important. For example, if GC health is GREEN for `gctime.sh`'s old and new metrics, then you can move on to the next item in the P.A.t.h check list. But knowing the history of GC performance provides key troubleshooting details that can help solve problems.

For example, if GC performance was fine for days but abruptly degraded, then your search for a slow memory leak should be put on hold, because an abrupt change like this is more likely to be caused by a one-time event, perhaps a single "poison-pill" request that led to an open-ended query with massive result set that used all available memory.

Heap trending can also be helpful during development to see if any memory leaks have sneaked into the code base. For instance, before the code is released, you could run a load test and make sure that the Used Tenured Heap metrics more resembles the sawtooth in Figure 12-3 than the memory leak in Figure 12-4. These figures show verbose GC data (see the second section of this chapter) graphed by the GCViewer, which is available from `https://github.com/chewiebug/GCViewer`.

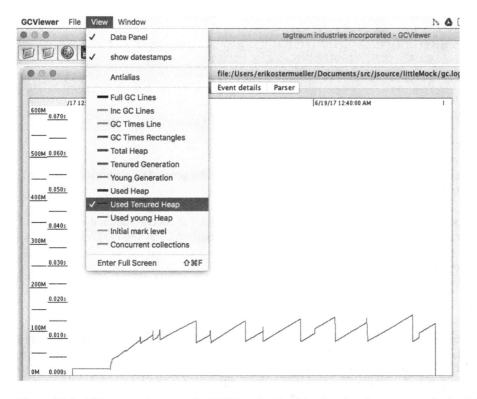

Figure 12-3. *This sawtooth pattern in GCViewer is a healthy sign that the system-under-load does not have any memory leaks*

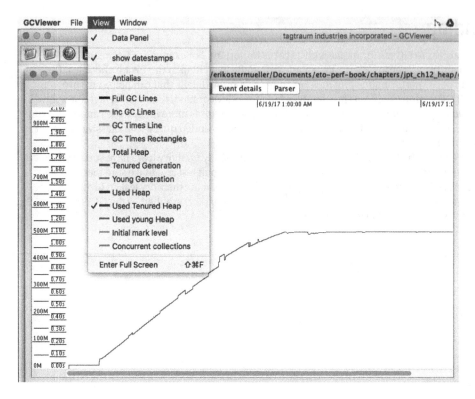

Figure 12-4. *When the Used Tenured Heap metric is missing a sawtooth, it generally looks like this, which is most likely a memory leak. Screenshot from GCViewer.*

The GC metrics available at http://gceasy.io are very helpful, but I'm not crazy about the "upload your GC data to our site or pay for your own server" business model. GarbageCat is another great option:

https://github.com/mgm3746/garbagecat

Using JVM Parameters to Size the Heap

In the world of micro-services, many more JVMs have to compete on a single machine for a fixed amount of RAM, which makes sizing the heap with the -Xmx parameter a critical task. Allocate too little RAM and starve yourself. If you allocate too much, you starve others.

I like to keep the min and max heap size parameters, -Xmx and -Xms, identical. For example, -Xmx1g -Xms1g is good, and I shy away from -Xmx1g -Xms512m. This makes things a bit simpler so I do not have to comprehend a heap that is perpetually expanding/contracting. Also, at JVM start-up time, keeping these two parameters the same makes an "early claim" to the operating system for every last drop of RAM that tests showed was needed.

This keeps other processes from staking a claim to RAM ultimately required by this JVM process. When more micro-service JVMs are playing in the same sandbox, someone is more likely to get sand in their eyes.

In my head, I use a shoebox metaphor to understand how to use JVM parameters to grow and shrink the old and new spaces. The -Xmx determines the size of the shoebox, and the shoebox has a cardboard divider that separates the old and new spaces. As shown in Figure 12-5, if I explicitly set the new size to a particular value, then the old space gets all of the remaining RAM, just as moving the divider to one side of the shoe box increases the size of the other side.

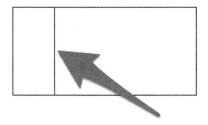

Figure 12-5. *The vertical line is like a divider in a shoe box*

Consider the parameters -Xmx512m -XX:NewSize=412m depicted in Figure 12-6. For starters, note that the -Xmx parameter does not use an equal sign and -XX:NewSize does—an important syntactical difference. Outside of that small detail, these parameters define a 512MB total heap and allocate most of it (412MB) as the minimum size of the new space. The JVM automatically allocates the remaining 100MB to the old space, as shown in the figure. This is my shoebox metaphor, and the line separating the two spaces is my cardboard divider.

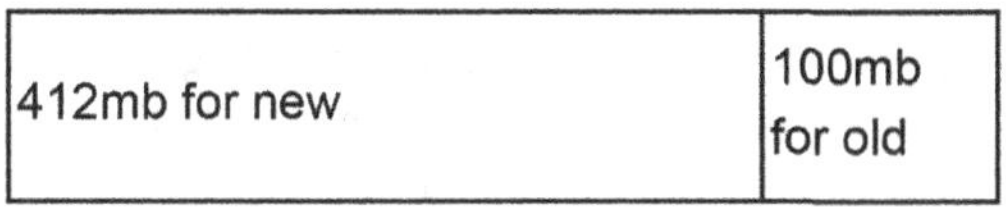

412mb for new	100mb for old

Figure 12-6. *Depiction of larger NewSize with JVM settings -Xmx512m -XX:NewSize=412m*

Changing the value of the -XX:NewSize parameter moves the divider inside the shoe box (Figure 12-7), but leaves the overall box size unchanged, like this: -Xmx512m -XX:NewSize=100m.

100mb for new	412mb for old

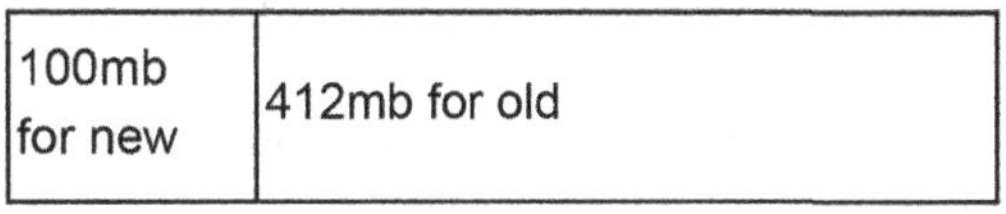

Figure 12-7. *Depiction of larger old size, with JVM settings -Xmx512m -XX:NewSize=100m. Changes to the -XX:NewSize parameter only move the shoe box cardboard divider. They do not change overall size of the heap.*

If I accidently (or mistakenly) ask for a -XX:NewSize larger than the entire heap (larger than the -Xmx), leaving no room for the old space, then the JVM will give you a not-so-helpful error message:

```
Invalid maximum heap size: -Xmx=512m
```

This basically says it is impossible to move the shoebox divider outside of the shoebox. Your shoebox divider, the -XX:NewSize parameter, must leave some room for both the old and new spaces.

So remember: the -Xmx parameter sets the size of the shoe box and the NewSize and MaxNewSize parameters are the divider, which in effect determine the sizes of both the young and the new generation.

Before finishing up this section I would like to quickly mention that the -XX:NewSize parameter is actually the minimum size for the new space.[1] To help keep the complexity down and to avoid twisting my brain into a knot, I like to set the -XX:MaxNewSize to the same value as -XX:NewSize. The -XX:MaxNewSize also provides a sanity check for invalid parameters. The 1.8 JDK allows the following, even though it doesn't make sense to have a new space that is twice the size of the entire heap it's supposed to be contained in.

```
java -Xmx512m -XX:NewSize=1024m Test
```

But if you add the MaxNewSize parameter, like this:

```
java -Xmx512m -XX:NewSize=1024m -XX:MaxNewSize=1024m Test
```

You get a warning telling you about the problem:

```
Java HotSpot(TM) 64-Bit Server VM warning: MaxNewSize (1048576k) is equal to or greater than the entire heap (524288k). A new max generation size of 523776k will be used.
```

Caution Using NewRatio

My shoebox metaphor approach explicitly sets a ratio between the old and the new spaces by setting absolute byte sizes with -XX:NewSize. The experienced GC tuner knows there is an alternative where the ratio is use instead of specifying integer sizes. That alternative is the -XX:NewRatio JVM parameter.

> *"Setting -XX:NewRatio=3 means that the ratio between the old and young generation is 1:3, the combined size of eden and the survivor spaces will be one-fourth of the total heap size..."*

> https://docs.oracle.com/javase/8/docs/technotes/guides/vm/gctuning/sizing.html

The JVM was designed to use either NewRatio or NewSize/MaxNewSize to size your old/new spaces, but not both at the same time. I ran a test, and NewRatio is ignored if it is supplied along with NewSize/MaxNewSize, which can be pretty confusing.

But it gets worse—a lot worse. In the new gen tuning we did for Listings 12-3 and 12-4, we shrank the old space to be pretty small compared to the size of the entire heap. In fact, the old space was just 1/7th of the entire heap when performance was at its best.

My point is that shrinking your old size to be less than 50% of your heap is a completely valid and often desirable approach, especially with stateless SOA systems, but unfortunately there are no valid values for -XX:NewRatio that let you do this, as shown in Table 12-1. For these reasons, I suggest avoiding -XX:NewRatio altogether.

Table 12-1. *Old Gen Percentages for Various NewRatio Settings*

NewRatio	Old size % (implicit)
1	50%
2	67%
3	75%
4	80%

---

[1]This link (https://docs.oracle.com/cd/E19900-01/819-4742/abeik/index.html) says: The NewSize and MaxNewSize parameters control the new generation's minimum and maximum size.

I have wondered why NewRatio is so limiting, and perhaps there are outdated, historical performance concerns might be at fault?

Some heap tuning tips have a short shelf-life. What's valid in one version of Java might very well be counter-productive in the next one. Old hands at Java will know this already, but newbies may tend to believe the advice they recently studied is going to be good for J8, J9, and so on.

I'd like to close this section with comments from Oracle tuning experts Charlie Hunt and Tony Printezis, who also stress the importance of the new generation:

> *"You should try to maximize the number of objects reclaimed in the young generation. This is probably the most important piece of advice when sizing a heap and/or tuning the young generation."*
>
> http://www.oracle.com/technetwork/server-storage/ts-4887-159080.pdf

Blindly Increasing -Xmx

A lazy way to try to fix a heap efficiency problem is by simply increasing the -Xmx value without understanding which GC space is having the problem. For example, consider test 12a in the javaPerformanceTroubleshooting tests.

If you search for 12a in pom-startWar.xml, you'll find this:

```
<profile> <id>12a</id> <properties>
<profile.specific.arg.01>-Xmx512m        </profile.specific.arg.01>
```

If you quadruple the size of the -Xmx value (to 2048MB), you get a little improvement but are still left with 10-15% New GC Overhead %. Try it. This happens because the space with the high overhead that is dragging down performance, the new space, never gets more RAM, because the shoebox divider was not adjusted when increasing the -Xmx—all the space goes to the old gen, and the stateless activity test 12a doesn't use the old gen.

Reclaiming Unused RAM

The previous section showed how under-allocation of RAM caused GC overhead that limited throughput by about 25%. Over-allocation may or may not cause performance problems, but it is a waste of RAM either way.

Here is a plug-it-in-now approach to detecting when you have allocated lots of RAM that your system never uses.

The jpt tests 06a and 06b get the same throughput, same response time, same CPU consumption. If all these metrics are the same, why do we care? The answer is that the *a* test achieves exactly the same throughput and response time as *b*, but it does so with less RAM, and the following data from JAVA_HOME/bin/jstat tells the story. jstat provides two metrics that are very helpful, OGCMX and OGC. As described at this URL:

https://docs.oracle.com/javase/8/docs/technotes/tools/unix/jstat.html

these values stand for "Maximum old generation capacity (kB)" and "Current old generation capacity (kB)," respectively.

The underlined data on the right in Listing 12-8 shows metrics that can help you discover RAM that is allocated but never used. The first data is from test 06a, and the second is from 06b of the javaPerformanceTroubleshooting examples.

Listing 12-8. jstat Metrics (Underlined) Help Discover Allocated but Unused RAM

```
jstat -gccapacity 94153 1s
 NGCMN    NGCMX    NGC    S0C    S1C      EC       OGCMN    OGCMX      OGC        OC        <SNIP!>
2097152.0 2097152.0 2097152.0 86016.0 89088.0 1915392.0  6144.0  262144.0  119296.0  119296.0
2097152.0 2097152.0 2097152.0 78336.0 82432.0 1928704.0  6144.0  262144.0  119296.0  119296.0
2097152.0 2097152.0 2097152.0 78336.0 74752.0 1944064.0  6144.0  262144.0  119296.0  119296.0

jstat -gccapacity 9344
 NGCMN    NGCMX    NGC    S0C    S1C      EC       OGCMN    OGCMX      OGC        OC        <SNIP!>
2097152.0 2097152.0 2097152.0 7168.0 7168.0 2082816.0  6144.0  1310720.0  118784.0  118784.0
2097152.0 2097152.0 2097152.0 7680.0 8704.0 2079744.0  6144.0  1310720.0  118784.0  118784.0
2097152.0 2097152.0 2097152.0 8704.0 8704.0 2079744.0  6144.0  1310720.0  118784.0  118784.0
```

Using the test data in Listing 12-8 from the command-line tool jstat, Figure 12-8 shows that test *b* wastefully allocates about 1GB of RAM that is never used, and its performance is no better than that of test *a*.

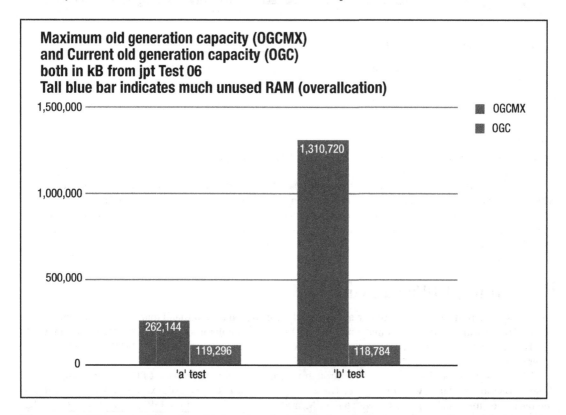

Figure 12-8. *Histogram of data from Listing 12-8. The tall blue bar shows RAM that is allocated but unused.*

Ultimately, it is up to you to determine how much RAM is considered wastefully allocated. But be careful here. If your performance tests somehow do not reproduce some condition where a great deal of memory is used in production, you could accidentally deallocate too much memory and run into an out-of-memory condition. But you can safely use jstat in production to gather these same metrics to help avoid this problem.

Also, the utility http://gceasy.io does a great job of providing charts that show this same thing—allocated but unused heap space, but it is not a plug-it-in-now tool. If you need to add JVM parameters for verbose GC collection, you need to add them and restart your JVM. Once verbose GC has been enabled, you will need to rerun your load test and then upload your verbose GC data file to someone's third-party website for the analysis. The jstat approach gets around all of these hassles!

Memory Leaks

The most common kind of memory leak is an ever-growing singleton of some kind, and these kinds of leaks often take hours, days, or longer to amass enough memory in the singleton to start causing problems. Imagine a singleton with a java.util.Map or a java.util.List, where memory continually grows over time as .put() or .add() is called until all of the allocated heap (the -Xmx JVM parameter) is used up. Fast leaks are less common, but are more dangerous, because they can lock up a JVM in seconds without warning. These happen when a defenseless piece of code is forced to process much more data than it was expecting, like mistakenly returning all the rows in a multi-million-row table to the end user.

Diagnostic data for troubleshooting memory leaks comes in a few layers that get increasingly more detailed:

1. The "Heap Trending" section earlier in this chapter will help you learn how quickly the heap fills before throwing out of memory exceptions. This is based on verbose GC data. This is great, but no class names are mentioned in this data, so it makes it tough to identify which class is leaking.

2. Identifying specific classes that have the largest instance counts and largest amounts of "referenced" memory, as there were at a single point in time. JAVA_HOME/bin/jmap -histo is one common source of this data. Glowroot provides this as well.

3. Understanding trends in the monitored data. For instance, which classes have instance counts that grow perpetually over time? Manual work can be done to compare jmap -histo output (histograms). A tool called heapSpank will do some of this processing for you.

4. Tracking ownership of proliferating objects back to the parents that store/ reference them. Sometimes you know which objects are littering the heap, but you don't know how they got there nor why the GC hasn't already discarded them. Locating exactly where the objects reside in the heap helps identify how they got there in the first place. Heap dumps and heap analysis tools like Eclipse MAT fill this role.

Keep in mind that capturing a heap dump is an expensive operation. It can shut down (basically pause) all activity in a JVM for dozens of seconds or more.

Troubleshooting Memory Leaks

Troubleshooting can be done using class histograms.

The JDK has a great plug-it-in-now approach to getting point-in-time instance counts of all classes loaded in the JVM. Just invoke JAVA_HOME/bin/jmap -histo <myPid> and redirect the stdout to a text file. Here is the doc:

https://docs.oracle.com/javase/8/docs/technotes/guides/troubleshoot/tooldescr014.html#BABJIIHH

If you have 2,000 classes loaded, the jmap -histo output will have one line for each class, showing instance counts of that class and also memory by class. This is the bulk of the output, and because a full heap dump dwarfs a histogram in size and complexity, capturing a heap dump causes much more overhead. That said, I have even seen jmap -histo pause a JVM for dozens of seconds. Sometimes important troubleshooting data is worth the temporary pause.

I suggest grepping the jmap -histo output for your package space. Keep in mind that Java primitives (arrays, int, long) and other types show up with the odd [I syntax shown in Listing 12-9. Generally knowing these primitive counts is only a little helpful, because there are no indicators in this data of what allocated the primitives. When class and package names show up, whether in your own package or a dependency's package, that provides some context to answer questions like, "Where might there be a singleton that would be amassing objects?" and "What user data would be collecting over time?" If you saw class names/packages dealing with session data, it would be worth your time checking whether HTTP session expiration was working as expected.

Listing 12-9. Very Top Lines of jmap Output

```
$ jmap -histo 29620
num   #instances  #bytes class name
--------------------------------------
  1:     1414     6013016 [I
  2:      793      482888 [B
  3:     2502      334928 <constMethodKlass>
  4:      280      274976 <instanceKlassKlass>
  5:      324      227152 [D
  6:     2502      200896 <methodKlass>
  7:     2094      187496 [C
```

The main limitation with jmap -histo is that it provides only point-in-time data. Capturing and reviewing jmap -histo multiple times can be helpful, but it is easy to drown in the data when you are looking for increases in object counts over multiple jmap -histo output files.

To get a better understanding of how class counts and memory consumption trends over time, I wrote heapSpank, available at heapSpank.org. This is a command-line tool that shows the percentage of time that byte counts are on the rise for the 15 classes most likely to be leaking.

I ran a littleMock test with this key to produce the memory leak:

X2,J25,K25,L0,Q,R,S,A4096,B65535,C120000,D240000

Figure 12-9 shows how heapSpank identified the leak class, but not the parent container; this is a nice head start.

```
● ○ ○                        target — java -jar heapSpank-0.09.jar 8985 — 150×50
                   ~/Documents/src/jsource/maphisto/JMapHisto/target — java -jar heapSpank-0.09.jar 8985
  0s    heapSpank memory leak detector pid[8985] [v0.09]
 LKY% #B-INC #JMH #I-INC #R-INC    BYTES     INSTANCES   NUM  CLASS
100.0%   4    5    4     1     562,051,584   35,128,224    1  com.github.eostermueller.littlemock.MyMemoryLeak
100.0%   4    5    1     1     173,043,448   13,769         2  [Ljava.lang.Object;
100.0%   4    5    3     3      14,809,032      198         3  [J
100.0%   4    5    4     4          25,680    1,070        70  java.util.concurrent.LinkedBlockingQueue$Node
100.0%   4    5    4     4          25,368    1,057        71  com.github.eostermueller.littlemock.OldGenerationRepo$OldGenerationData
 75.0%   3    5    1     0      12,645,680   88,896         4  [C
 75.0%   3    5    3     2         248,152    6,742        18  [Lorg.glowroot.agent.shaded.h2.value.Value;
 75.0%   3    5    3     2         166,720    5,210        21  org.glowroot.agent.shaded.h2.result.SimpleRow
 75.0%   3    5    3     3          84,096    3,504        31  org.glowroot.agent.shaded.h2.value.ValueLong
 75.0%   3    5    3     3          61,000    1,525        40  org.glowroot.agent.shaded.h2.result.Row
 75.0%   3    5    3     3          54,280      294        43  [Lorg.glowroot.agent.shaded.h2.result.SearchRow;
 75.0%   3    5    3     3          19,296      268        90  org.glowroot.agent.shaded.glowroot.common.model.MutableProfile$ProfileNode
 75.0%   3    5    3     3          15,240      124       105  [Lorg.glowroot.agent.shaded.h2.result.Row;
 75.0%   3    5    3     4          14,720      184       107  org.glowroot.agent.shaded.h2.index.PageBtreeLeaf
 75.0%   3    5    3     4          12,984      541       117  org.glowroot.agent.shaded.h2.store.Data
===============================================================
```

Figure 12-9. *heapSpank from heapSpank.org has detected the littleMock memory leak. See how the MyMemoryLeak class bubbles to the top of the display?*

Heap Dump Analysis

Early in the chapter, I mentioned the layers of metrics that are available. jstat provides instantaneous metrics to assess health. The verbose GC logs and the trending tools like GCViewer help show trends over time. These indicate whether you have a slow leak building over time. jmap provides counts of classes, and then heapSpank helps understand overtime whether those specific class counts and byte counts continue to rise over time.

All that data is very helpful, but sometimes even all of this is not enough information to fix a memory leak. Let me explain. Just because instances of one or a few objects grow over time doesn't point you to the exact spot where they are accumulating or even why they are accumulating. Always with chagrin we ask why the Garbage Collector hasn't already recycled a particular set of objects highlighted by jmap, heapSpank, or Eclipse MAT.

Analyzing a heap dump helps answer these questions.

Capturing a Heap Dump

Especially with a heap filled to capacity with leaky objects, capturing a heap dump can be a high-overhead operation. It can halt JVM activity for seconds or even minutes. That said, some problems just have to be fixed. So I never capture a heap dump unless the jstat and verbose GC data indicate there is an upward trend of byte counts and/or instance counts. If there have already been out-of-memory errors, forget about the overhead and capture the dump.

I simulated a memory leak using this littleMock key—the same one used in the previous section.

X2,J25,K25,L0,Q,R,S,A4096,B65535,C120000,D240000

I let this test run for just a few minutes. Then I captured a heap dump using the command shown in Listing 12-10.

Listing 12-10. One of Many Ways to Capture a Heap Dump

```
jcmd <myJavaPid> GC.heap_dump /path/to/myDump8.dat
```

Don't forget to use these among the JVM start-up arguments for your application that will automatically capture a heap dump when an out-of-memory error occurs:

```
-XX:+HeapDumpOnOutOfMemoryError and -XX:HeapDumpPath=/some/path/in/production
```

Using Eclipse MAT to Find Memory Leaks

Generally if you are going to fix a leak, code changes will have to be made. The goal is to find all the leaks that won't be collected by the garbage collector, but mainly to figure out *why* the objects are not being collected. Invariably, the answer lies in the object hierarchy—which classes own and hold instances of the classes littering the heap. This is essentially a search for parentage—who owns whom.

This section will use Eclipse MAT to find the source of a leak. The IBM Heap Analyzer is an OK alternative. It sometimes has better auto-leak detection, but the Swing GUI is slower and the navigation around the object graph is more difficult and displays less information than MAT, which is coded in Eclipse RCP/SWT. Let's get back to MAT.

Download and install MAT from this URL: http://www.eclipse.org/mat/. I then chose the File ä Open Heap Dump menu option and pointed to myDump8.dat that I captured in Listing 12-10.

Running MAT on your desktop takes a lot of heavy processing, especially with heaps larger than 1GB.

I suggest getting 32GB RAM on your desktop and allocating perhaps half of that to MAT in the -Xmx parameter in MAT's MemoryAnalyzer.ini.

Eclipse MAT Automatic Leak Detection

MAT has three reports that basically do automatic leak detection. Don't ignore these reports. They are:

> Heap Dump Overview
>
> Top Components
>
> Leak Suspects

I will say there is significant overlap between their functionality and purpose.

When Eclipse opens your heap dump, it asks if you want to create a Leak Suspects report. I chose that option, and MAT displayed Figure 12-10. The Leak Suspects view is not a very interactive pie chart, but the Details hyperlinks in the bottom do allow you to explore the object graph of the heap.

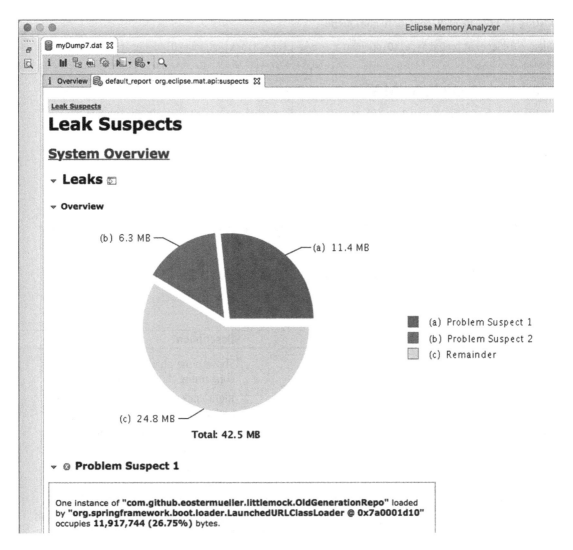

Figure 12-10. *Eclipse MAT Leak Suspects looking at a heapDump from littleMock. In perhaps a third to a half of the heap dumps I have seen, this screen points reasonably close to the the leaky instances and/or the object containing them.*

In fact, this screenshot in Figure 12-10 has already found the container holding all the leaked objects. See the OldGeneratioRepo at the bottom? littleMock stores all the MyMemoryLeak objects in a this object, and the exact collection is in Listing 12-11. This queue is the object storing all the leaked objects, taken from source code of OldGenerationRepo.java in the littleMock github repo.

Listing 12-11. The OldGenerationData Queue

```
Queue<OldGenerationData> allOldGenData = new LinkedBlockingQueue<OldGenerationData>();
```

Exploring in Eclipse MAT

Right under the name of your dump file is a nice set of icons that I rely on heavily (Figure 12-11).

Figure 12-11. *The usability of Eclipse MAT is OK. I normally rely on the icons here to help me find my way around.*

Table 12-2 details the location, name and purpose of each icon in Figure 12-11.

Table 12-2. *Eclipse MAT Icons Displayed in Figure 12-11*

Location on toolbar	Name of Report	Description
Leftmost icon	Overview	Shows a pie-chart with biggest consuming classes/packages.
Icon second from the left	Histogram	Right-click to drill down into incoming and outgoing references.
Icon third from the left	Dominator Tree	Very much like histogram but with left-click drill down.
Icon fourth from the left	Object Query Language	SQL-like language that lets you query the object ownership tree.
Icon fifth from the left	Double Gears / Thread Overview	Basically includes a fancy thread dump that also shows allocations in thread and thread local storage. Very helpful for finding the stack trace in progress of creating a fast memory leak.
Icon sixth from the left	Reports	Leak Suspects and other reports.
Icon seventh from the left	Database Can / Query Brower	Provides the same right-click drill down options available in Histogram view.
Icon eighth from the left	Search / Magnifying Glass	Find objects by hex object address.

The Histogram in Figure 12-12 looks very similar to jmap output, but it is very interactive. For instance, the MAT GUI does an excellent job of managing massive lists of objects. It displays a single screenful and allows you to Click for More. But Figure 12-12 uses a different feature to manage the massive quantity of objects—a simple filter. See at the top-left, where I entered a regular expression to find all objects matching *stermueller*?

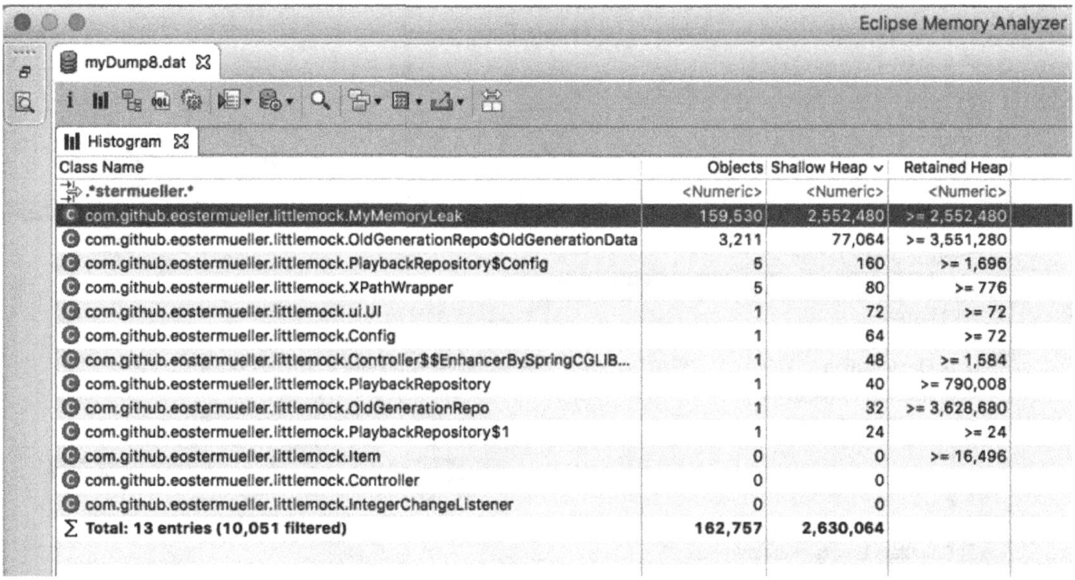

Figure 12-12. *Eclipse MAT Histogram that shows counts and byte counts of all instances. Note that the MyMemoryLeak class shows up right at the top. This is very much like* jmap, *but interactive. You can sort it in various ways and easily right click and drill down to see all the objects this class points to, and all the objects that point to the selected class.*

That is a very handy feature. In this screenshot, MAT has already detected the 2-3MB of data in my package space that is causing the leak. This is an indispensable tool.

In Figure 12-13, I am right-clicking and drilling down to see what "container" class might be holding references to me, keeping "me" from getting collected. This is called looking for GC roots. In my simple example, we already know the answer to this question. But perhaps half the time I am looking at very unfamiliar code and need this feature very much.

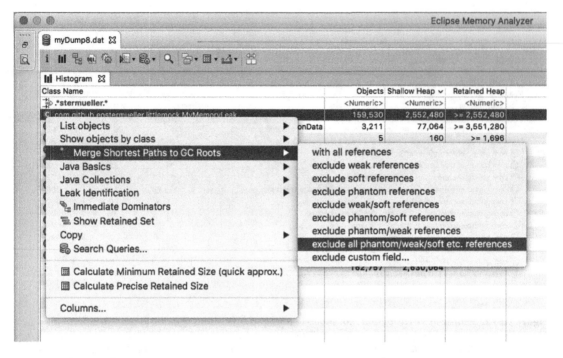

Figure 12-13. *I right-clicked a leaky object to find the "roots"—what object is keeping this from getting collected*

The result is this very nice tree view in Figure 12-14, where we finally see the gory detail of the object parentage that we have been seeking.

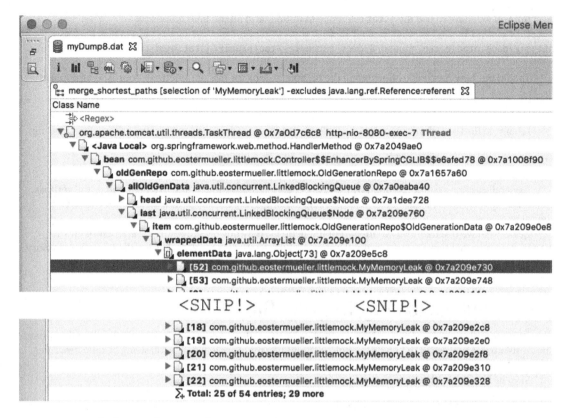

Figure 12-14. The 'Merge Shortest Path to GC Roots' screen from Eclipse

Kinds of Leaks

Eclipse MAT does a great job at finding garden-variety leaks, like the MyMemoryLeak shown earlier. This is in part because that leak is anchored to a singleton—the GC root. Imagine a small, stateless process that queries all the rows in a multi-million-row database table. There are no GC roots in this case. So I have created one of these for you to experiment with.

Invoking this URL will essentially crash any jpt JVM by selecting millions of rows from a database table:

```
https://localhost:8675/crashJvmWithMonsterResultSet
```

Perhaps MAT could be improved by trying to find the leak in the heap dump created by this scenario. Perhaps I just missed it.

Meta-space leaks are also difficult to solve, but I can provide you with a little head start in the troubleshooting. The following command will show meta-space capacity, to see if you are close to filling up the space or not:

```
jstat -gcmetacapacity <myPid> 1s
```

But you will have to use the jstat reference to understand all the field names:

`https://docs.oracle.com/javase/8/docs/technotes/tools/unix/jstat.html`

To find out how much you allocated in the first place, look for this parameter in your JVM arguments:

`-XX:MaxMetaspaceSize=1g`

Finally, to find out what class might be leaking, use these instructions to turn on verbose class loading:

`https://dzone.com/articles/how-use-verbose-options-java`

Generally after a system has been warmed up, class loading should come to a near halt. If the verbose class loading continues to show activity, especially loading a few classes or more a second, you have a meta-space leak.

Leaks we have discussed so far are part of the heap used by our Java programs. Back before Java 7, we saw a number of memory leaks in the C program (I think) that is the JVM. This is called a native memory leak and is not easy to debug; it is well beyond the scope of this small book.

Heap Troubleshooting, Step-by-Step

I generally troubleshoot heap issues by first checking to see if there are easy solutions. Only when those easy solutions are not successful to I go on to explore things like memory leaks. The following outline describes this rough, troubleshooting progression.

Start by abiding by these general rules:

- -Xmx must not exceed available RAM.

- Avoid NewRatio.

- Love the one you're with: stick with your favorite GC algorithm (except serial).
  If you're on IBM J9, then only use gencon (default) or the new Balanced, which is a 'regional' algorithm, similar to G1.

Basic GC troubleshooting steps follow:

1. Start out with a not-huge heap, something between 512MB (perhaps for micro-services) and 4GB.

2. While under load, assess GC generational overhead. Use jstat and gctime.sh or gctime.cmd.

3. If one or both of the generations have sustained red and/or yellow overhead, configure an additional chunk of RAM (perhaps 256MB?) for that generation; then restart and retest. Repeat until GC overhead percentage results are in the desired range.

4. If infrequent but long old gen pauses (slower than 5 seconds) are unacceptable, consider moving to one of the following:

   1. Hotspot / G1, because old gen collections are broken up into smaller collections yielding smaller pauses. Here is the detailed G1 tuning doc:

      `http://www.oracle.com/technetwork/articles/java/g1gc-1984535.html`

2.   For IBM J9, use the Balanced collector, whose "regional" approach is very similar to G1.

Advanced GC troubleshooting steps follow:

1.   If old gen continues to have yellow or red or out-of-memory errors, check for memory leaks.

    1.   Use jmap -histo and/or heapSpank to assess whether there are one or more classes whose byte counts or instance counts are continually on the rise.

    2.   Use PMAT or GCViewer to check verbose GC. Check the graphs in these tools for upward trends in old gen memory consumption. Consider the amount of time the graphs show that it takes to fill the heap. If the heap fills in a matter of seconds or minutes, I consider that a fast leak and look for individual requests that allocate massive amounts of data. A massive JDBC result set is once example. If instead, it takes hours or days to fill the heap, look for a small number of objects that collect in a java.util collection that is held in memory by a singleton.

    3.   If heapSpank doesn't provide enough data to find cause of the leak, capture heap dump, try one of the following:

        1.   MAT leak suspects.

        2.   Histogram.

        3.   Use MAT to find GC Roots.

2.   Metaspace leaks. Look for "MC", "MU", "CCSC", and "CCSU" from the output of "jstat -gc <myPid> 1000".

3.   Sometimes, a single huge allocation of memory can fill the heap and crash your JVM. To learn how to troubleshoot this situation, invoke the following URL from any browser during any jpt test:

    `https://localhost:8675/crashJvmWithMonsterResultSet`

    This executes a JDBC query that returns a massive result set.

    The brower will hang and the JVM will produce "java.lang.OutOfMemoryError: Java heap space" errors. Create a heap dump using "jcmd <myPid> GC.heap_dump myDump.bin". Use MAT to detect the leak.

4.   Look for failure messages in the verbose GC logs. Normally, I use PMAT or GCViewer to 'look' at my logs. But when I'm working on a real tough GC problem that defies explanation, I get out my text editor and look through the logs for errors like "[ParNew (promotion failed)". Be sure to do an internet search for similar errors.

Don't Forget

The world of micro-services is coming, where many more JVMs will run on a single operating systems instance. Instead of 4-8 JVMs on a single machine, perhaps there will be 10 to 30. All of this will require tighter memory management, discovering heap over-allocations, and watching the performance health of many more processes.

For these reasons it would be prudent to learn some of the heap troubleshooting techniques in this chapter. Earlier in this chapter I said that diagnostic data for troubleshooting heap issues comes in a few layers that get increasingly more detailed. Being cognizant of these layers helps you understand troubleshooting data you have missed. For example, plug-it-in-now GC data from gcstat is great for immediacy, but PMAT and GCViewer are better for capturing trends, and those trends indicate whether you have a fast or a slow memory leak.

That is the end of the P.A.t.h. Checklist. What's next is getting real-world practice learning how to turn Dark Environments into environments with good visibility, and to teach your co-workers how to use these plug-it-in-now techniques to make that happen.

CHAPTER 13

■ ■ ■

Conclusion

Other disciplines take more of a walk-before-you-run approach to engineering and the validation of production readiness. For example, airplane aerodynamics are vetted in a wind tunnel before the first test flight. Before the full-sized bridge is built, a scale model is fabricated to assess load-bearing capacity.

Yet even today, we continue to write software that is unprepared to handle a production load, as if onesie-twosie functional testing nearly approximated a production workload. It doesn't. Our deliverables include the part about handling a production load.

To address this gap, you need to first understand a common misperception, one that I encourage you to discuss with your friends and coworkers. Don't be shy about it.

Here is the misperception: Getting performance right is nearly impossible, because you must have a massive computing environment and expensive monitoring to solve problems that only performance experts can fix. We also think of many environment as having little monitoring—the Dark Environments. That Dark Environments exist is antother misperception, because as this book has shown, there are lots of plug-it-in-now tools available in every JDK in every Dark Environment.

But really, like the code samples in this book, the majority of performance defects can be reproduced and detected in just about any environment using open source or freely available monitoring tools. It just takes a little guidance from a methodical approach (like the P.A.t.h. Checklist) to help you locate the most common and pernicious defects.

Ultimately, before going into production, system performance must be vetted in a full-sized environment under the full production workload. But attempting to tune everything at once in a large environment normally results in a half-baked performance rush-job. It is an expensive and horrifically slow endeavor, because of the lack of access and high maintenance required, like code redeployments that take half a day or longer.

Contrast that to the easy access of a small environment where you can get perhaps ten fix-test tuning cycles in a single day. Finally, the early feedback you can get in a small environment helps avoid costly retreats from approaches with unacceptable performance.

Steps for Getting Started

Getting started now to tune your system is pretty straightforward. Follow these steps:

1. Create a Modest Tuning Environment (Chapter 2) using existing hardware. A massive amount of fast, expensive performance hardware is not required.

2. Let's fix the problem of undersized databases in development. Whether you rent it or buy it, make a modest investment in extra hard disks for the various Modest Tuning Environments in development. The cost of ten single terabyte drives is small. The lack of a production-sized dataset is an obstacle to locating performance defects. It often takes a lot of data from a large disk to exacerbate GC and other problems. You'll also need to give the team 40–80 hours to work on a repeatable solution to generate a production-sized database. This is a modest ask for a huge benefit.

© Erik Ostermueller 2017
E. Ostermueller, *Troubleshooting Java Performance*, DOI 10.1007/978-1-4842-2979-8_13

3.   Ensure good performance visibility in every single environment. The plug-it-in-now tools demonstrated in this book go a long way here. Sure, SQL performance metrics are still required, but you can easily use the open source Glowroot or similar for that.

4.   Apply load to your code on a regular basis to identify obvious issues. Remember, the "under load" thing is part of our deliverable. Most of the examples in this book were able to demonstrate performance issues with just three threads of load and zero think time. I call this "3t0tt." Chapters 4, 5, 6 and 7 focus on load generation.

5.   Use the P.A.t.h. Checklist as a reminder of where to look to find the most common defects. See Chapters 9, 10, 11 and 12. Chapter 1 on the Main Performance Anti-Patterns will also help. Whether you are fighting performance fires in production or you have other development priorities, there is only so much time to troubleshoot performance. To minimize troubleshooting time, you can easily make one pass at P.A.t.h. Checklist in 30 minutes or less.

Using this Book with Large Monitoring Tools

For all of my talk about small, free monitoring tools, I have nothing against sophisticated monitoring tools—not even commercial ones. Java profilers, APM tools, network trace tools, and so on. They're a mainstay in my day job as a performance engineer; I occasionally use one tool that has a $75k license. New, open source APM tools like Glowroot are maturing and there are a few good commercial ones, too. I'm OK with large tools that work.

But these tools are absent from perhaps half or more of all environments, and this happens because of high license cost, fear of high overhead, and other reasons.

I hope the plug-it-in-now, small-tool tuning techniques presented in this book can shed enough light on these issues in Dark Environments to keep the performance technical debt at bay.

But the load generation techniques, the Main Performance Anti-Patterns, the P.A.t.h. Checklist and other tuning approaches in this book can provide value with any monitoring toolset in any environment, Dark or not.

For example, if stack traces in a Java Profiler or APM tool indicate during a load test that some slowdown is caused by a rarely executed business process, you'll know to remove that process from the load test, because it's not a challenge that will be encountered (at any significant load) in production. That's Main Anti-Pattern 3, Overprocessing.

Here is a second example. Quality APM tools are capable of serving up the vast sea of metrics that I outlined in Chapter 3 where I talked about the three reasons for metrics (checking whether we've met our performance requirements, assessing whether our resources are all used up, and identifying the component responsible for a slowdown). This vast sea of metrics can be overwhelming, knowing which ones to focus on. Well that's easy. As a starting point, make sure you have some focus on each of the items in the P.A.t.h. Checklist. To get a little more specific, the P.A.t.h. Checklist should guide decisions on which metrics to place on APM "dashboards." A dashboard is a user-arranged screenful of performance graphs/metrics.

The plug-it-in-now tool mentality is certainly lacking one big thing: a repository. When you are there troubleshooting a system, plug-it-in-now is a great approach. But systems go bump in the night, and its great to have an APM tool with a repository that captures great data while your not there. This lack of a repository is perhaps the Achilles heel of the plug-it-in-now toolset. The said, the plug-it-in-now is always there as a last resort for Dark Environments.

Finally, remember that Chapters 4, 5, 6, and 7 are on load generation, which is required regardless of the server-side monitoring tools that you use. So, when you care enough about scalability to actually test to see if your product has it, the Scalability Yardstick is the test for you.

3t0tt (3 Threads of Load, Zero Think Time)

I think we are very close to the point where all code should get at least a light performance vetting before being checked in. Here is one way to accomplish this: stipulate to your developers that:

> All changes to components as big as or bigger than a SOA service should be
> examined under the stress of exactly three threads of load with zero think time.

When I say, "bigger than a SOA service", I am trying to avoid the complexities of micro-benchmarking. Towards this end, 3t0tt should only include components that have at least one I/O—like one or more database hits, or one or more other network requests. It also makes sense to exclude "really fast" code from 3t0tt testing, again to avoid the complexities of micro-benchmarking. Perhaps lay out 'required 3t0tt', 'optional 3t0tt' and 'never 3t0tt' response time landmarks. Choose your own thresholds, but I would choose numbers like never do 3t0tt testing for 25ms and faster; 25ms to 100ms would be optional, and 100ms and higher would be required.

Why three threads of load and not 42 or 95 threads of load? The idea is that we need enough activity to reproduce issues, including multi-threaded ones, but not so much activity that it risks overwhelming modest-sized tuning environments, the most productive place to tune code.

In my experience, three threads are sufficient to flush out the vast majority of all multi-threaded issues. Applying this amount of load to a multi-threaded or re-entrant bug, you will see between 00.001% and 10.000% of all requests end in errors errors/exceptions. Ignore this "errors" metric at your own risk. The JMeter Summary Report and JMeter Plugins Synthesis Report (a better "Summary Report") label this simply as "errors." Also, if your code makes a regular practice of catching and ignoring exceptions, you are short-circuiting a wonderful feedback process that will help you find fixable bugs using this 3t0tt technique.

One Last Word

Have you ever heard coworkers say these things?

- It would cost too much to create a performance environment that matches the size of production.

- The network people won't let us load test on that network.

- Is the firewall causing performance issues?

- It will take one day to get that code redeployed.

- It will take two days to get an exception for that firewall rule.

Actually, you'd never hear that last thing because you could never get a firewall changed that quickly. But outside of that, this is just a sampling of all the daily impediments to load testing. These are all legitimate issues, but they don't excuse us from asking developers to be accountable for their own deliverables, which should include acceptable performance under a production workload.

Index

© Erik Ostermueller 2017
E. Ostermueller, *Troubleshooting Java Performance*, DOI 10.1007/978-1-4842-2979-8